LEGENDARY LOCALS
OF
BUCKEYE
ARIZONA

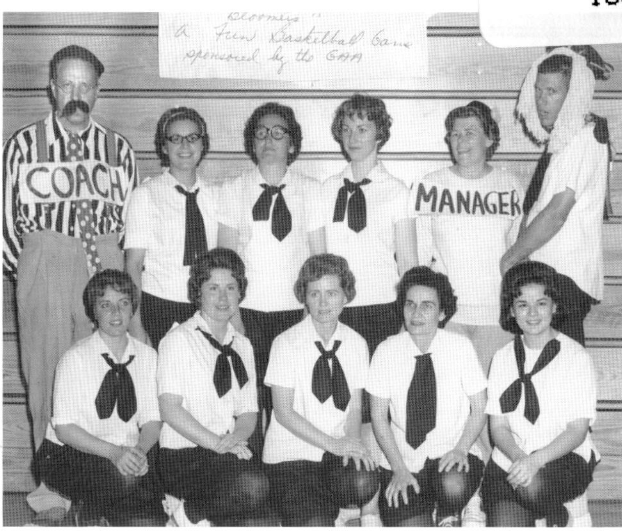

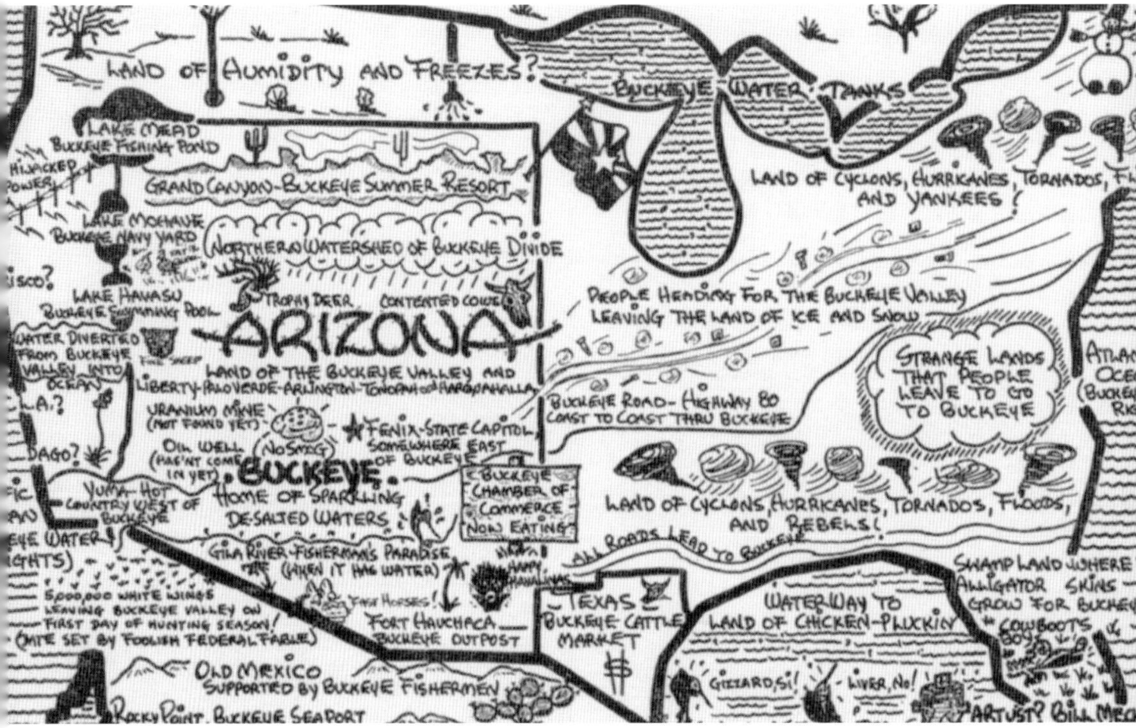

Buckeye Map

In 1962, Bill Meck drew this map of the United States with Buckeye, Arizona, as the focus. Meck's story is featured on page 26. (Courtesy of author.)

Page 1: Bloomers

A fun basketball game in 1964 featured Buckeye Union High School faculty and staff members (see page 110). (Courtesy of BUHS Archives.)

LEGENDARY LOCALS

OF

BUCKEYE

ARIZONA

VERLYNE MECK

LEGENDARY LOCALS

ISBN 978-1-4671-0200-1

Legendary Locals is an imprint of Arcadia Publishing
Charleston, South Carolina

Printed in the United States of America

Library of Congress Control Number: 2014951888

For all general information, please contact Arcadia Publishing:
Telephone 843-853-2070
Fax 843-853-0044
E-mail sales@arcadiapublishing.com
For customer service and orders:
Toll-Free 1-888-313-2665

Visit us on the Internet at www.arcadiapublishing.com

Dedication
To those who came before us, to those here now, and to those who are to come. Thank you Janene Van Leeuwen for this powerful thought.

On the Front Cover: Clockwise from top left:
Robert A. Saide, MD, family doctor (Courtesy of author; see page 99), Fernando Carrera, barber, and his wife, Stella (Fisher) Carrera (Courtesy of author; see page 46), W. Bruce Heiden, cotton farmer/cattleman (Courtesy of author; see page 37), Margaret (Makin) Jackman, essay writer (Courtesy of author; see page 8), Irene (Hunter) Makin, BUHS administrator assistant (Courtesy of BUHS Archives; see page 81), Art Arnold, professional rodeo roper (Courtesy of author; see page 70), Clyde Cobbin, local personality (Courtesy of author; see page 82), W.H. Olsen, teacher/administrator/coach (Courtesy of BUHS Archives; see page 74), Larry and Jerfee Eng, grocery-store owners (Courtesy of Eng family; see page 47).

On the Back Cover: From left to right:
Legendary cowboys (Courtesy of Jack C. Gable; see page 120), 1957 Helzapoppin Rodeo Parade announcer Bill Meck (Courtesy of the author; see page 26).

CONTENTS

ACKNOWLEDGMENTS

Once again, a Buckeye book would not be possible without the help of others. I am very grateful for their support and expertise. The vision and leadership of Edith Mae Christian for the *Buckeye First 100 Years* book laid the groundwork for three Arcadia projects. Thank you, Arizona historians Jack August and Marshall Trimble, for encouraging me to author the first book: Images of America: *Buckeye*. Meeting Nancy Crandall, great-great-granddaughter of M.M. Jackson; Dorothy (Clanton) Hudman, great-granddaughter of T.N. Clanton; and Margaruite (Hegi) Rains and Lilly Predmore, Hegi descendants, brought to me a reality of Buckeye pioneers. Others who shared time and expertise were the following: Esther (Woody) Walls, June (Benedict) Dean, Marion Ratlief, Don Balmes, Kathy Ratlief, Loren Ratlief, Sharon (Beyer) Hinkle, Jane (Way) Thomas Miller, Linda (Armstrong) Davis, Margaret (Makin) Jackman, Jane Fricke, Ray Hinshaw, Ken Wood, and Jim Grosbach. For my adult children, Teresa (Meck) Kennedy, Sara (Meck) Faccio, and Jackie Meck Jr., I am so thankful for the joy and expertise you provided to me. You are the best. Also, this book would not have been published if Karen (Williams) Goins had not given hours and hours of computer techie expertise. Thank you Arcadia Publishing and Erin Vosgien for this opportunity to write again about Buckeye. Last, but not to be forgotten, is my wonderful, loving, and encouraging husband, Jackie Meck.

I, Verlyne Meck, hope that within these pages you will find photographs and words to help capture the spirit of the Buckeye Valley.

INTRODUCTION

The introduction of this Legendary Locals book began about 70 years ago. Margaret Makin, a Buckeye Union High School freshman, wrote an essay for her history class, taught by Bill Olsen. He assigned the students to write an essay on a pioneer of Buckeye. Makin's essay was found around 2012 by her granddaughter Christine Jackman. Christine, with the help of grandmother Margaret (Makin) Jackman, wrote an informative prelude to the essay. It goes as follows:

> I chose Mrs. H.E. Kell (maiden name Cora Clanton). On a Saturday morning, I got on my bicycle and went up to Kell's. They lived south of the canal on Fourth Street. Their house was white with a large wooden front porch that extended the entire length of the house. I had called so that Mrs. Kell would know to expect me. I knocked on the door and she hollered from the kitchen asking who it was and I told her and she said come in. I walked down the hall that was the length of the house and the kitchen was on the right and Mr. Kell's office was on the left. Mrs. Kell was at the sink doing dishes as she had just finished making her famous sugar cookies. There was a window above the sink and looking out of it, you could see huge aluminum tanks that held water for their Water Company. To the right of the sink was the stove where Mrs. Kell did all of her baking and on the stove was a large tank that held water that was always hot for her to do her dishes. She would dip a pan into the water and then into the sink. Across the room was a round kitchen table, where she told me to sit. I told her what I was there for and because of Mrs. Kell I compiled an essay. This is part of what I turned in. "In 1885, the first ten miles of the Buckeye Canal was started and completed. The man who was in charge of the canal was from Ohio, which is known as the Buckeye State; therefore he named the canal after the Buckeye State. The post office which was called Buckeye was established in 1888. Cora J. Clanton (Mrs. Kell) was the first post mistress. The post office was named Buckeye, after the canal. One of the men that helped to lay out the town later, conceived the idea of calling the town Sidney, but the post office has always been called Buckeye. After a while, the name of Sidney was dropped and officially the town was called Buckeye. The first letters received bears the mark of May 18, 1888. T.N. Clanton was the founder of Buckeye. Nick Hurley opened the first grocery store, and he was the second postmaster for Cora J. Clanton served for only one year. Ms. Clanton later married Ed Kell and was residents of Buckeye. The first hotel was built by W.B. Long and his brother Ed. The first butcher shop was owned by J.S. Gowett. Tom Shoultz ran the first newspaper. The first automobile, an Oldsmobile (which was operated with a lever instead of a wheel), was owned by Dr. Thayer. In 1920, my folks arrived in Buckeye.

Thank you, Margaret (Makin) Jackman, for giving us a glimpse of what Buckeye was like many years ago. You preserved history by writing it down.

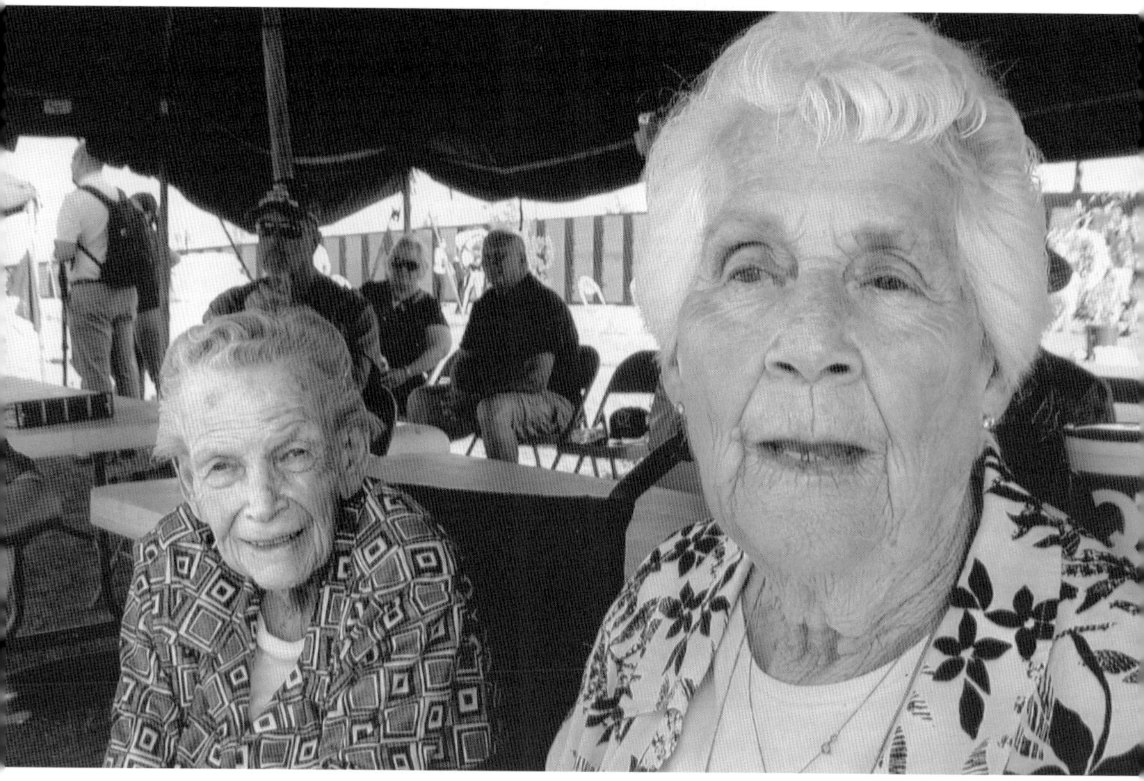

Margaret (Makin) Jackman

Shown here on May 8, 2013, are Margaret (Makin) Jackman (right) and her sister-in-law Irene (Hunter) Makin (see page 81). They attended the Vietnam Traveling Memorial Wall in Buckeye. Margaret's nephew and Irene's son, Allen Makin, was killed in the Vietnam War. Margaret was born in Buckeye on June 9, 1925. She graduated from Buckeye Union High School (BUHS) in 1944 and became a registered nurse at St. Joseph's Hospital in Phoenix. After marrying John Jackman, Margaret moved to San Diego, California. She still resides there, living in the same home for the past 60 years. (Courtesy of author.)

CHAPTER ONE

Early Legends and Visionaries

Charles A. Mitten, son of the *Buckeye Valley News* founder, wrote the following information in the *Buckeye Printer* in 1971:

> In the first issue of the *News* (February 12, 1912), the Buckeye Valley was described by C.M. Zander. Basically, he wrote that people in the late 1800s became founders and visionaries. Their stories are told in this chapter. Legendary people such as J.L. Spain, M.M. Jackson, Junius Brewster, T.N. Clanton, and James Wilson Davis laid Buckeye's foundation. Others in this chapter, such as Marshall Long, Nate Sanders, John Beloat, Hugh Watson and Uncle Hi Parkman, added much to Buckeye's storied beginning.

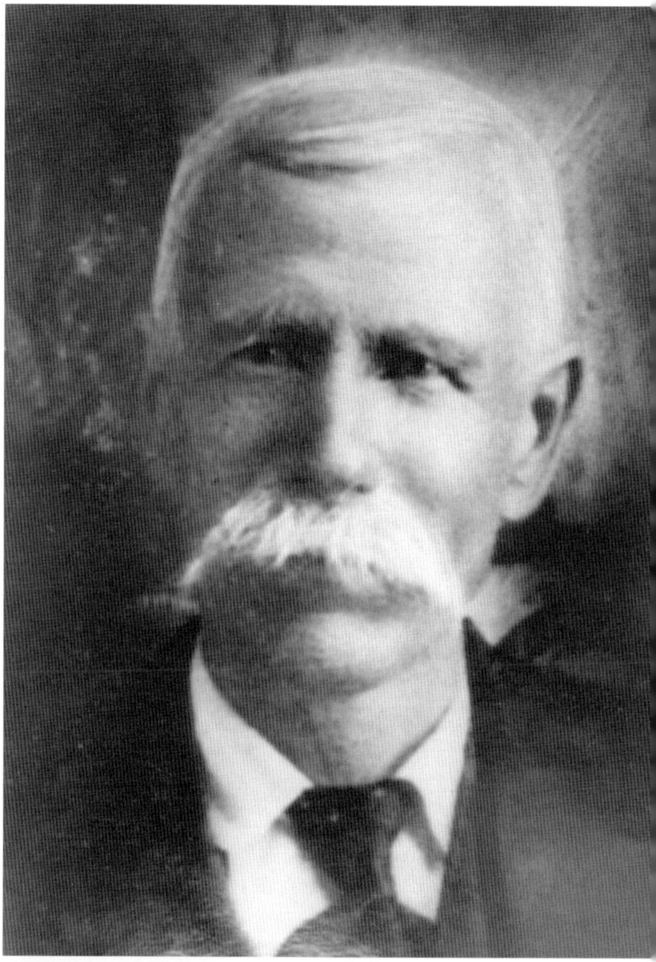

Joshua Leonides Spain

Joshua Leonides "J.L." Spain was the valley's first settler, in 1885 in Liberty. Spain was born in North Carolina on December 10, 1838. At an early age, he moved to Illinois, where he met and courted Sarah Moody. They married in 1867 and moved to Arkansas. In 1875, they started for the West Coast by covered wagon. In due time, they arrived in California, and after a couple of years, they came to Phoenix. In 1885, Spain, M.M. Jackson, and Henry Mitchell located the Buckeye Canal and organized a company to build and operate it. He built a home in Liberty in 1886 and farmed there until 1905. The family home (pictured), east of Liberty School, is the oldest surviving building in the valley. In 1917, J.L. and Sarah moved to Watsonville, California, where J.L. died on December 9, 1932. Sarah Spain lived to the ripe old age of 102 years, dying at the home of a grandchild in Prescott, Arizona. The present-day homeowner is Paul Mansanares, a 1977 BUHS graduate. In 2014, Paul began restorations to the former Spain home and property. (Both, courtesy of Buckeye Museum.)

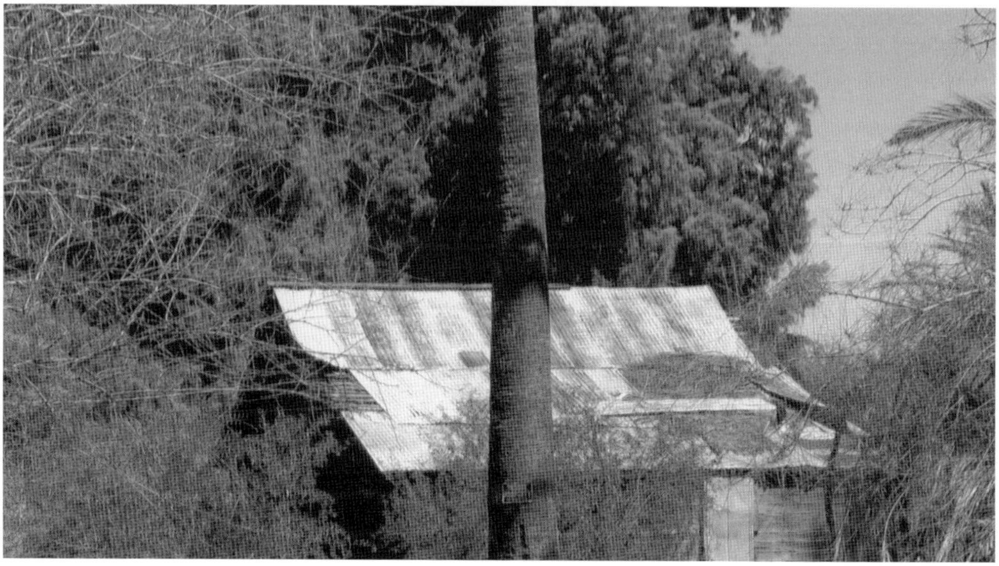

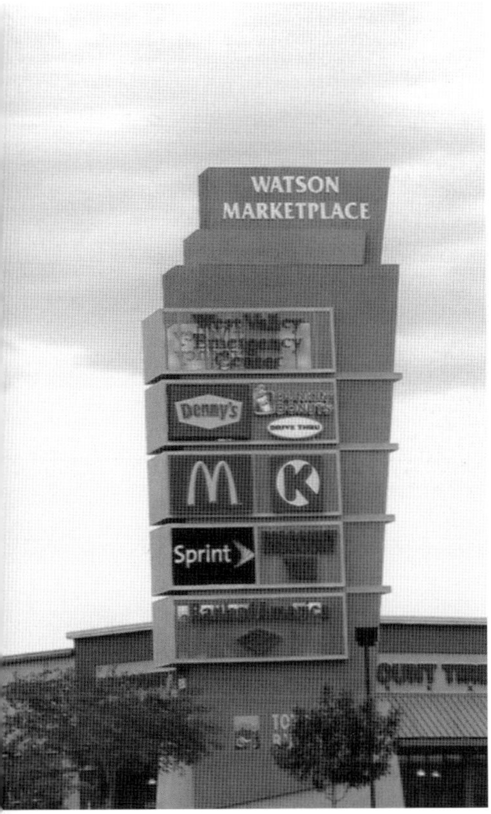

Hugh M. Watson Sr.

Hugh Miller Watson was born on September 22, 1881, in Denton, Texas. He moved to Arizona in 1910. After leaving Texas, he went to Clifton, Arizona, where he worked as postmaster and later decided to run for the territorial legislature. He then moved to Duncan, worked for Phelps Dodge, started a bank, and was making a political speech when a train arrived from Texas bearing Marjorie "Madge" Eason. That night, at a Duncan hotel, the smitten Watson hired a Mexican band to play under Madge Eason's window. After they were married, Hugh sold his bank, and the couple moved to Yuma, where Watson was a manager of the First National Bank. They came to Buckeye, and he started the Buckeye Valley Bank with a capital of $25,000. He served as cashier until 1928. He became president and moved the bank into a new building. He was instrumental in Buckeye's 1929 incorporation and later served as Buckeye's first mayor. Hugh Watson planned for the pavement of Monroe Avenue, organized Buckeye's Helzapoppin, and helped students by giving high school scholarships. He was a member of the Masonic Lodge for 50 years, IOOF, AZ club, El Zaribah Shrine Temple in Phoenix, and First Baptist Church in Buckeye. Watson Marketplace (left), on Watson Road, is named after him. (Left, courtesy of author; below, courtesy of Buckeye Museum.)

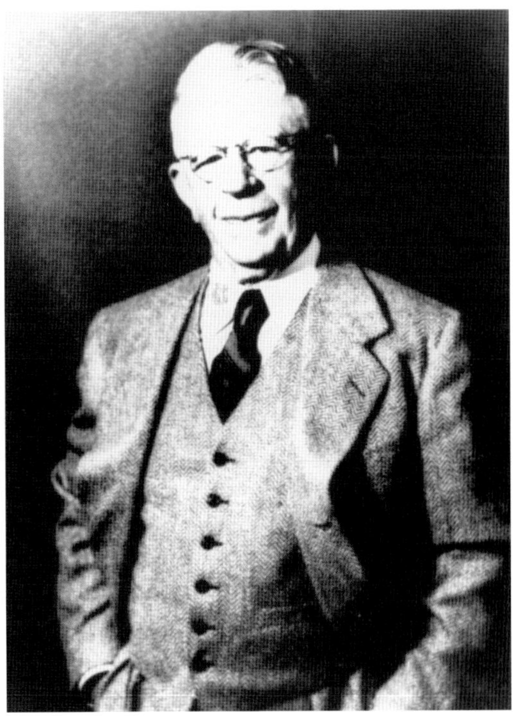

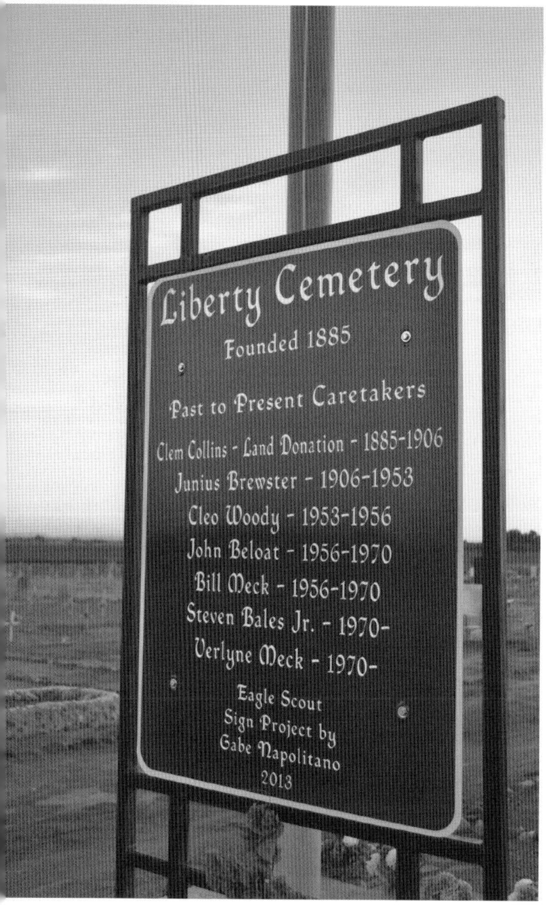

Liberty Cemetery Caretakers

Junius Brewster moved to the Liberty area with his parents, Edward and Kate (Savage) Brewster, in 1898. The family was direct descendants of William Brewster, a passenger on the *Mayflower*. Junius married Myrta Ina McDonald on November 19, 1906, in Phoenix. Her parents were William and Sara (Hazelton) McDonald.

After Junius and Myrta married, they took over the management of her parents' farm. Junius passed away on June 17, 1953, and Myrta died on May 23, 1961. The 130-year-old Liberty Cemetery is located on Tuthill Road (207th Avenue), south of MC Highway 85. The land, donated by Clem Collins in 1885, was located next to the Free Methodist Church. The first burial, in 1885, was for Norma Jones, daughter of W.W. Jones. There are approximately 590 interments, with the last burial being Jose Ruan in 1992. Buckeye pioneer Thomas Newton Clanton is also buried there. Junius Brewster, the first caretaker, gave 50 years of devotion and service. Shown below are caretakers Junius Brewster (left) and Cleo Woody. Other caretakers are listed on a sign erected in 2013 (left). The sign was an Eagle Scout project by Gabe Napolitano. In 2012, an outstanding restoration project was undertaken by Buckeye VFW Post No. 12098, led by Dennis Barnwell. (Left, courtesy of Lara Serbin; below, courtesy of Esther [Woody] Walls.)

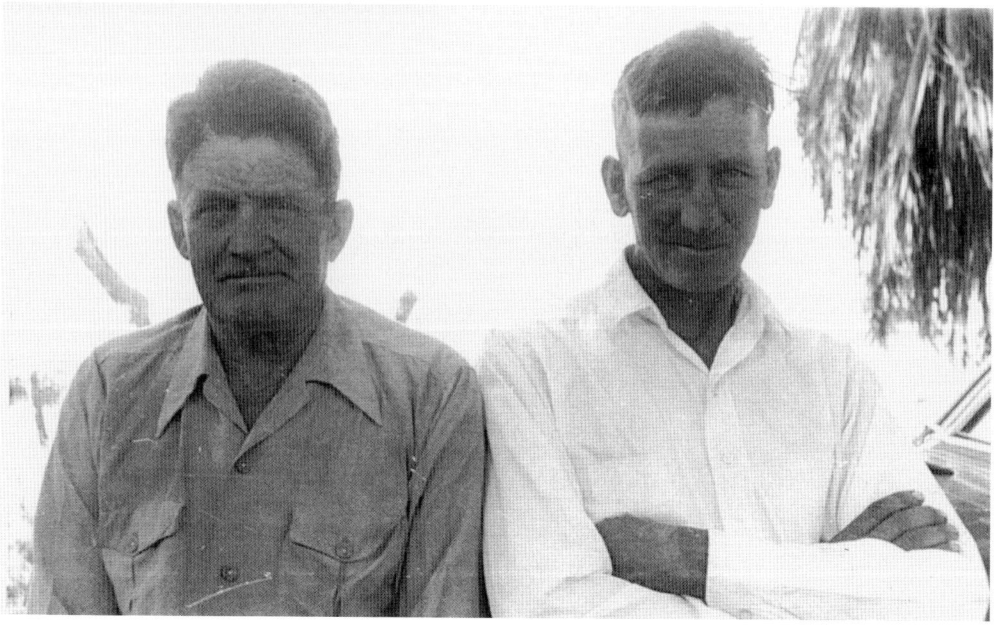

Malie Monroe Jackson

Buckeye's history began with the words "location notice" written by a quill pen fashioned from a willow branch. The writing fluid was a strange mixture of ink: black gunpowder and water. Malie Monroe Jackson (pictured) was the writer. He was a member of the family that had produced a US president, Andrew Jackson. Born in Ohio in 1834, M.M. Jackson had already experienced 42 years of toil and service, including pioneering in Wisconsin, Missouri, and Arkansas and serving in the Union army during the Civil War. A daughter, Angie Case, who died in 1953, related some details of his life in 1936: "With his wife and six children, Jackson crossed the plains in a prairie schooner drawn by oxen. Sometimes there were 30 wagons in our train, sometimes less, as they would intermittently turn off to go into Texas, or to some other goal. We always had a large herd of cattle, belonging to families, bringing up the rear." Case said her father discovered the Buckeye district's potential while prospecting with Joshua Leonidas Spain in 1884.

Case continued: "Jackson and Spain were returning to Phoenix after a trip to the White Tank Mountains. Along the Gila River, they noted the levelness of the sagebrush country and the fertility of the river bottom lands. At a point two miles below the mouth of the Agua Fria River, they came on a good site for a canal intake and camped at the point overnight. Before leaving the next morning, my father posted a location notice . . . covering 30,000 inches of water." In 1886, the first water was turned into the canal. M.M. Jackson died on July 23, 1926, in California, at the age of 92. He is buried in Phoenix Greenwood Cemetery. (Courtesy of Buckeye Museum.)

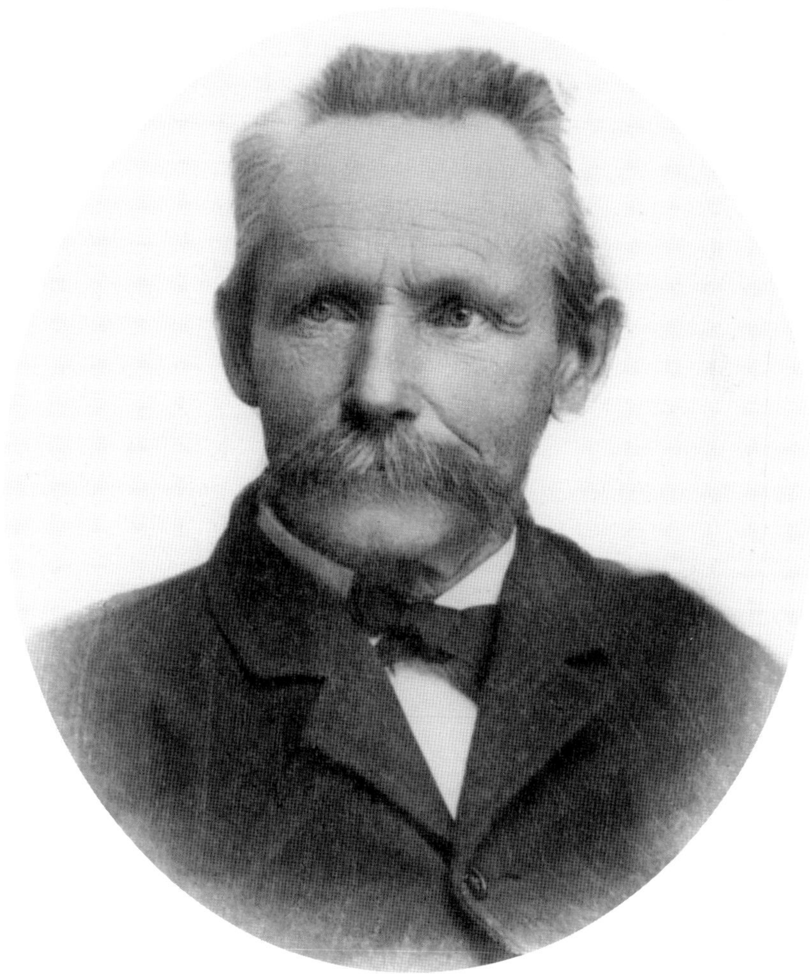

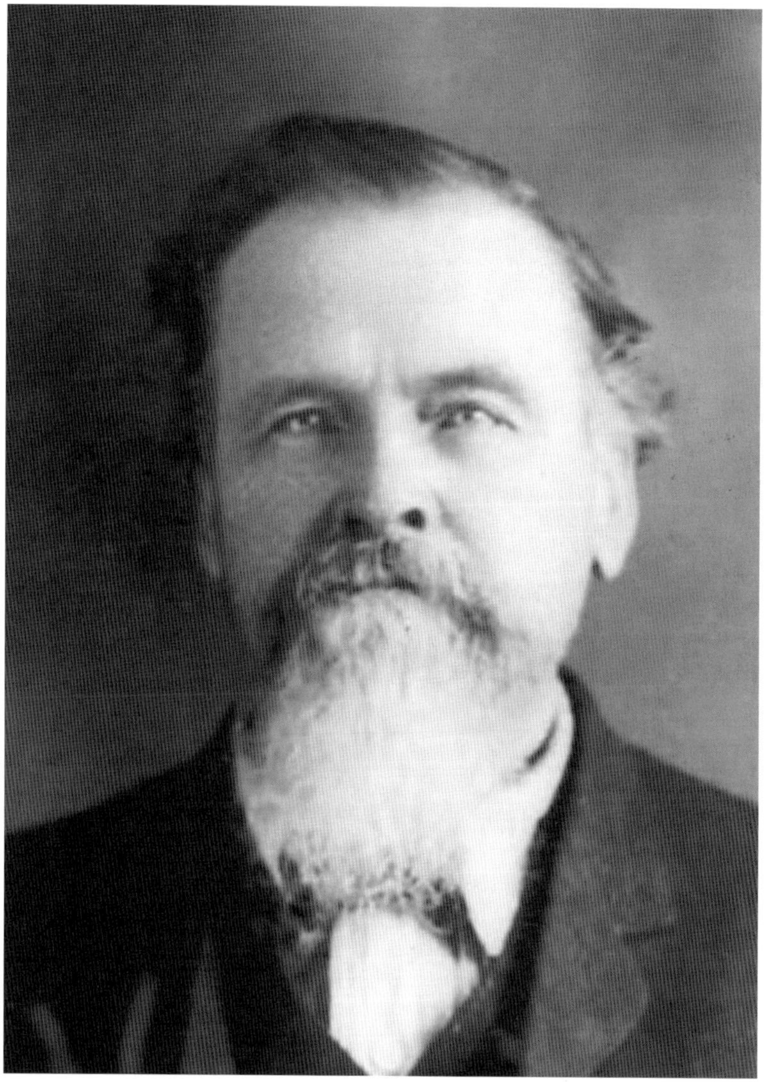

Thomas Newton Clanton

Sidney was the name originally filed for a new community west of Phoenix when O.L. Mahoney and T.N. Clanton decided to subdivide 120 acres of their land into lots and create a townsite. Clanton (pictured) dutifully filed the land plat for the town of Sidney on September 3, 1888, and was given a receipt for money paid, but the county recorder did not file the map. Clanton filed again on October 24, 1902.

T.N. Clanton and his family moved to the area in 1887, making them the first settlers in what is now Buckeye. Named for the Buckeye Canal, the Buckeye Post Office was established a half-mile from the town of Sidney on March 10, 1888, with T.N.'s daughter Cora J. (Clanton) Kell as postmistress. An article in the November 1910 *Arizona Republican* reported that most people were referring to the growing community as Buckeye, except for the people who had bought their land in Sidney. T.N. Clanton collected the signatures of all the property owners he could reach to petition to have the name of the town changed to Buckeye. The petition was filed with the county recorder with the approval of the county board of supervisors. As of 2014, the families of Dan, Don, John, and Frank Drew, current Buckeye residents, are related to the pioneer Kell family. An answer to an often-asked question, "Was T.N. Clanton related to the Clantons from Tombstone?" is "no." (Courtesy of Buckeye Museum.)

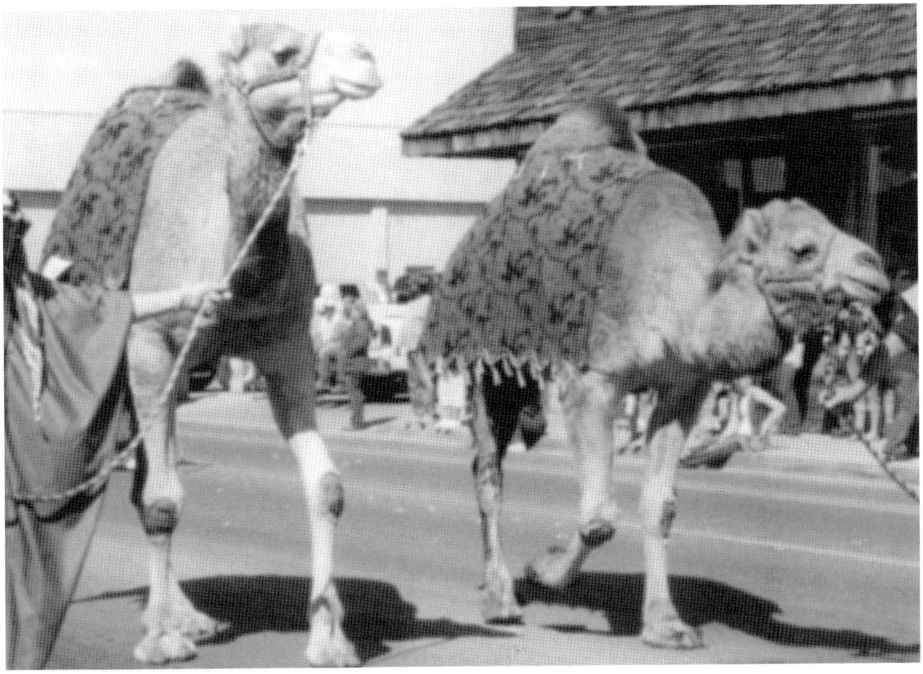

James Wilson Davis

Were camels ever in the Buckeye Valley? A story written by I.H. "Uncle Hi" Parkman from *Old Timer Tales* in 1972 discusses the camels:

> In the early 1870s, James Wilson Davis, from Denton County, Texas, had been hearing about a wonderful little valley, west of Phoenix, along the road to Yuma that was as flat as a floor. It was described as being covered with mesquite trees as much as three feet thick through the base, and waist-high grass in abundance. Since his lease on a south side farm in Phoenix was about to expire, Jim Davis decided to take his family with dairy cows and settle on some of that rich land. In 1878, he moved into this little paradise and made camp at the base of a large malpai rock mesa, about half a mile southeast of the present Arlington schoolhouse. The Davises let the cows roam around during the day to feed on grass and mesquite beans and corralled them at night. Butter and cheese were made from the milk. Once or twice a month, Davis would pack a load on the back of a horse, get on a saddle pony, and lead the pack horse to Phoenix. There, he traded his merchandise for such things as his family needed. The trip would take three or four days. One day, Davis ran into five camels while rounding up his cattle. As the humpbacked animals kept hanging around and seemed quite tame, he caught a gentle one, a female, and led her home for his wife and children to see. He conceived the idea of using her to carry his butter and cheese to Phoenix. In two days, he was back home. The camels had been brought from Africa to the United States under an 1855 act of Congress. On May 1, 1856, a ship arrived on the coast of Texas with 33 Bactrian camels and dromedaries. The camels were turned over to Lt. Edward F. Beale, who made the trip to Arizona in 1857. Due to tender-footed reasons, the experiment was pronounced a failure. The camels were turned loose on the desert near Yuma to fend for themselves. Many of them wandered up the Gila River and it was from this bunch that Davis picked up his camel. The Davis family moved back to Phoenix in 1879.

Were the camels in the 2006 Pioneer Days Parade (pictured) decedents of those in the book *The Last Camel Charge*, by Forrest Bryant Johnson? (Courtesy of author.)

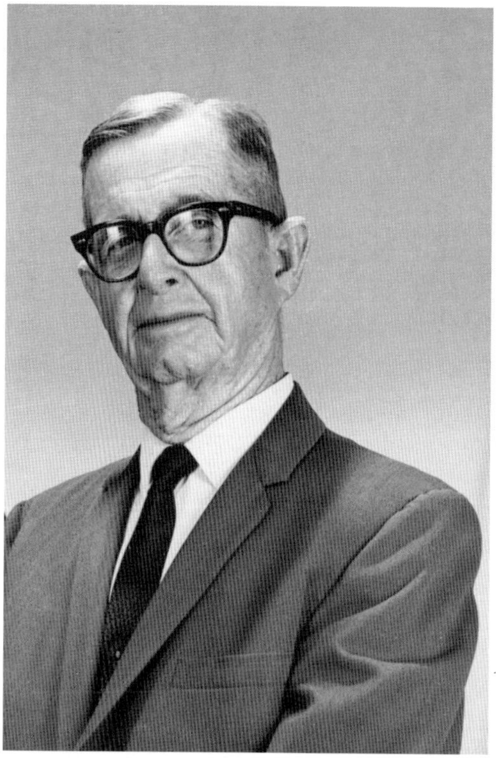

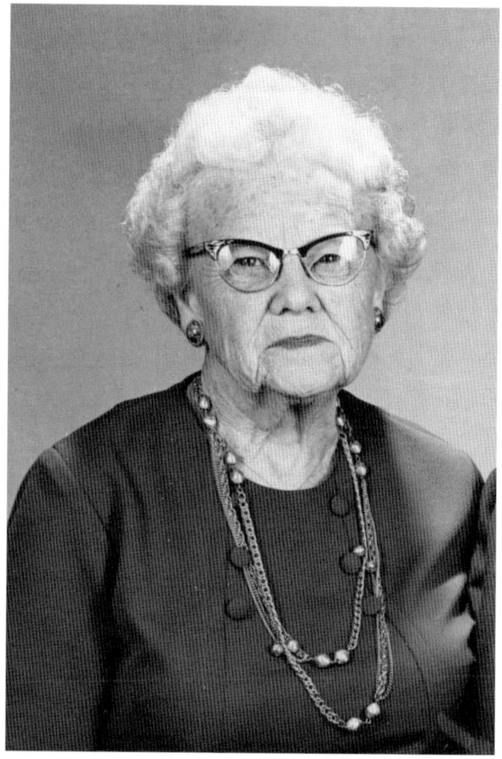

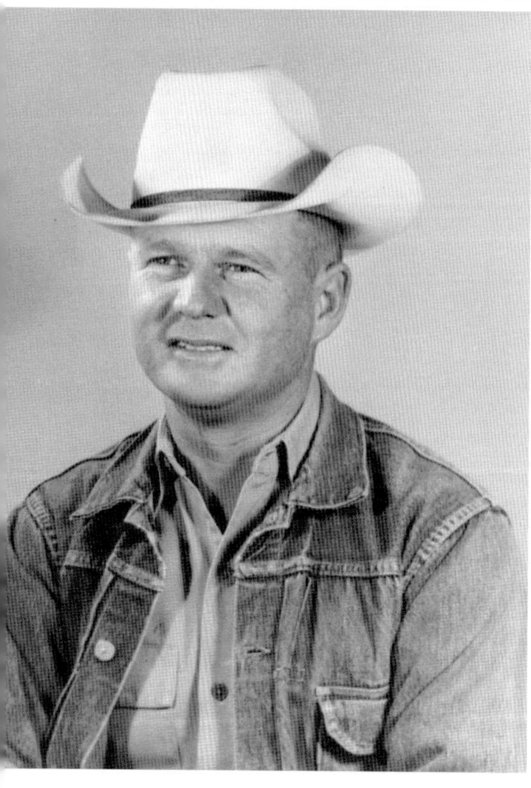

Marshall Long Sr., Neva Long, and Marshall Long Jr.

William B. Long and Nellie (Hurley) Long homesteaded the Long Bros. Farms when he began taming 160 desert acres in 1890. The Long Bros. Farm & Dairy marked the site of the Long's Hotel, Livery Stable, and Blacksmith Shop, built in 1908 near Centre and First Streets. The couple had five sons and one daughter. In 1913, Nevada "Neva" Mae Miller (above, right) and her family, from Nebraska, settled in the desert north of Buckeye. In 1915, she became an operator for Mountain States Telephone & Telegraph Company in Buckeye. On January 7, 1920, Neva Miller married Marshall Long Sr. (above, left) at Saint Mary's Catholic Church in Phoenix.

In the following years, Marshall Long Sr. and his only son, Marshall Jr., expanded the farm by adding sheep, chickens, feeder cattle, hogs, milk cows, and peacocks. Marshall Jr. (left) became an avid collector of antiques. Buckeye citizens through the years enjoyed his collections. Buckeye lost three wonderful citizens when Marshall Jr. died in 1973, Marshall Sr. passed away in 1976, and Neva died in 1985. (All, courtesy of Buckeye Museum.)

Isaac Hiram Parkman

The branch of the Parkman clan responsible for the writing of *Old-Timer Tales* had its origin with a rural wedding in the hollows of central Tennessee shortly after the Civil War. Isaac Parkman was the youngest. Before he was six months old, his father loaded his family of seven children into a covered wagon and headed for Hickory County, Missouri. After eight years there, the mother contracted tuberculosis. It was decided to take her to Carthage, 100 miles south, while the father stayed on the farm. After about a month, the mother died. In 1893, a family member went to Arizona, and letters arrived in Carthage telling about frontier wonders. Soon, Isaac (pictured) came to Arizona. In 1900, he married a Mesa girl, Amy Stewart, and went to work for a well-known cowman on the banks of the Hassayampa River. After moving from place to place, he bought 80 acres and went into farming. He served his community as school trustee, notary public, deputy tax assessor, postmaster, and justice of the peace. "Uncle Hi" was instrumental with others in organizing the Palo Verde Baptist Church in 1903 and the Buckeye & West Gila Valley Old Settlers Union in 1934. He was the founder of the Buckeye Archeological and Historical Museum in 1952 and was voted Buckeye Valley's Man of the Year that same year. Parkman was a steady contributor to the *Buckeye Valley News*, beginning with the third issue, and he contributed hundreds of articles to the *Arizona Farmer-Ranchman*. He researched and compiled the first *History of the Buckeye Canal* around 1957. Uncle Hi died on November 23, 1972, three weeks before *Old Timer Tales* was published. (Courtesy of Buckeye Museum.)

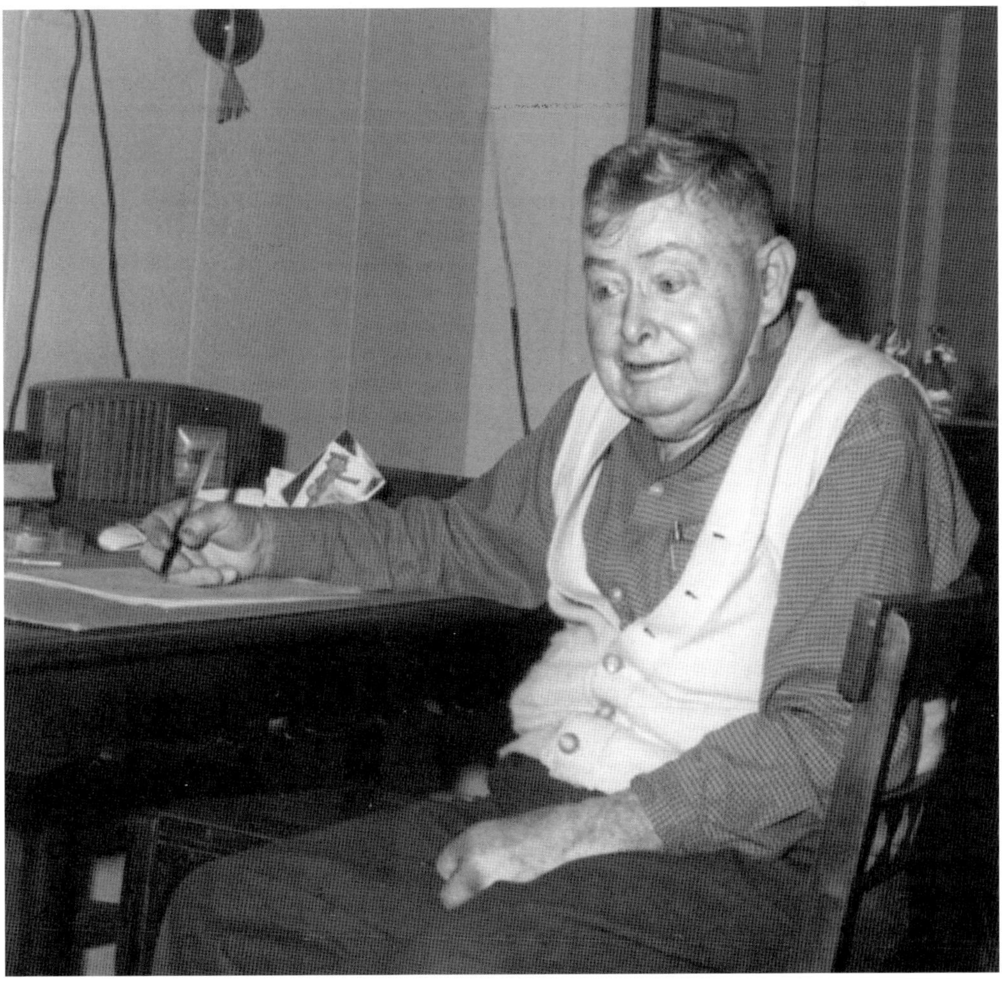

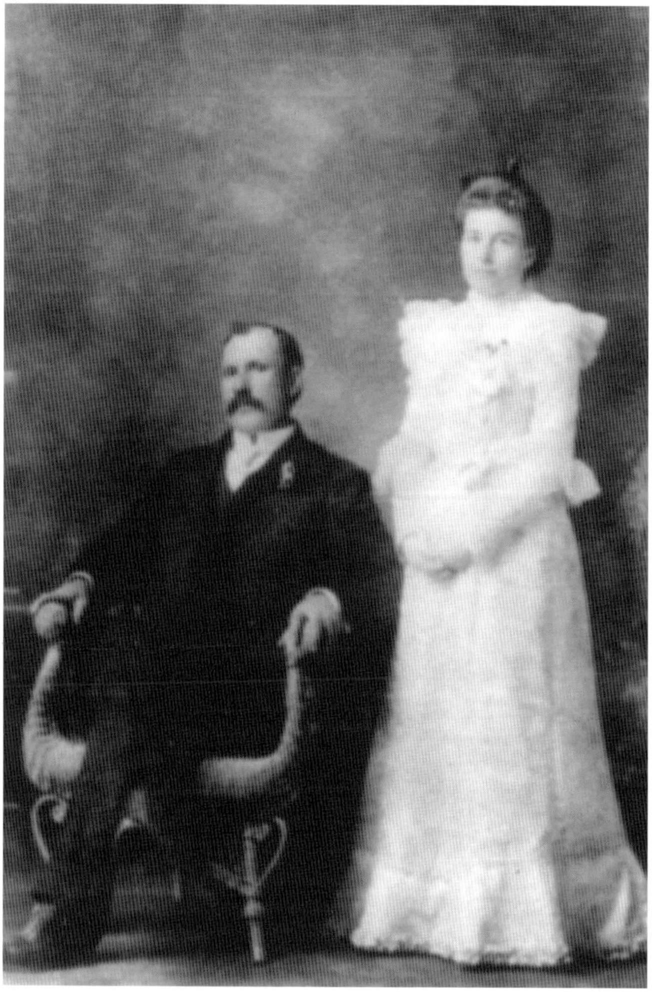

Nathaniel and Lee Annie Sanders

Nathaniel "Nate" Anthony Sanders was born on September 11, 1868, in Harrison, Arkansas. He was the 10th child born to James L. Sanders (1827–1874) and Anna Roy (1831–1872) in Pope County, Arkansas. He was orphaned as a child and raised by his Uncle John H. Roy and his wife in Harrison. In 1887, Nate Sanders came to a growing area called Phoenix, Arizona (about 4,500 people). On November 17, 1901, he married Lee Annie Charlton in Glendale. In Liberty, Sanders purchased a 320-acre farm and cattle ranch. The Sanderses were in the cattle and farming business at this location for 23 years. Lee Annie and Nathaniel had eight daughters in Liberty. Family legend has it that Nate named each of the not-yet-born children George Washington in hopes of having a son. Instead, the first grandson was named George. In 1908, Nate and Lee invited neighbors to their home for ice cream and cake and discussed the need for a church in Liberty. Largely due to the efforts of Nate Sanders, the Methodist church was organized around 1909 and established just west of Liberty School. A prime mover in Democratic Party politics, Nate Sanders served as chairman of the Maricopa County Democratic Committee. In other significant achievements, he participated in the removal of the state capital from Prescott to Phoenix. For a number of years, he was president of the Buckeye Irrigation Co. and served on the Liberty School Board. The Sanders family moved back to Phoenix in 1927. Nate Sanders died on June 9, 1937. Lee Annie (Charlton) Sanders died on November 28, 1952. (Courtesy of Kellie [Cambron] Haworth.)

Dr. George C. Rubel

One of the well-known doctors in the Buckeye Valley was George Rubel, who came to the valley with his family in 1912. He homesteaded two miles north of Palo Verde. In 1918, Dr. Rubel moved his family and house to Buckeye, at 213 East Monroe Avenue. George Rubel, as doctors did in those days, made house calls, traveling by horse and buggy from Liberty to Arlington. The average fee for prenatal care and home delivery of a baby was $25. The Bill Kaufman family, plus many others, remember office calls, which usually cost $1. Dr. Rubel was the second mayor of Buckeye, from 1933 to 1937. He is pictured here around 1935, dressed for Buckeye Helzapoppin Days. Dr. Rubel continued his practice in Buckeye until his death in 1945 at age 70. He had a hobby of drawing trees and other vegetation. In the 1930s, he developed a nursery, which is still growing on Baseline Road, north of the canal and east of Apache Road. (Courtesy of Buckeye Museum.)

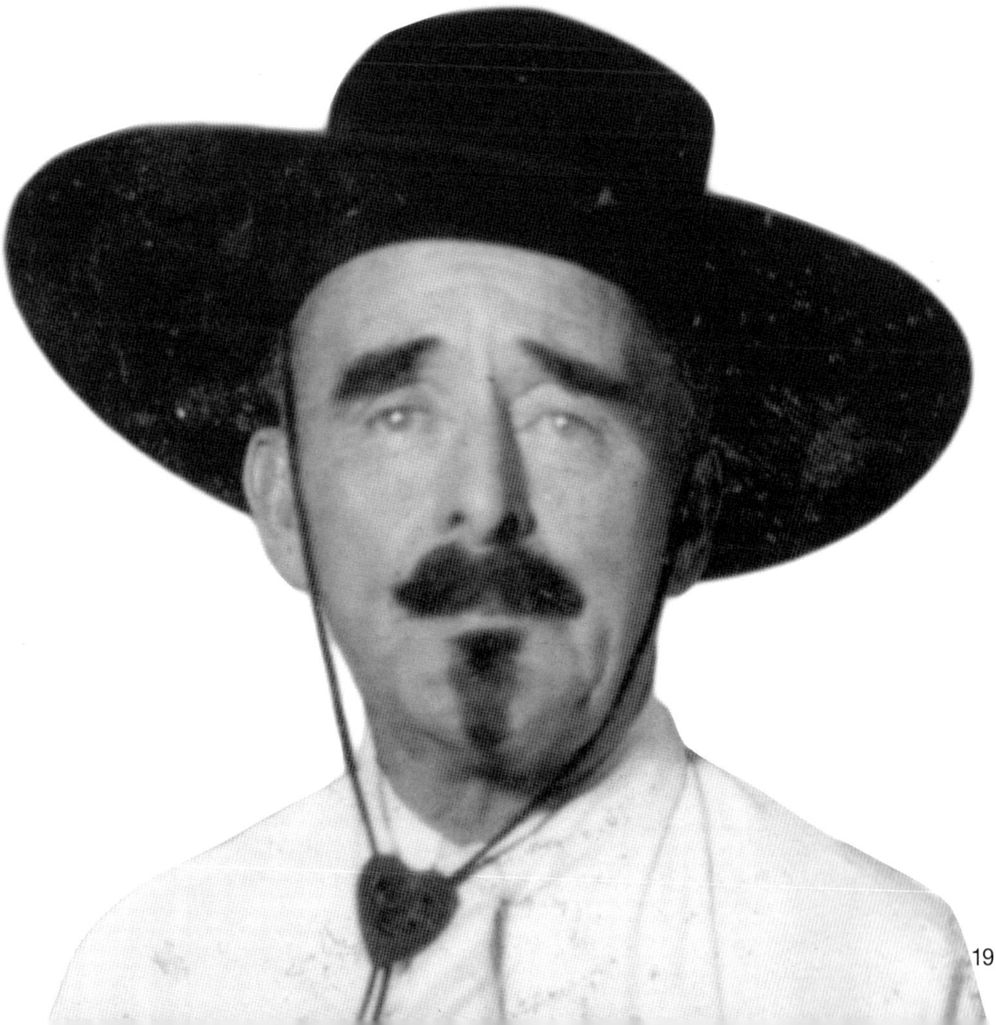

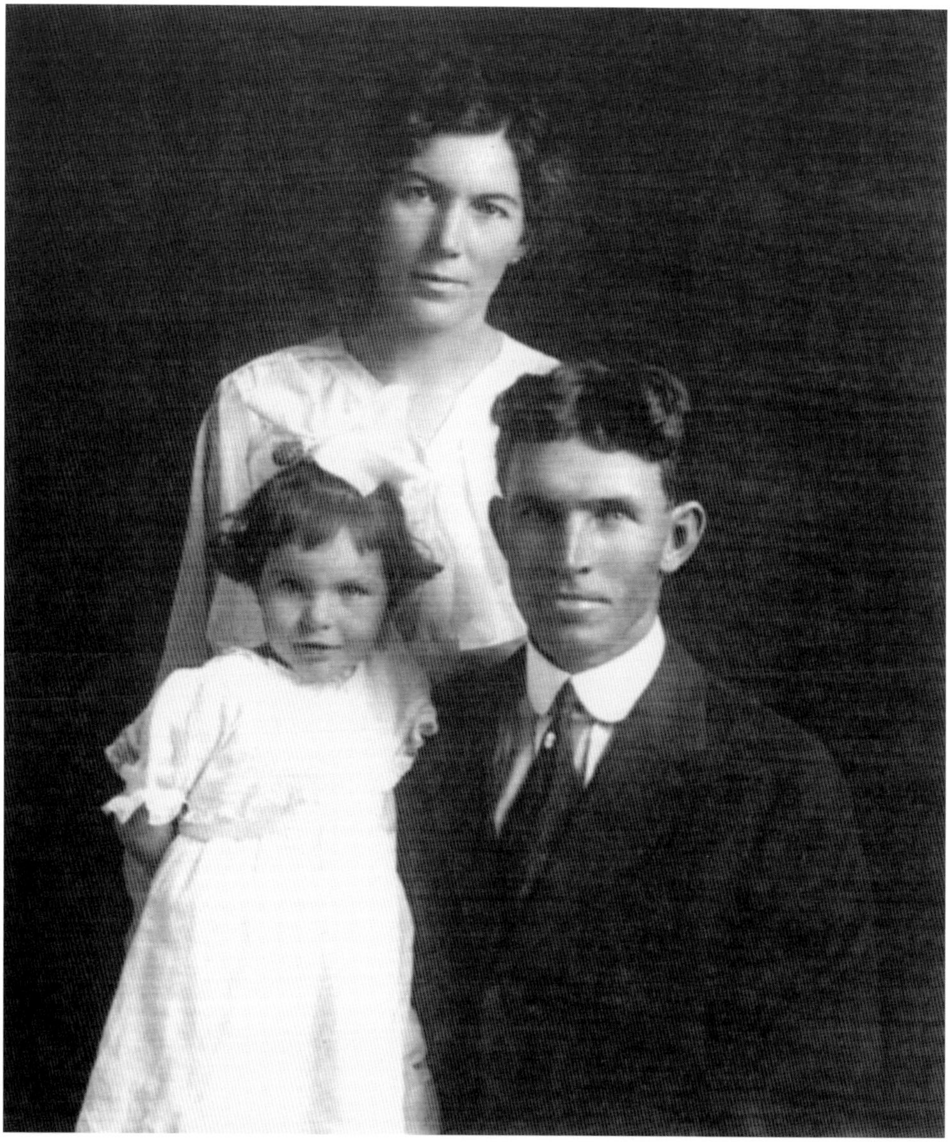

John and Loretta Beloat
John Beloat, one of 14 children, was born in 1892 to Bob and Mary Elizabeth (Wright) Beloat in Liberty. John purchased the only meat market in the valley early in 1913 from J.E. Wish and, a few weeks later, purchased a Ford Runabout to deliver fresh meat. Loretta Parker, one of 12 children, was born in Palo Verde in 1893 to Charles and Jane Parker. John and Loretta were married at the home of her parents on April 23, 1913. The *Buckeye Valley News* reported on April 17, 1913, the approaching marriage of the couple, who announced a public dance in the Joslin Hall (3H Mercantile Building) for the wedding. The *Valley News* of April 24, 1913, carried a detailed account of the wedding. The Beloats moved to Buckeye in 1958, becoming active residents of the town. John was elected to the town council and served as mayor (1961–1962). He was also a life member of the Odd Fellows Lodge, active in the Cattlemen's Association, and served on the Arizona Livestock Board. He died in 1977 at the age of 85. Loretta served as president of both the Buckeye and Liberty Woman's Clubs. She died in 1978 at the age of 84. Their daughter, Alberta (Beloat) Bales, is pictured here with them. (Courtesy of Barbara [Sanders] Bales.)

CHAPTER TWO

Military and Law

In 2008, the Buckeye Elks Lodge sponsored an Americanism Essay Contest. A Palo Verde Elementary School sixth-grade student, Sarah Rohrback, submitted her entry, "What Is an American?" Her Americanism essay can be summarized in this way: An American is someone who is an American citizen, someone who has freedom, and someone who is thankful to be an American.

This chapter recognizes military and law-enforcement legends. People such as John C. Butler, Charlie Post, Al Makin, Bill Meck, and Eldon Towner did much for the town. Residents should not forget those who served and gave their lives. The Vietnam Traveling Memorial Wall and Benbow Veterans Memorial Park provide remembrances. Buckeye is grateful for all of its veterans.

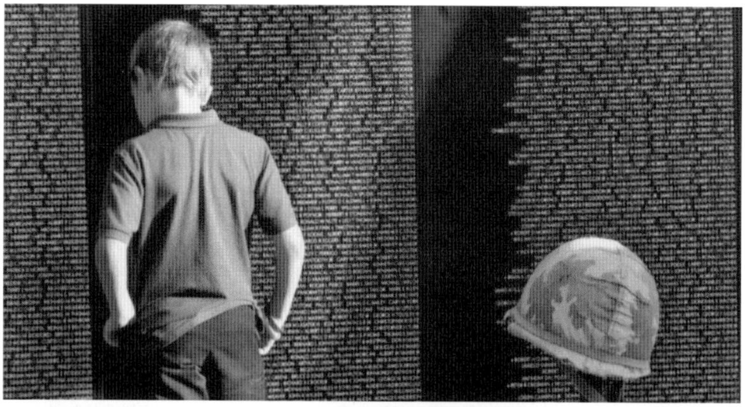

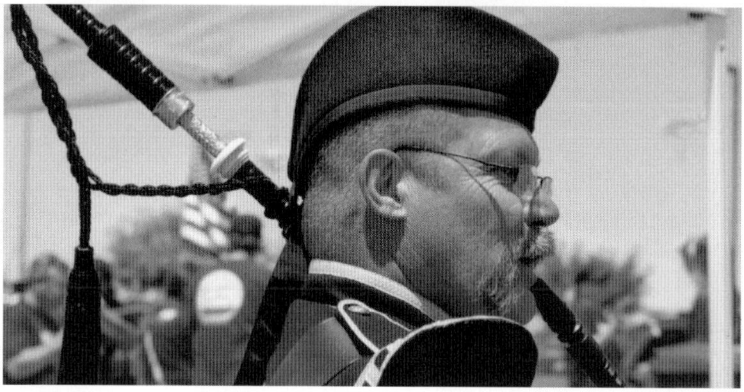

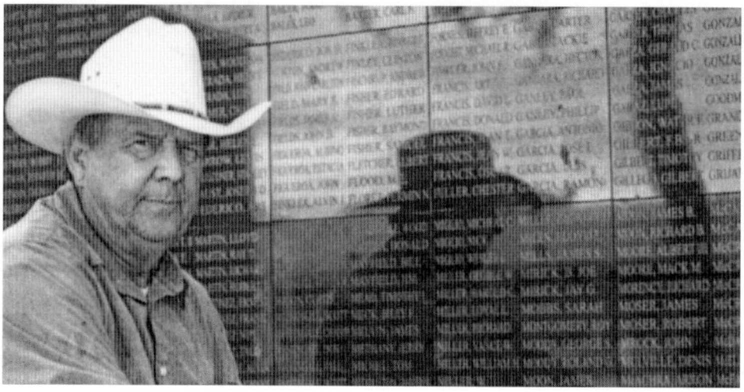

Traveling Tribute and Memorial Park

The Vietnam Traveling Memorial Wall came to Buckeye on May 9–12, 2013. At top, Liam Henry, son of Russell and Susi Henry, reads the wall. The local young men that died during this conflict are as follows: James Dale Laser of Arlington, US Navy; Donald Robert Elmore of Buckeye, US Marine Corps; Geronimo Lerma of Buckeye, US Army; Allen Theodore Makin II of Buckeye, US Army; Herman Serna of Buckeye, US Army; and Darrel Monroe Pickett of Buckeye, US Army.

The memorial wall at Benbow Veterans Memorial Park lists 950 Buckeye veterans who served in the military. Mike Malcolm (middle) plays tributes on the bagpipe. Ron Noble (bottom), of Main Street Coalition, organized the May 9, 2012, dedication event. An Honor Roll booklet, titled "On the Land, in the Air and at Sea" was published in 1944. It listed Buckeye Valley men and women in the armed forces of the United States. These booklets are treasured today by many Buckeye families. (All, courtesy of author.)

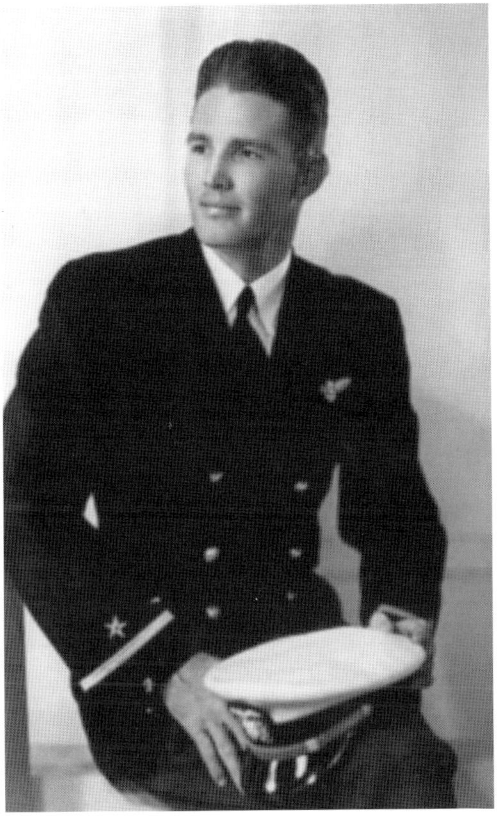

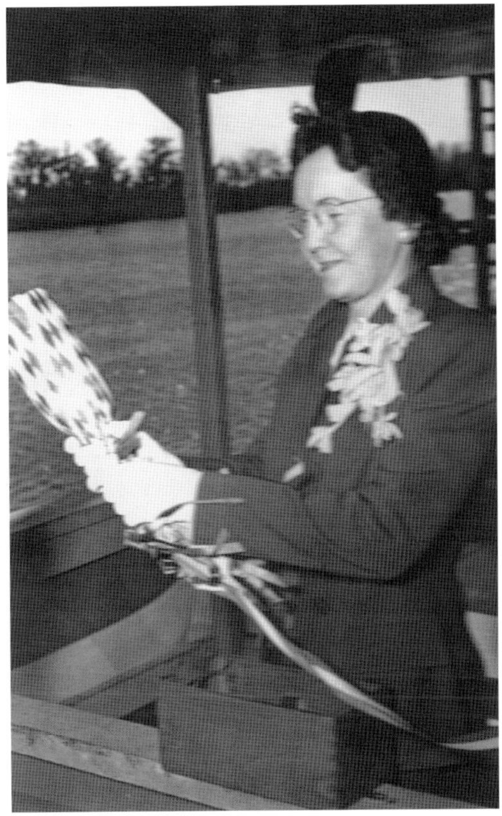

John Clarence Butler

John Butler (above, left) was born on February 2, 1921, in Liberty to Walter and Irene (Beloat) Butler. He enlisted in the Navy Reserves in February 1941 and was appointed aviation cadet on April 3. After flight training, Butler reported to Bombing Squadron III on the carrier USS *Yorktown*. In the Battle of the Midway, on June 4, 1942, Butler and his squadron attacked a Japanese carrier group and, despite heavy opposition, succeeded in sinking three of the vital enemy flattops. His plane, however, did not return. Butler was declared "lost in action" on June 5, 1942. For his part in this gallant attack, which did much to turn the tide of the war in the Pacific, Ensign Butler was posthumously awarded the Navy Cross. The citation noted: "His gallant intrepidity and loyal devotion contributed in large measure to the success achieved by our forces and were in keeping with the highest traditions of the United States Naval Service." Butler's exploits in the Battle of Midway led him to be highly decorated and to have a ship, the *John C. Butler*, named for him. The ship was christened by his mother, Irene, in 1944 (above, right). Buckeye's American Legion Hazelton-Butler Post No. 53 is named for John C. Butler. Recently, Buckeye Municipal Airport officially dedicated the airfield as Ens. John C. Butler Memorial Field. (Both, courtesy of Leslie [Butler] Krumtinger.)

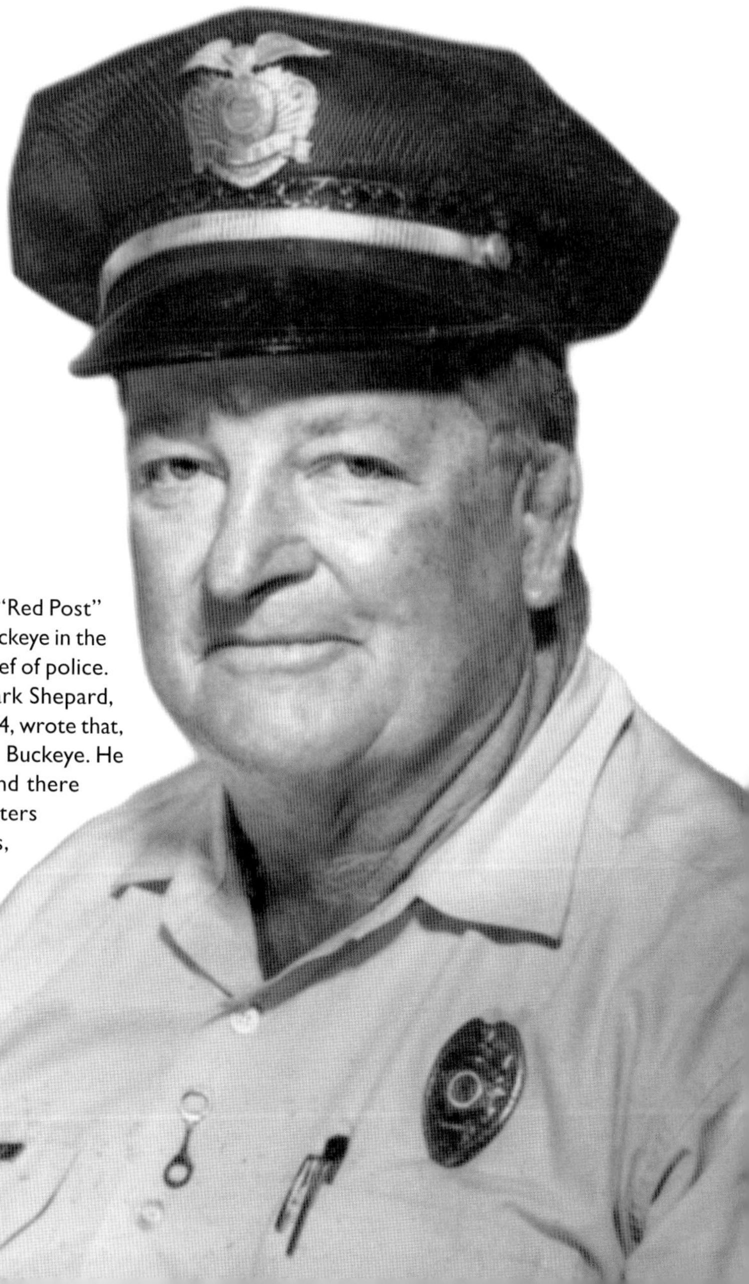

Charlie Post
A professional wrestler named "Red Post" from New York City came to Buckeye in the early 1950s and became the chief of police. His name was Charlie Post. Mark Shepard, *Buckeye Valley News* editor in 1994, wrote that, in the 1960s, Post was the law in Buckeye. He and one patrolman did it all, and there were some pretty tough characters around at the time. In the 1960s, teenagers would drive up and down Monroe Avenue and turn garbage cans upside down. Chief Post would slip up behind one of the boys and toss him into the garbage can—justice was served. (Courtesy of author.)

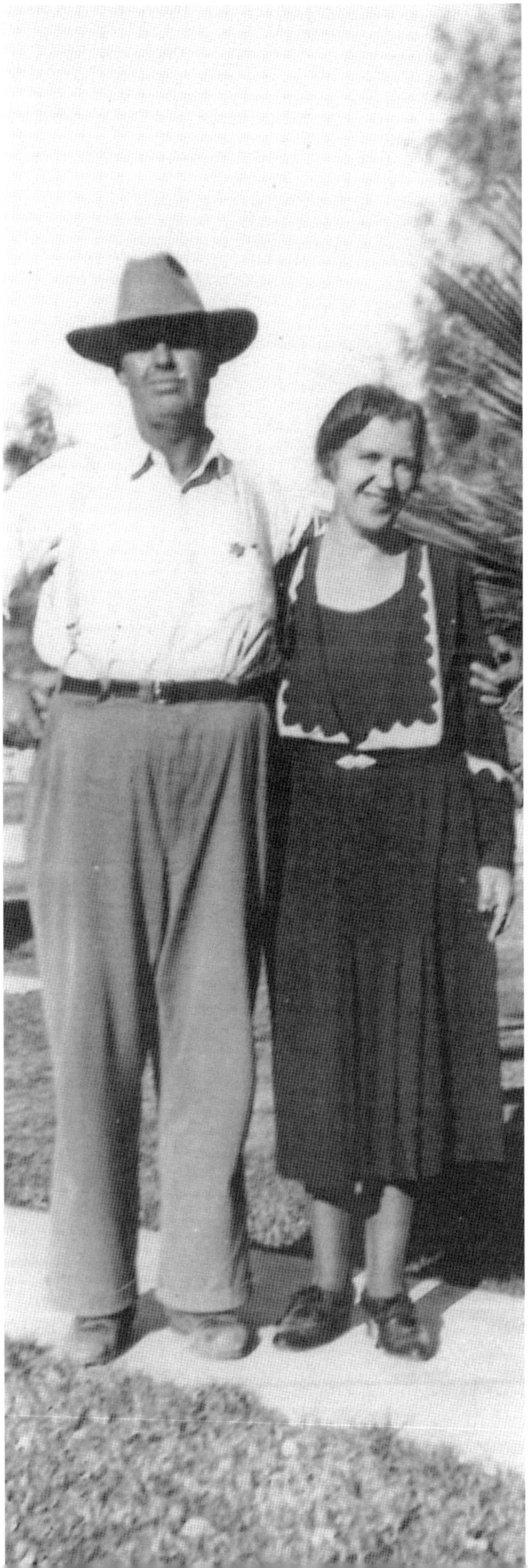

Allen (Al) Makin

In 1920, Al Makin moved his family to Buckeye after securing a job with Webster's Creamery. His job was to pick up cream from farmers and haul it to the creamery in Phoenix. His territory included the farmers from Liberty to Arlington. It was said that he was so strong he could pick up a 10-gallon can of cream in each hand and load them into the back of the truck. People soon nicknamed him "Big Al." When Al and Florence moved to Buckeye with their five children, Mark, Alice, Edith, Florence, and Margaret, there was no available housing. They purchased a tent and camping equipment and made a temporary home under a tree at the edge of the Butler Elementary School (BES) yard. A house became available next door to the H.E. Kell's Mercantile Store on Centre Street. Everyone encouraged Al Makin to go into politics and run for constable. Al was a Republican in a Democratic state. He ran and won, becoming one of two Republicans elected in the whole state. He was also a deputy sheriff in Maricopa County. Beginning around 1930, and for the next 20 years, he kept law and order in the town of Buckeye and surrounding vicinity. Al Makin was a gentle but a firm man, as many teenagers found out. When Buckeye obtained a fire engine, all the firemen were volunteers. The town needed a system to alert firemen in the case of a fire. Makin came to the rescue. From his days working for the creamery, he knew where everyone lived. So, when a fire broke out, residents called his home. He decided that three rapid pistol shots would signal a fire. Al taught his wife, Florence, how to shoot a pistol. When three rapid shots were fired, volunteers called, and Florence would relay the fire's location. If Al was home, he would go to the fire station and there relay the message. Al Makin passed away on his 62nd birthday. Florence was appointed to finish out his term after his death, and she became the first woman constable of Buckeye. Al and Florence Makin pose here in 1939. (Courtesy of Jo Anne [Makin] Van Liere.)

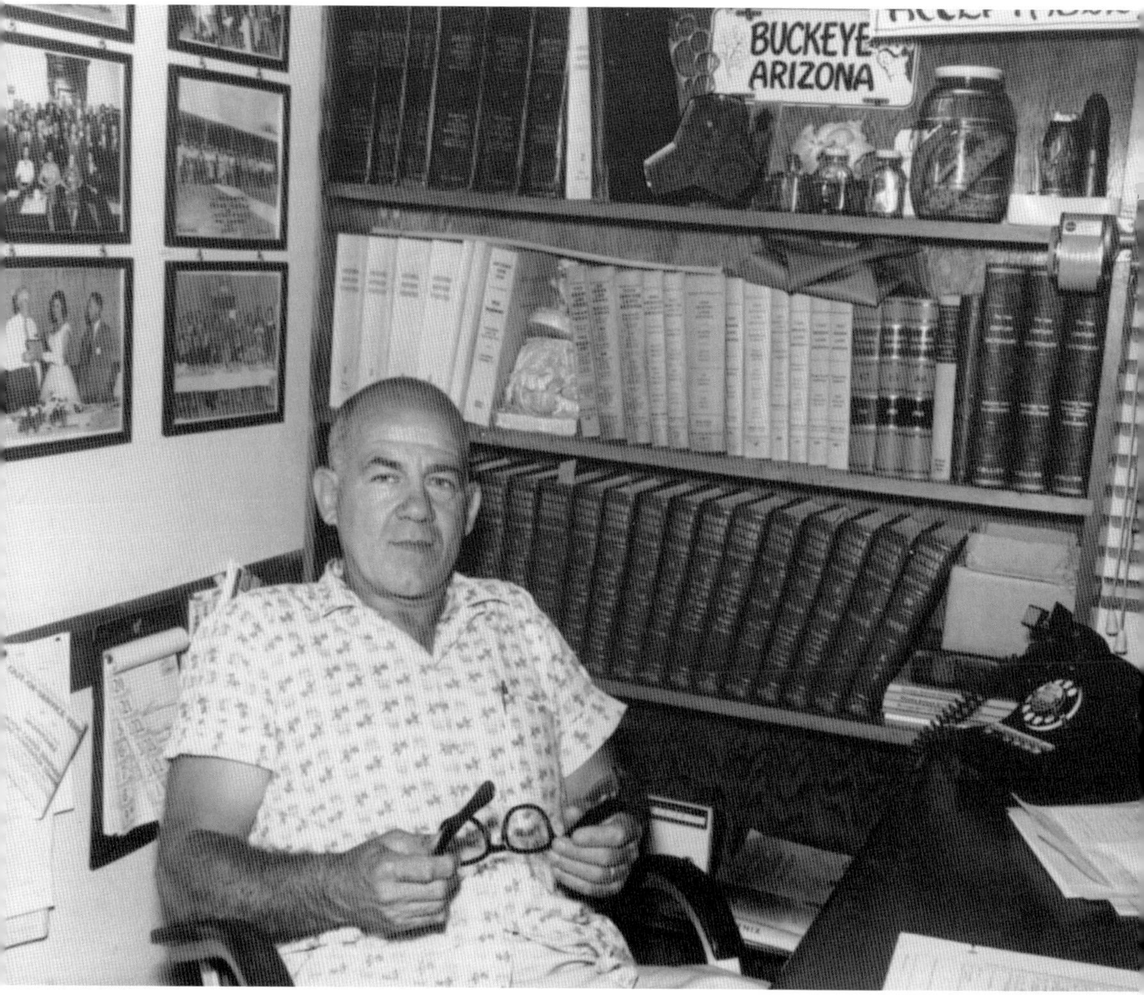

Bill Meck

Judge Bill Meck was widely known as "Law West of the Agua Fria." The precinct embraced most of Maricopa County on the sunset side of the Agua Fria River. Meck, ex–prize fighter and farmhand, ran for office in 1946 because a German shell in Italy had given him a weak leg that made him unfit for hard labor. Billy said, "I didn't know anything more about law than a snake knows about a left uppercut." He prepared himself by reading manuals on how to operate as a justice of the peace and took his responsibilities seriously. In all proceedings, he enforced strict order, with no one speaking without permission. He wore out two or three gavels. One time, a dispute got completely out of hand in spite of all he could do. Wearily, Meck sat back and listened to accusations and contradictions shouted by the residents of a cotton camp where several persons had been hurt in a free-for-all. "And you know," he smiled, "in a few minutes I had the whole story, just the way it happened. Since then I don't stop arguments; I start 'em going." He was Buckeye Valley Chamber of Commerce Man of the Year in 1969. With a booming voice, Bill Meck was the announcer at local parades and Fourth of July celebrations. Halloween Carnival signs were done in his distinguished writing style. Buckeye lost an outstanding citizen with his death on January 1, 1970. (Courtesy of author.)

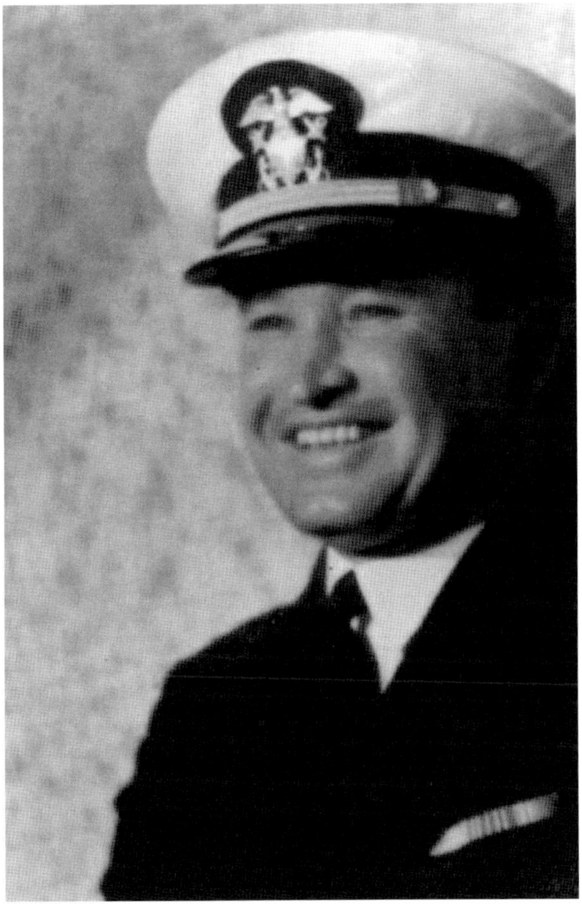

Eldon Towner
Eldon Hillyer Towner was born in Buckeye on April 21, 1914. The Towner family had relocated to Buckeye from Oregon around 1910. Eldon's father, Carl, and grandfather Hillyer each had 160 acres located at what is now the southeast corner of Apache Road and Monroe Avenue. Eldon attended Buckeye Elementary School. In 1922, the wanderlust again struck the Towner families, and they left for Southern California. In 1928, the folks who had bought the Towner holdings could no longer make the payments, and they gave the land back to them. Eldon, by this time a teenager, would accompany his father and worked many summers at the ranch, driving a team of mules and windrower, retrieving newly mown hay from the field. He never forgot the climate shock of trying to sleep in screened-in rooms during Arizona summers, with wet sheets hung and hoping for a good breeze. Trips across a board highway west of Yuma, back and forth to California, were remembered. The board highway had only one lane, with turnarounds every two miles. Eldon Towner graduated from USC, passed the California bar exam, then took a job with the Traveler's Insurance Company. Towner's time with Traveler's provided him the opportunity to meet a "dark-haired beauty," Elsie Mae Short. After December 7, 1941, Towner was assigned to the Office of Naval Intelligence in the Los Angeles area. Elsie Short and Eldon Towner reconnected and were married in March 1945. Together, they made the decision to relocate to Buckeye. Eldon rented office space for a law practice. Today, the space is the Buckeye Elks Lodge. Eldon and J.D. "Clyde" Wilson combined their practices. Wilson & Towner, Attorneys at Law, moved into their office at Third Street and Monroe Avenue. Eldon Towner served as Buckeye's town attorney beginning in the early 1950s until 1983, when he retired. He was active in Hazelton-Butler Post 53 of the American Legion and the Rotary Club. Buckeye lost Towner on January 16, 1986, when he passed away. (Courtesy of Bob Towner.)

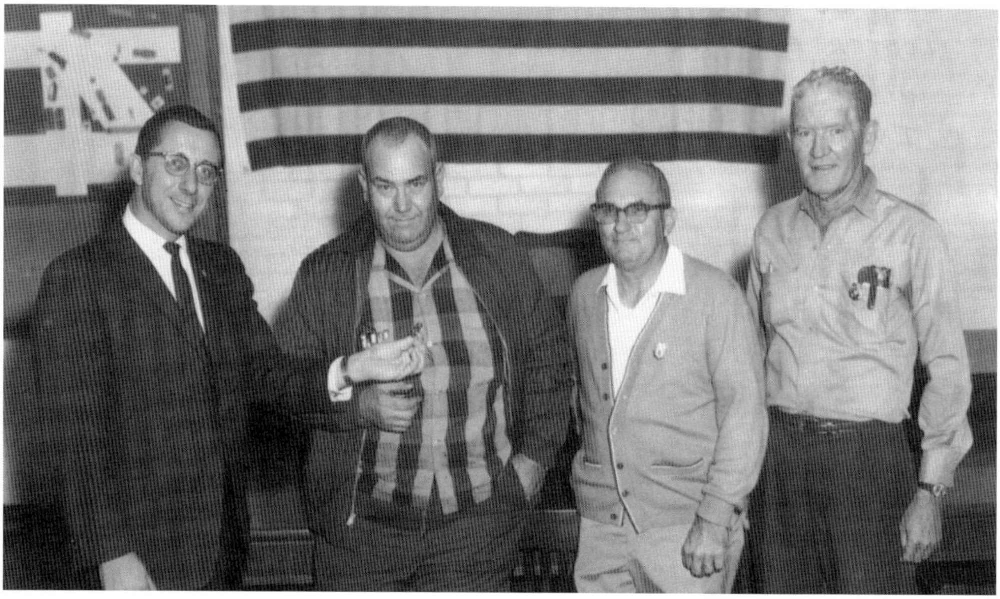

Buckeye Fire Department

Beginning around 1940, service for the Buckeye Fire Department was provided by volunteers. They rushed to calls when the downtown siren sounded. As seen in the above photograph, in 1966, three volunteers received 25-year pins from Mayor Bob Bonnes (left). Those retiring were Lester Currens (second from left), Wilbur Weigold (third from left), and Ivan Hendrick (right). Records indicate that the volunteer fire department began in 1936. The transition from an all-volunteer department to one manned by career firefighters took place in 1999–2000. The nonvolunteer department, Buckeye Fire-Medical Rescue, is under the leadership of Capt. Bob Costello (below). As of 2014, the department has 88 sworn fire personnel. Captain Costello came to Buckeye in July 2004 and has been the fire chief since 2007. In 2012, he was inducted into the Arizona Fire Service Hall of Fame. (Above, courtesy of Buckeye Museum; below, courtesy of author.)

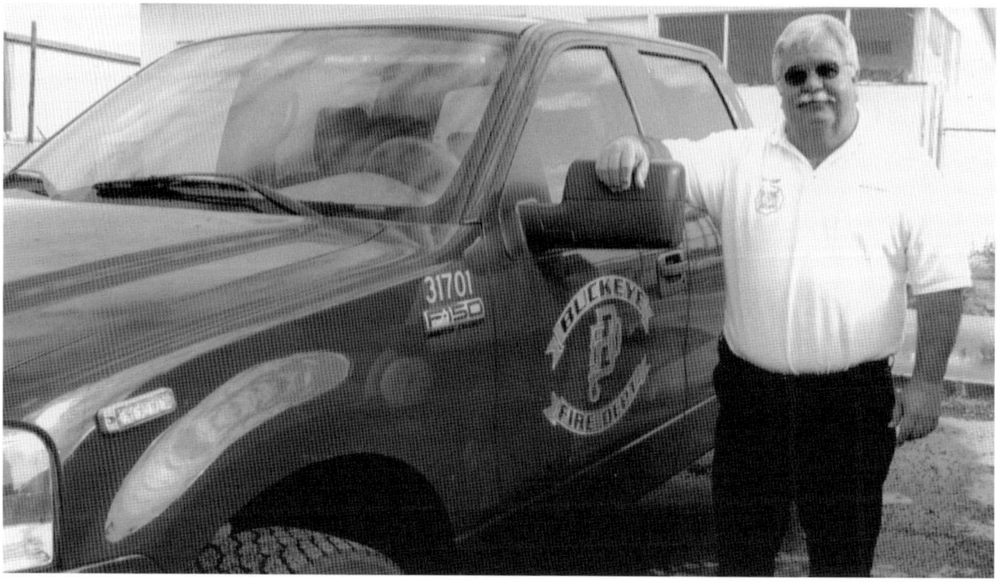

CHAPTER THREE

A Growing Community

Founded in 1888 and incorporated in 1929 as a 440-acre town, Buckeye had a land area of 660 square miles in 2014, making it, geographically, the largest city in Arizona. While driving around the valley, folks often ask "Where am I?" and "I remember when so-and-so lived there" and "That's where so-and-so lived." On an October 2014 drive around town, former resident Kemp Biddulph identified homes from days past, occupied by families such as the Bartyllas, Aulwurms, Sissons, Loudermilks, Ames, and Van Denburghs. Many of Buckeye's roads are named for pioneers and families. Never to be forgotten are the following names: Amabisca, Beloat, Bruner, Butler, Clanton, Dean, Fisher, Hazen, Jackson, Johnson, Mahoney, Miller, Monroe, Narramore, Patterson, Roberts, Rooks, Rovey, Shepard, South, Thayer, Turner, Watkins, and Watson. Yet another remembered aspect is Jackrabbit Trail. Was it named after fast-moving creatures that ran through the desert environment before houses were built?

***Buckeye Valley News* Publishers**

The *Buckeye Valley News* has had 18 different publishers. It folded three times in a 114-year span, but the paper is still here! History has been told and preserved. The paper's publishers, along with the ownership time span and the paper's name during that tenure, are as follows: Park Richards Mitten (1912–1926), *Buckeye Valley News;* William Ryan, George Corn, Harold Wrenn, and Miller Cattle Co. (1926–1932), *Buckeye Review Years;* Otto Paulson (1933–1950), *Buckeye Valley News;* Charles Crouch (1950–1951), *Buckeye Valley News;* Paul Hieronymus (1951–1952), *Buckeye Valley News;* Lyall Dawkins (pictured) (1952–1961), *Buckeye Valley News;* Ted Mauntz (1961–1963), *Buckeye Valley News;* Richard David (1963–1966), *Buckeye Valley News;* Lyall Dawkins (1966–1968), *Buckeye Valley News;* Mark Shepard (1968–1990), *Buckeye Valley News;* Tom Thompson (1990–1992), *Buckeye Valley News;* Steve Morris (1992), *Buckeye Valley News;* Sharon Butler (1992–2006), *Buckeye Valley News;* Mark Shepard (2007–2009), *Buckeye Valley News;* and Marlene Turner (2010–present), *Buckeye Valley News.* The longest-serving publisher was Mark Shepard (25 years). (Courtesy of *Buckeye Valley News.*)

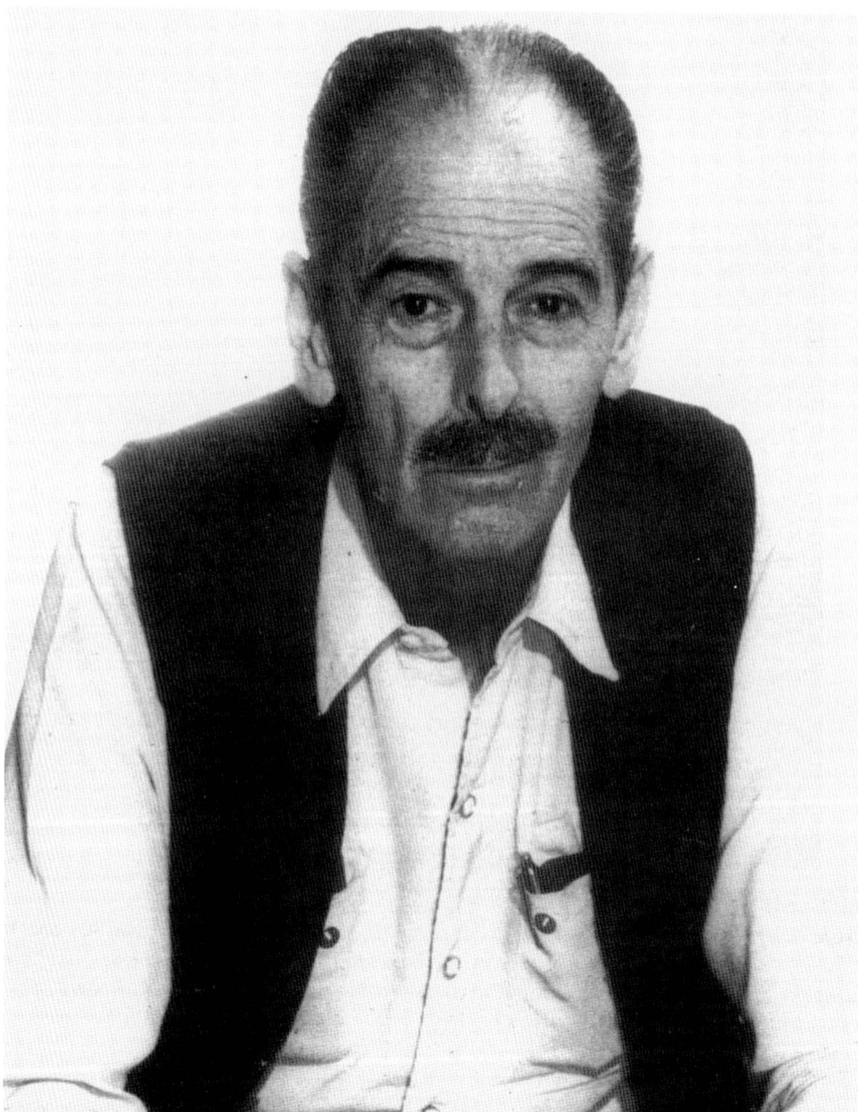

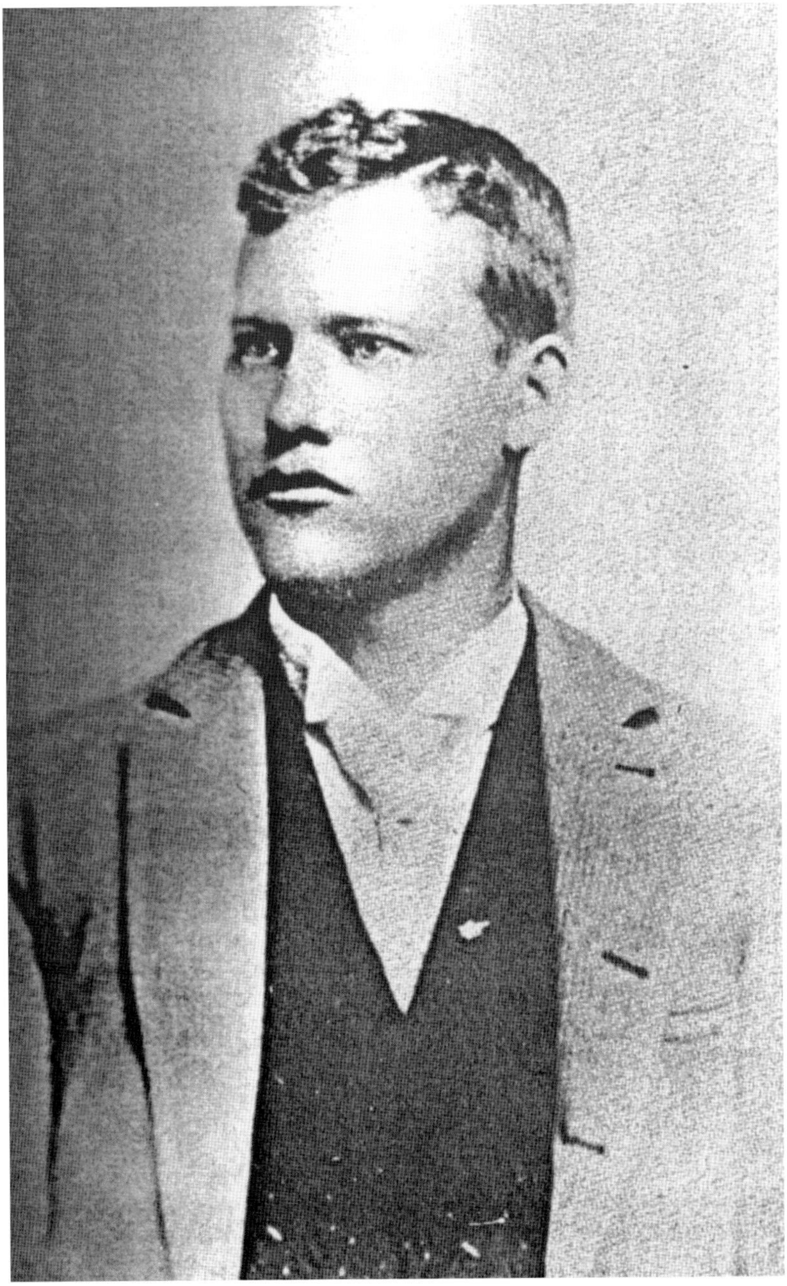

Park Richards Mitten

The *Buckeye Valley News* was 100 years old on February 12, 2012, making it older than Arizona. In 1890, Thomas Schultz started the first newspaper in the Buckeye Valley, the *Buckeye Blade*. The newspaper lasted 42 weeks, and then, as a result of some businesses being destroyed by flood, the newspaper folded. In 1912, Park Mitten (pictured) came to the Buckeye area. He decided to start another newspaper, the *Buckeye Valley News*. The *News* served the area under the direction of Mitten until 1923, when he moved his presses and equipment to Chandler, Arizona. He continued to publish from Chandler by correspondence. By 1926, subscriptions dropped and changes began happening. (Courtesy of *Buckeye Valley News*.)

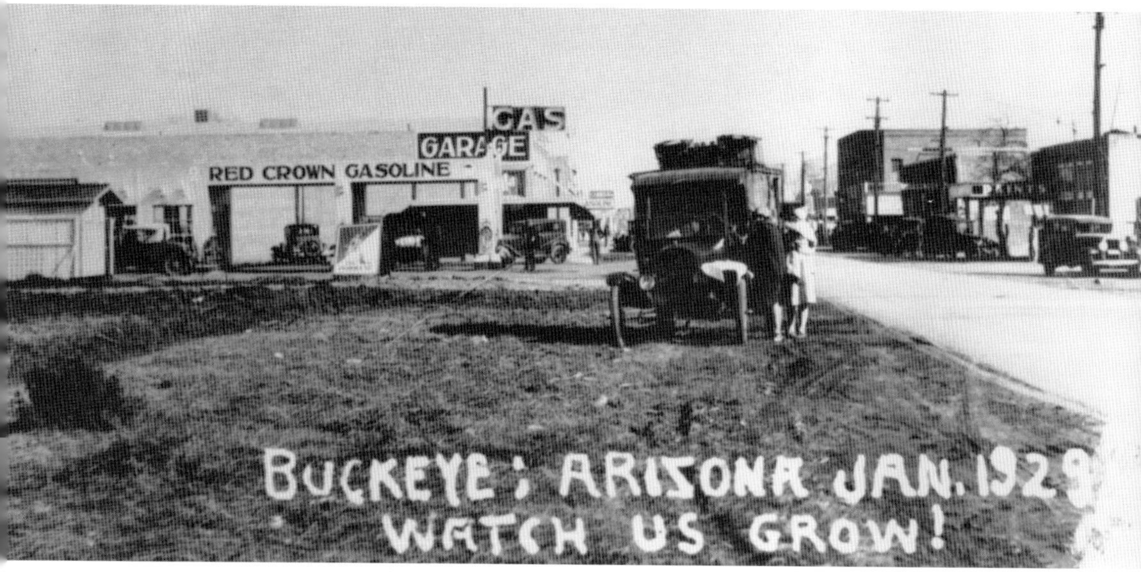

Buckeye Mayors Watson and Meck

"Watch Us Grow!" was the mantra of Buckeye, Arizona, at the time of the above photograph, taken in January 1929. The town of Buckeye was incorporated on May 8, 1929, with Hugh M. Watson as the first mayor. On January 13, 2014, a transition was celebrated by citizens and city officials as the "CITY" portion of the new city hall sign was unveiled in downtown Buckeye (below). The city of Buckeye's mayor, Jackie Meck (standing, third from left), thanked generations of the community as well as previous town officials, whose work would be continued by future leaders. Meck stated that the city was no longer in the shadows and in fact was working to create shadows of its own. (Above, courtesy of Buckeye Museum; below, courtesy of author.)

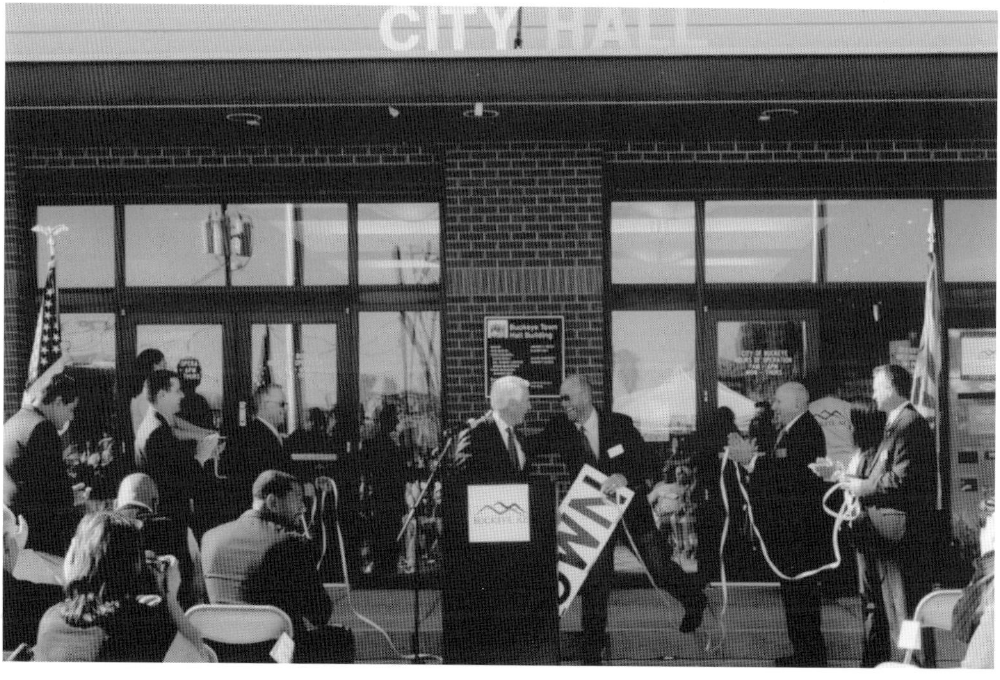

Ben Youngker Sr. Family

"Bennie" Youngker Sr. was one of Buckeye's early pioneers. He cleared and leveled the desert terrain, drilled wells in order to spring up life where it had not existed before, and contributed to one of the early farming operations in the valley. It was through the efforts and hard work of Bennie, his wife, Martha Jane, and his sons Charles F. Youngker and Ben F. Youngker Jr. that the 55-acre site at Apache and Lower Buckeye Roads was established. This location was one of the Youngker family's first cotton fields, and now it is the site of Youngker High School. Here, Grace Youngker (left), Charles F. Youngker (center), and Martha Jane Youngker (right) turn the shovels and break ground on April 17, 2006. (Courtesy of author.)

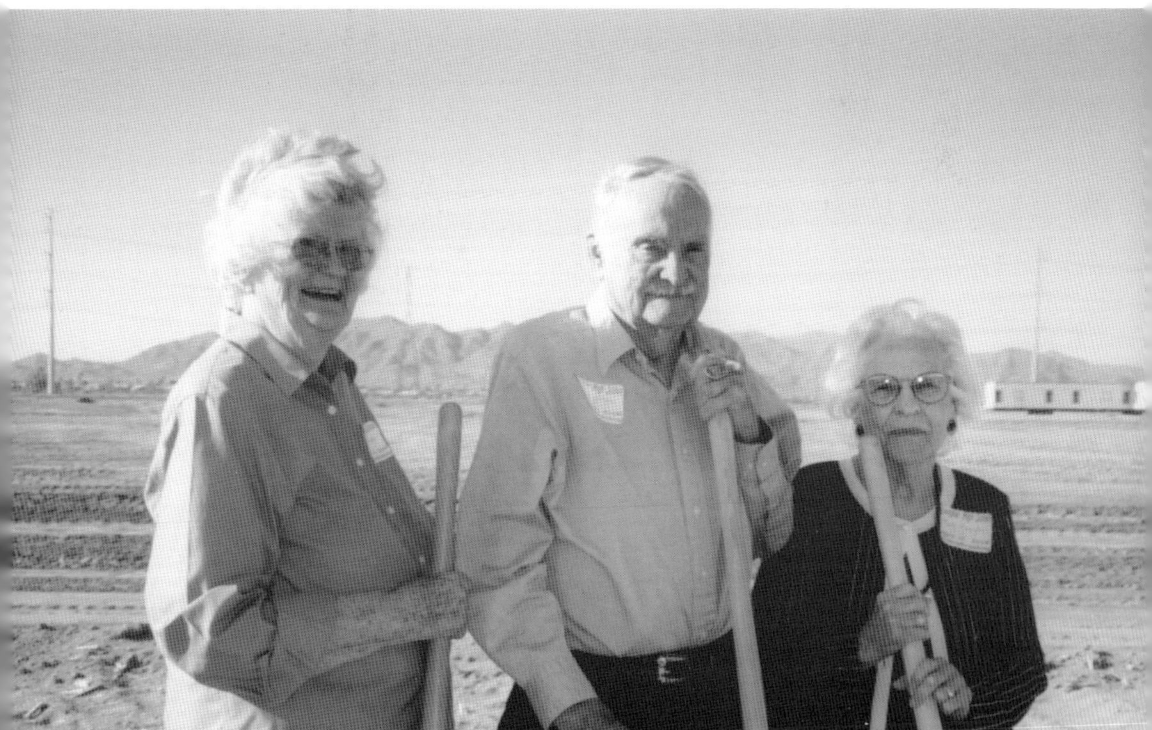

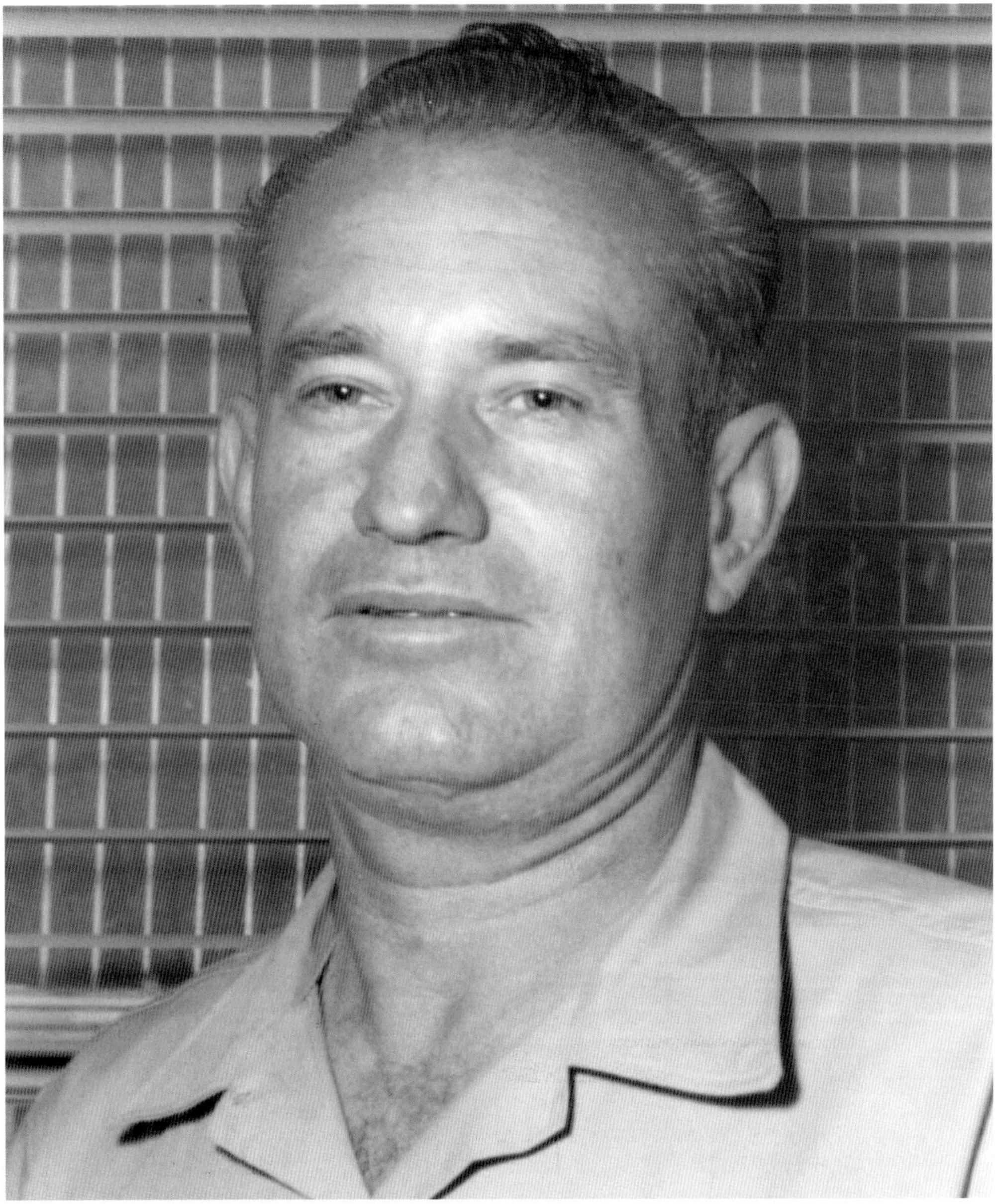

Lanier Calvert

Lanier Calvert, 91, of Buckeye, died on June 11, 2013. He was born on January 22, 1922, in Hawley, Texas, and moved to Liberty in 1935. He attended Liberty Elementary and graduated from Buckeye Union High School in 1940. Calvert joined the Coast Guard in 1942 and served until 1946 in the Southwest Pacific. He married Peggy Butler in 1947 in Liberty and started working for Shell distributor L.D. McDonald two years later. Calvert purchased the business in 1968, forming Calvert Oil Co., later expanding into retail gas sales and a self-service car wash. Lanier's volunteer service to Buckeye included serving on the town council (1962–1972) and his 63 years in the Lions Club. (Courtesy of Buckeye Museum.)

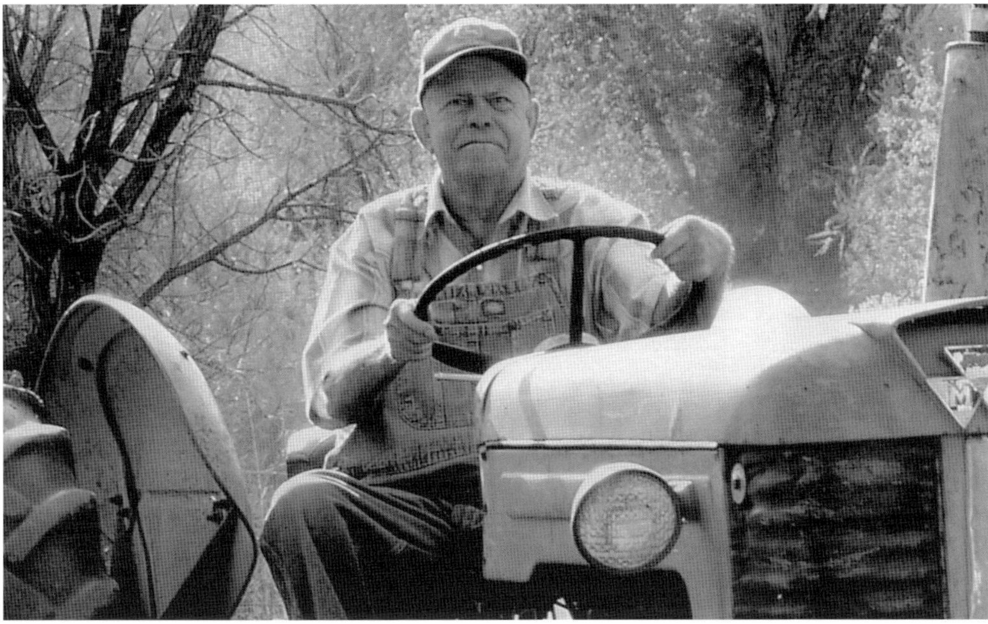

Roy F. and June Dean

Roy F. Dean Sr. came to Phoenix, Arizona, at the age of one. After Roy's brother Roland was born in 1931, the family moved to Buckeye. Roy Sr. (above) attended BES and BUHS. The family then moved to the Liberty area. In 1949, Roy married June Benedict in Liberty. Roy started his own business, repairing farm machinery and welding in the late 1940s for $2.50 per hour. A local country road was named Dean Road. Roy began his house-moving business in 1950. He moved various structures statewide, including churches and historic buildings, and he provided homes for people by moving a house to their property. John Marsden remembers Roy knocking down the 1929 BUHS gym with a crane and a heavy, pear-shaped ball in 1955. Roy's multitalented wife, June, wrote historical articles for the *Buckeye Valley News* for two and a half years beginning on March 16, 2008. Her favorite topics were territorial Arizona, floods in Buckeye Valley, and old cars. June (below) cochaired Pioneer Days, and the Dean family constructed more than three prize-winning floats for Pioneer Days parades. Roy and June have preserved history by saving the first car that came to Buckeye. Roy died in 2008. (Both, courtesy of Gretchen Hardison.)

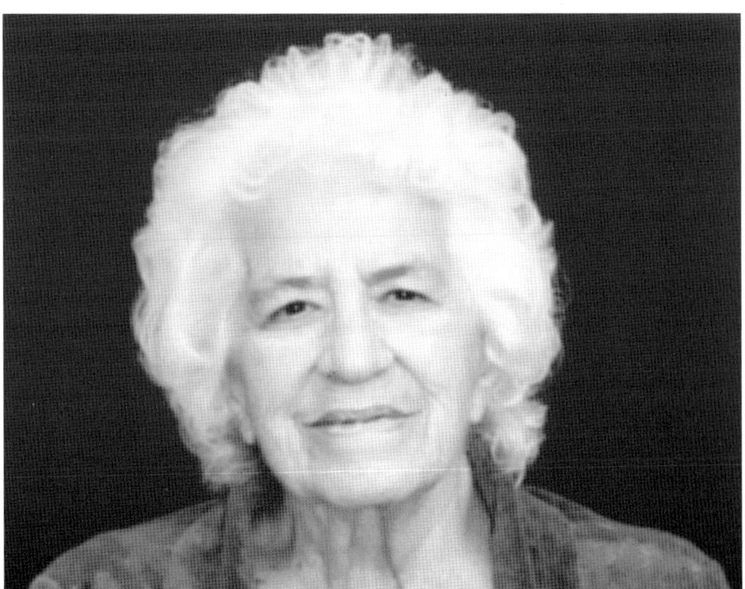

Ralph A. Watkins Sr.

Watkins came to Phoenix penniless and alone at the age of 16, hoping to find relief for a respiratory condition. After finishing high school, he married Ruby Lena Formby. The couple moved to Buckeye in 1927 and opened a bulk plant for Lockart's Rio Grande Oil Company service stations. Watkins was the first volunteer chief of the Buckeye Fire Department and the first chairman of the Buckeye and Maricopa County Housing Authority. In 1936, he served as president of the Buckeye Chamber of Commerce. He founded Watkins Chevrolet in 1939. Watkins was also one of the founders of Arizona Television Company, the firm that started Channel 3. Always interested in politics, Ralph worked for many of Arizona's Democratic candidates and was a trusted government advisor. He also served four times on the platform committee of the Democratic National Convention, and he ran for governor of Arizona twice. (Courtesy of Buckeye Museum.)

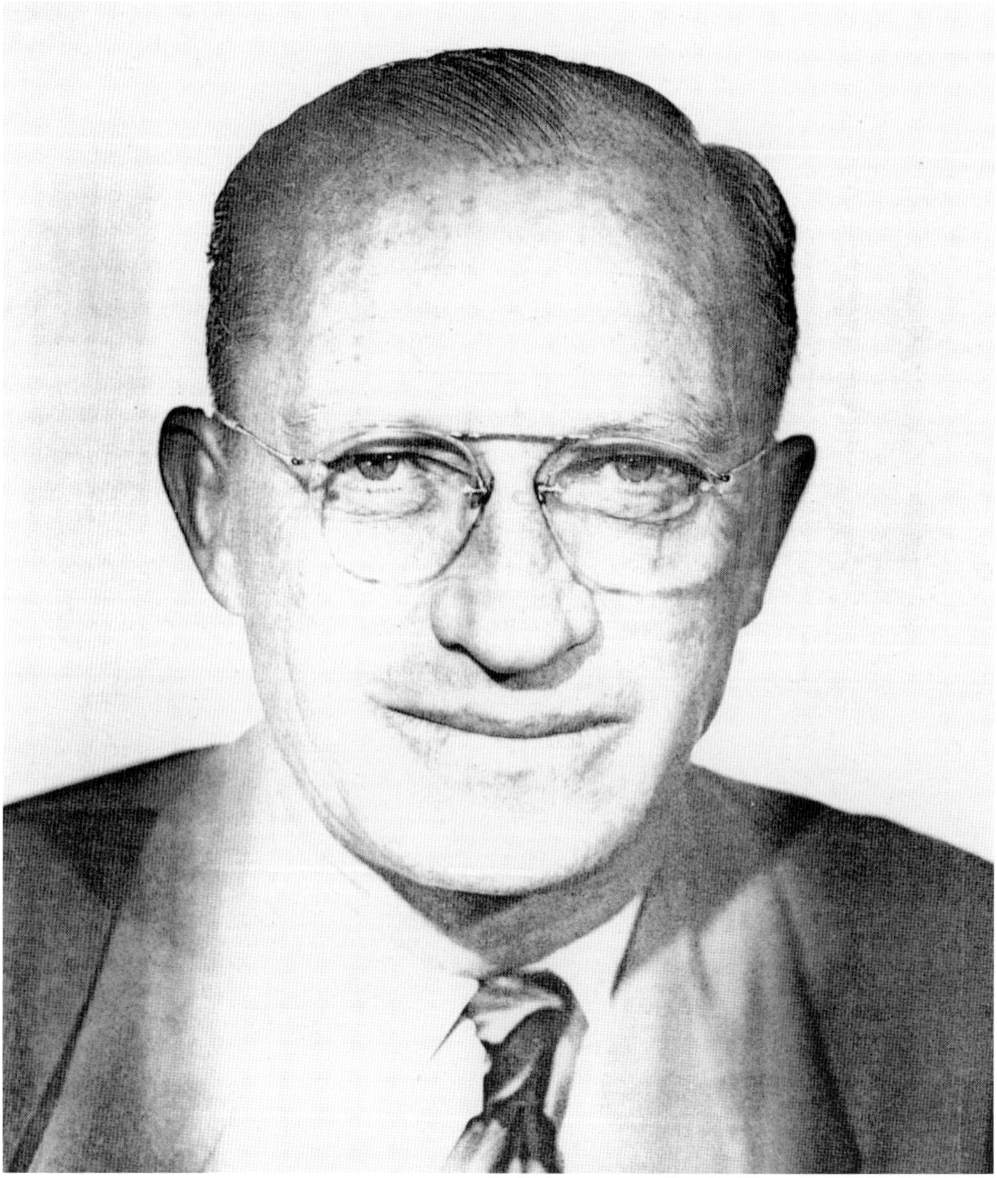

W. Bruce Heiden
Heiden was born in May 1934 in a house on Narramore Avenue, across from the First Baptist Church. While at Buckeye Union High School, he had his eye on a lovely young woman named Helen Holly. They married not long after graduation in 1952 and have been partners for over 60 years. Since Heiden had always been interested in farming, it was natural for him to join his father following graduation from high school. He continues to farm cotton, alfalfa, wheat, and corn silage, and he raises cattle. Bruce and Helen's four children, Art, Les, Hal, and Holly, all have special responsibilities in the H-Four Farm. Through the years, Bruce Heiden has been a leader in agriculture at the local, state, and national levels. In addition to operating his farm, cattle-feeding operations, and Paloma Gin Properties, he has been active on the boards of a number of organizations, including the Roosevelt Irrigation District, Arizona Cotton Growers Association, Calcot, Ltd., National Cotton Council of America, Buckeye Medical Center Development Project, Buckeye Elementary School Board, Buckeye Community Church, and Paloma Irrigation and Drainage District. He has earned many awards, the most recent being in March 2014, when he was inducted into the Arizona Farming and Ranching Hall of Fame. His first award was in 1979, when the Future Farmers of America named him Man of the Year for Arizona Agriculture. (Both, courtesy of author.)

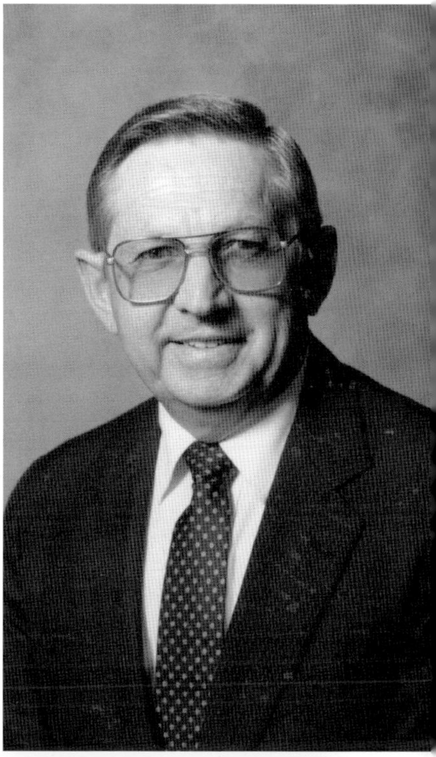

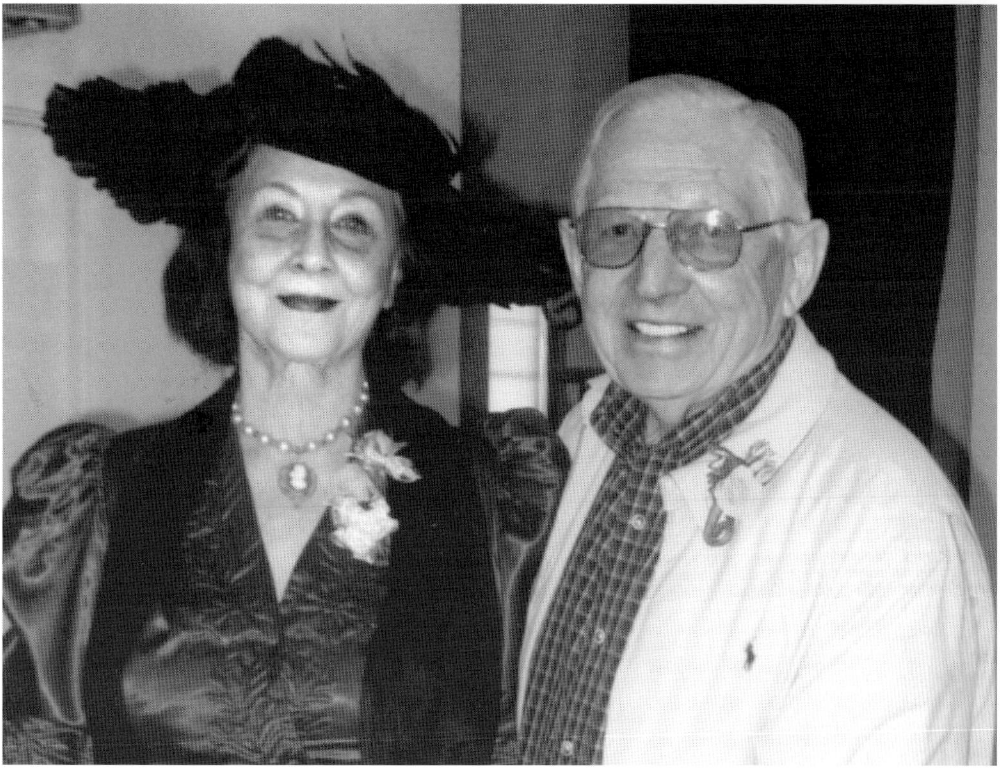

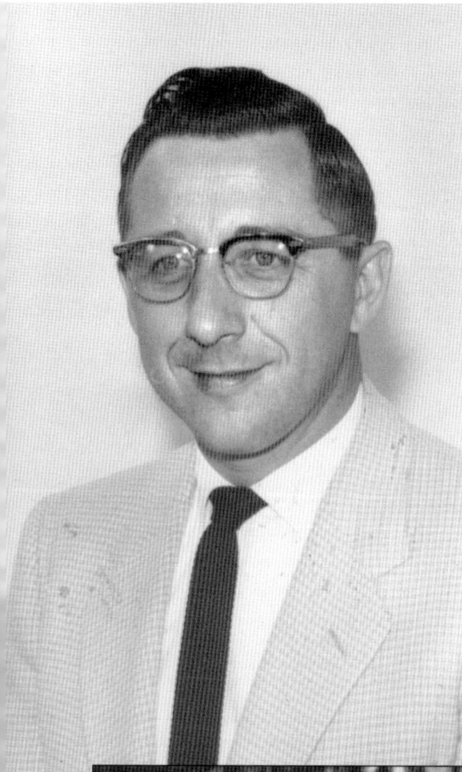

Robert Bonnes

Bob Bonnes wrote his story of coming to Buckeye. "I interviewed for a teaching job at Buckeye Union High School, in the summer of 1950, in a cotton field, with the president of the BUHS School Board. I had a job at Peoria High School, had signed a contract when the superintendent went on vacation right after he signed three of us to teach. The Korean War got hot, and three farmers on the Peoria Board told the school secretary they were not going to take a chance with young men who might be called into service. So, I called George Hamner, a naval shipmate of mine during World War II, talked it over, and he said I should come to Buckeye and interview. I did, and G.V. Stanley offered me a job at BES." Bob Bonnes was the Buckeye Elementary School superintendent and teacher for 16 years. The below photograph shows his first BES fourth-grade class in 1951–1952. He served as Buckeye's mayor from 1966 to 1972 and was the chamber of commerce president in 1957 and 1990. In 1990, he was chosen Buckeye Valley Chamber of Commerce Citizen of the Year. In a May 20, 2004, *Buckeye Valley News* article, Bonnes commented, "Our hearts have never left Buckeye. After 41 years as a resident, 16 years at BES, 6 years as Mayor of Buckeye, and 14 years in the AgCom Insurance Agency, how could it be any other way???" (Both, courtesy of Bob Bonnes.)

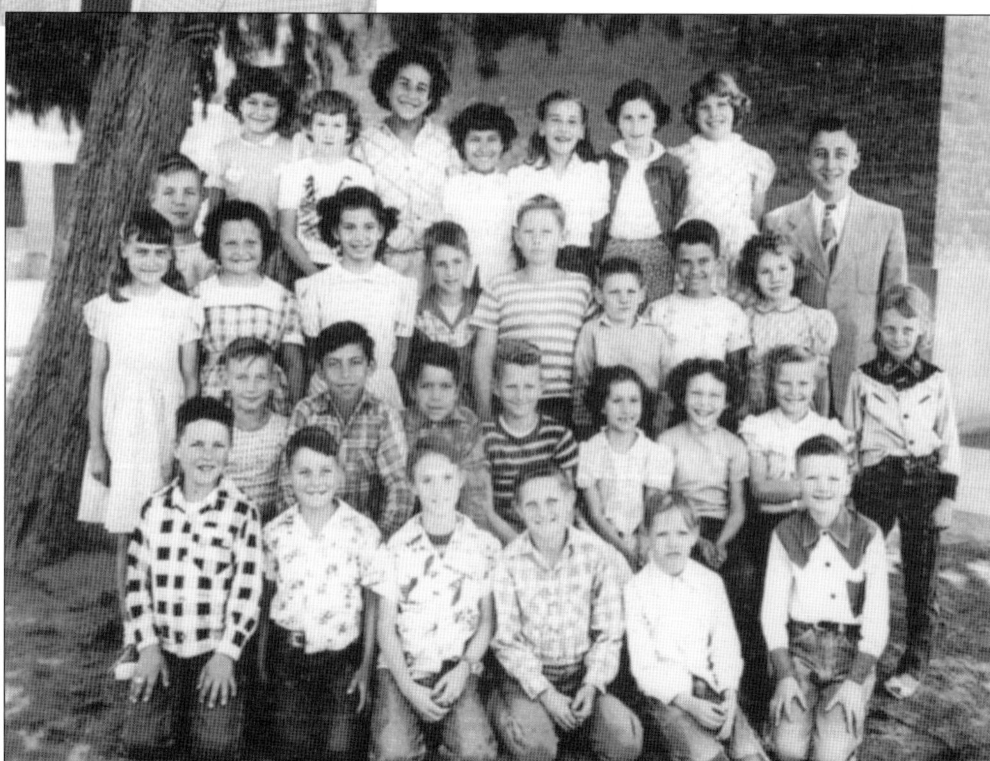

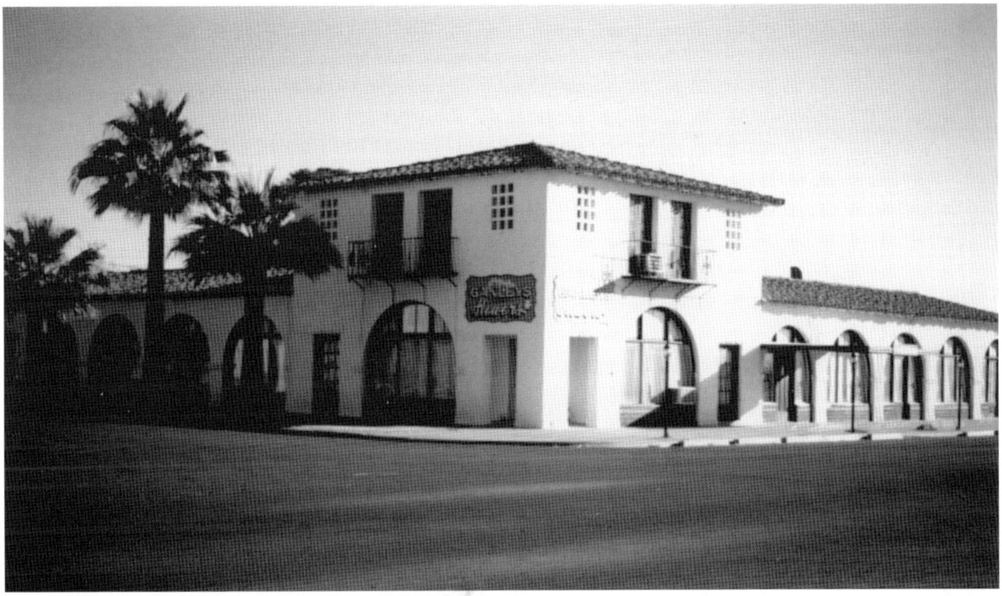

Paul Ganley

From the time he moved to Buckeye in 1939 until he passed away in 1994, Paul Ganley was the one who prepared the bodies of loved ones. In his quiet manner, he took care of many details, smoothing weary paths. Paul Melvin Ganley was born on May 17, 1903, in New Castle, Colorado. While in high school, he supplemented his income by working in a local mortuary, and he decided that would be his profession. He received his embalmer's license in Colorado and moved to Phoenix, where he worked 13 years for the H.M. Maus Mortuary. In 1939, he moved to Buckeye and established the Buckeye Funeral Home, located on the corner of Baseline Road and Central Boulevard in Valencia. It is pictured here in 1998. In 1929, Paul married Mary Catherine LaBranch of Phoenix. Everyone remembers Mary for her friendly and beautiful floral arrangements from Ganley's Floral Shop. Phil Ganley, who was born on Paul's 30th birthday, continues to manage the family business. Phil recalls that, as a young boy, he helped his dad make grave markers. Also, one of his first jobs was cutting weeds at the Buckeye Cemetery. On Saturdays, he would go there, take a jug of water, and just chop weeds. Grandson Steve Ganley, son of Phil, is following in the family footsteps. (Courtesy of author.)

G.R. and Molly Jolley

The Jolley family has been in the Buckeye Valley since 1946. G.R. Jolley and his wife, Molly "Tiny" Jolley, and their six children moved from Crockett, Texas, to work in cotton fields. They lived in cotton camps and settled in Hodges Camp 25 at Broadway Road and Airport Road (now Verrado Way). G.R. Jolley soon became the "camp boss" and the cotton contractor, taking people to and from the fields in his school bus. In 1955, he purchased 20 acres of farmland between Jackrabbit Trail and Tuthill Road on Broadway Road. The Jolley Trucking Company hauled alfalfa hay, barley, wheat, sugar beets, cottonseeds, and other locally grown farm produce. When Jolley passed away in 1981, Fay moved home to care for her mother for six years. Fay says, "perhaps that's how the Jolley Family Assisted Living Care Home was started." So Fay and her husband, Sam Webster, began the journey to build a care home. They now have two homes in Buckeye on Broadway Road, the first dedicated on October 22, 2000, and the second on October 22, 2007. That October day is special, as Fay's parents were married on October 22, 1938. These homes are in their honor. (Both, courtesy of Fay [Jolley] Webster.)

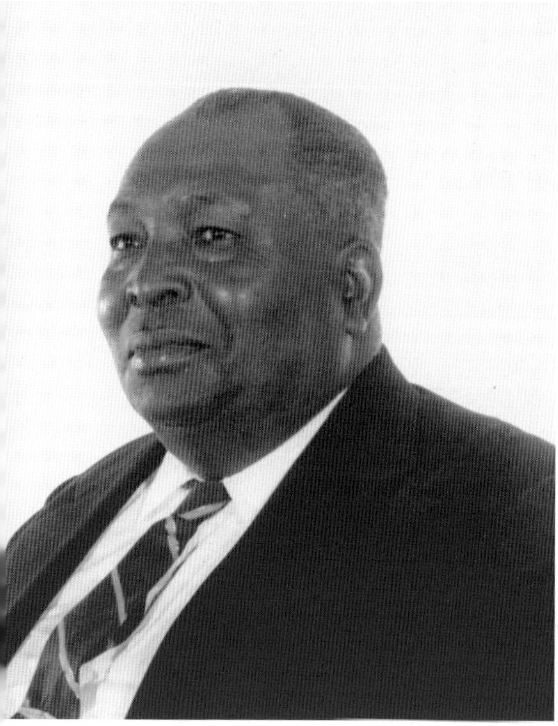

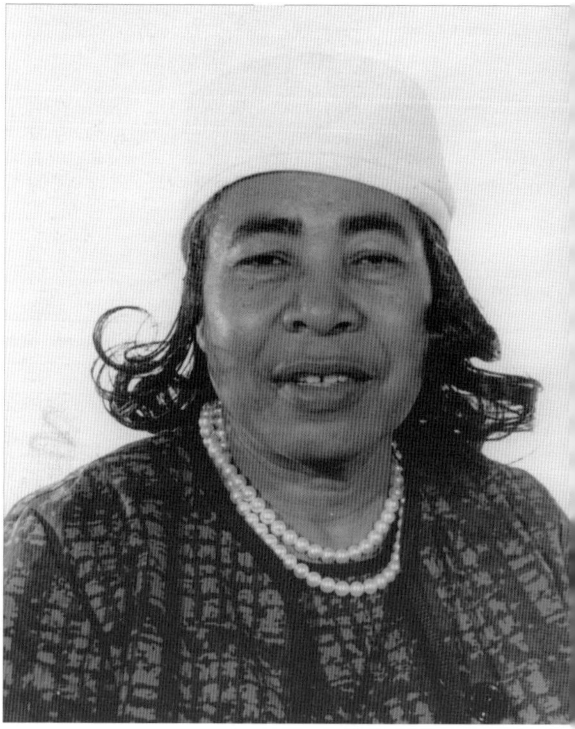

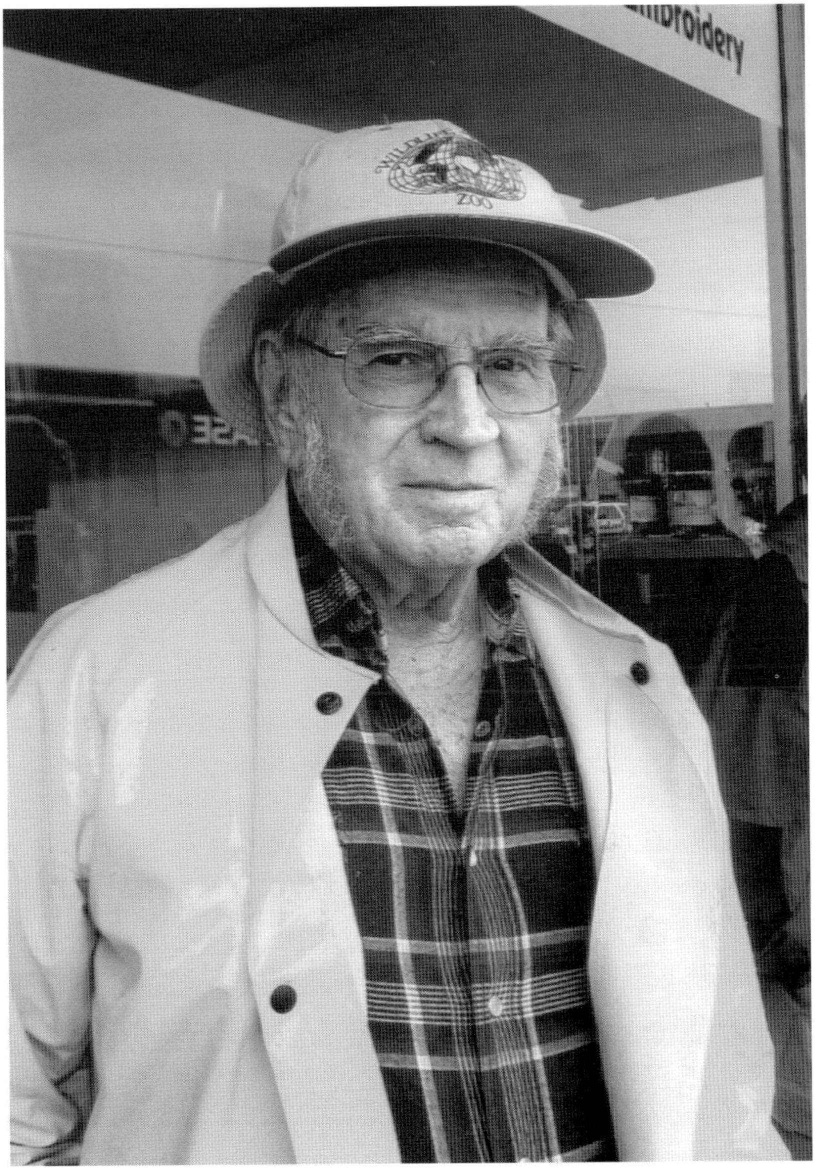

Bootleg Miller

This Buckeye legend was told to Verlyne Meck by Buckeye native Richard Roglin (pictured) on November 17, 2007. Miller Road, on the west end of Buckeye, was named after Bootleg Miller. He made bootleg whiskey and also kept cattle and horses at a desert site north of the present I-10 on Miller Road. He hid the whiskey under a bed, and his Native American wife, who spoke Spanish, spent a lot of time in bed, so the home was not searched. Miller Road gave Buckeye Miller Wash, north of I-10, which has always been a favorite gathering place for families and a site of "teenage parties." A Miller Wash memory involves a large group of teenagers enjoying a party. A large bonfire was burning, and there was lots of beer drinking. Suddenly, two cop cars showed up with lights flashing. One stopped in the middle of the road, blocking the exit. So four teenagers who did not have cars took off running into the desert. The cops did not chase them, so the youth spent the rest of the night working their way back to Buckeye. (Courtesy of author.)

Travis Curry

Travis William Curry was born on August 27, 1906, in Durango, Texas. He arrived in Buckeye at age 25 and worked on a farm for his cousin John Liles. He then drove a truck for Wayne Rainey, who helped him get started in 1939 as operator of the Texaco service station, later the Buckeye service station. He bought the station and operated it for 19 years. Travis proudly wore the 1940s Texaco slogan, "You Can Trust Your Car to the Man Who Wears the Star." He met Mildred Golling in 1931 at the Silver Moon Dance Hall in Buckeye, where folks danced on Saturday nights. They married in Prescott on June 17, 1937. Travis also opened a Goodrich Budget Store connected to the service station in 1952. Although he did not engage in farming, Curry was certainly part of the farming community. He not only supplied tires for tractors and other farm equipment, he was capable of doing mechanical work on farm vehicles. He often had to drive out to Tonopah or Rainbow Valley to fix flats and get the farmer up and running again. The station was not just for the farmers, as it sold appliances, televisions, and bicycles. Local kids knew they could always drop by for bike repairs and be treated to an ice-cold Coke. Travis and Mildred moved in 1958 to Sedona, where he died in 1977. The couple had four children: Diane England of Safford, Arizona; Nancy Brainard of Laguna Beach, California; James of Albuquerque, New Mexico; and Steve of Sedona. (Courtesy of Nancy [Curry] Brainard.)

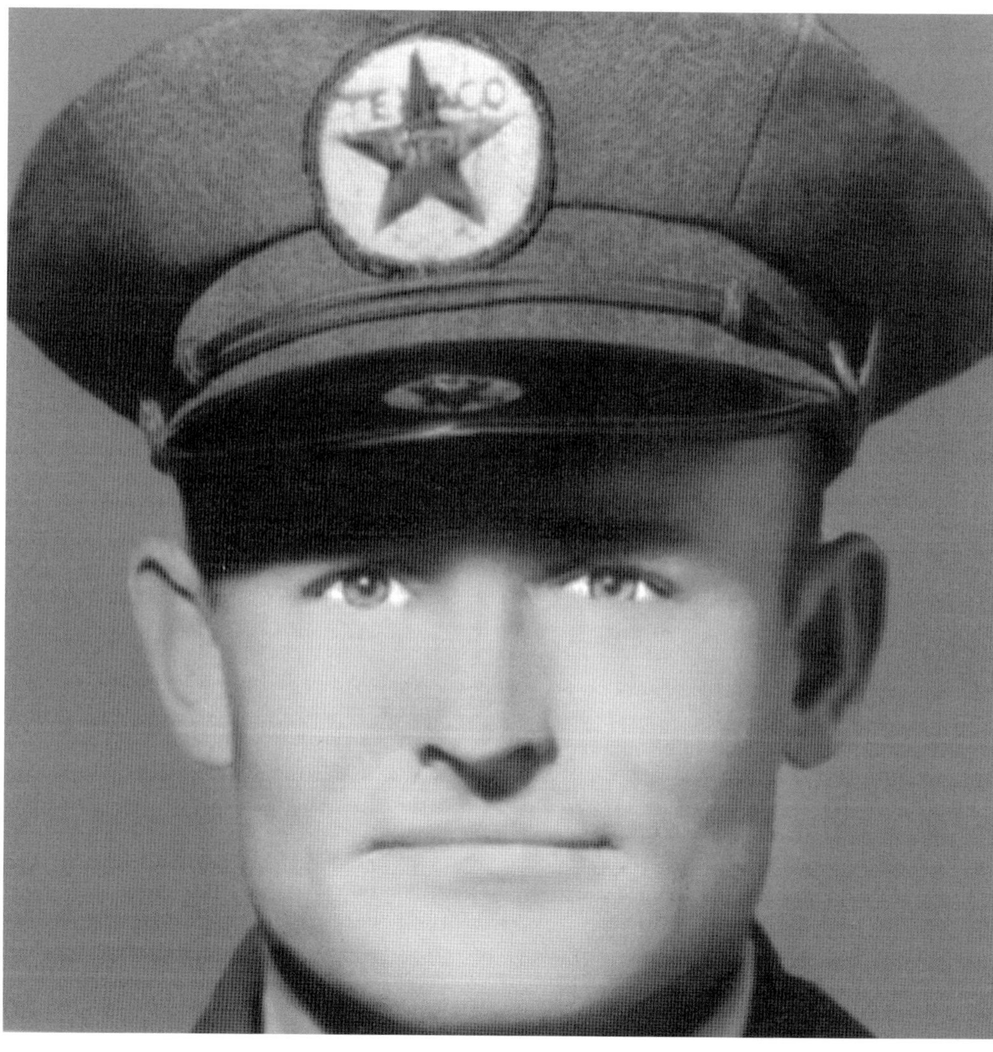

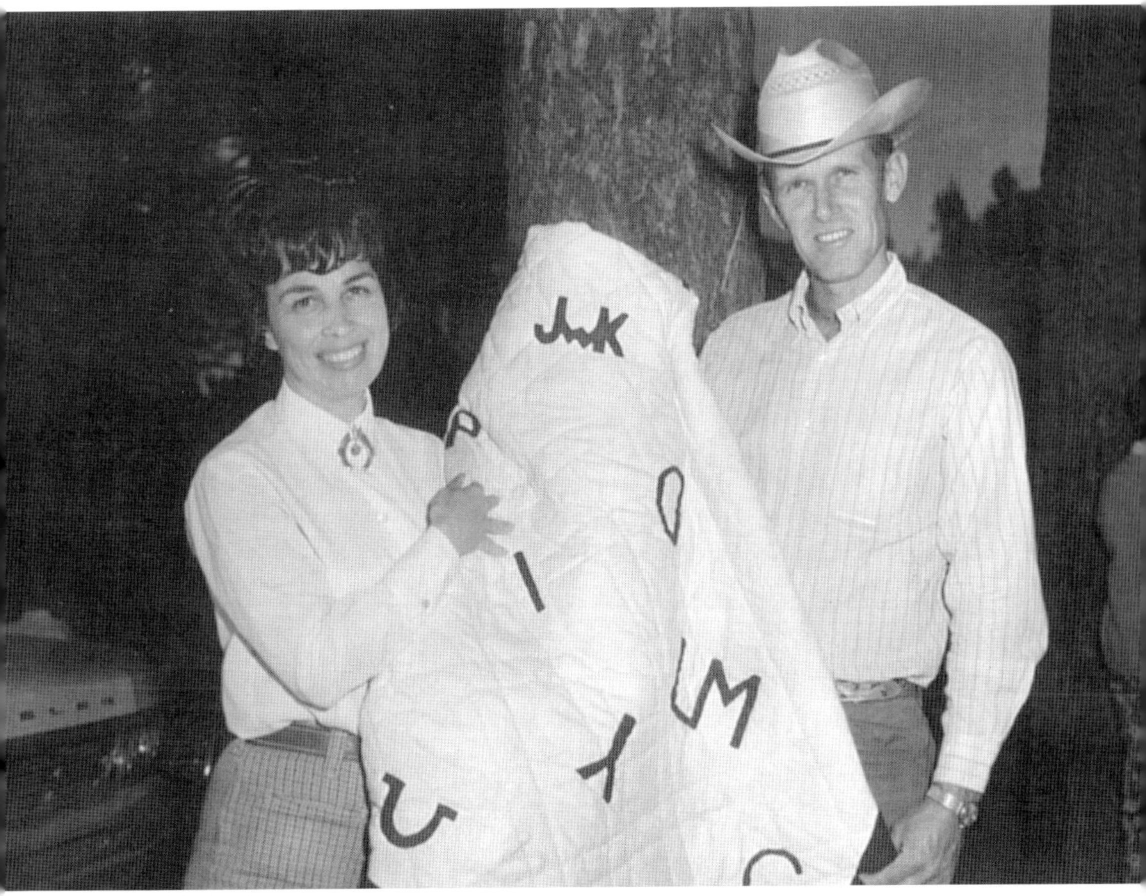

John and Bobbie Kerr

The Kerrs were inducted into the Arizona Farming and Ranching Hall of Fame on February 27, 2010. When the couple married in 1950, they rented John's family farm for a few years then bought it from his dad and added purebred Cheviot, Dorset, and Shropshire sheep to the inventory. In the early 1950s, while in Tempe, John Kerr was instrumental in the formation of the United Dairymen of Arizona. He was a member of the first board of directors and continued serving for 36 years. As their three sons grew and became involved in 4-H, John and Bobbie volunteered as livestock superintendents at the Maricopa County 4-H Show and served as superintendents in the sheep and dairy goat departments at the Arizona State Fair. John and Bobbie began a lamb auction at their Tempe dairy for 4-H youth.

In the early 1970s, they moved to Buckeye, where they established a larger dairy at 8200 South Dean Road and continued the lamb auction. They initiated the Purebred Sheep Show and Junior Market Lamb Show at the Arizona National Stock Show and started the popular Li'l Buckaroo Rodeo Show for young children. In 1975, Bobbie was a founding board member and commissioner in establishing the Maricopa County Fair. In 1989, the couple retired from the state fair, but in a few years, John returned as the first livestock director and Bobbie began the Farm Tour Program. The Kerr family sheep and dairy operation is now in its fifth generation. Their impact on Arizona agricultural industry, especially in Buckeye and Maricopa County, will continue to be felt for many years to come. Their son Jerry said, "John and Bobbie Kerr are truly ambassadors for agriculture, and pioneers that helped shape today's farming and ranching in Arizona." Here, Bobbie and John display a quilt with their cattle brand and other ranch brands of Arizona. (Courtesy of Bobbie Kerr.)

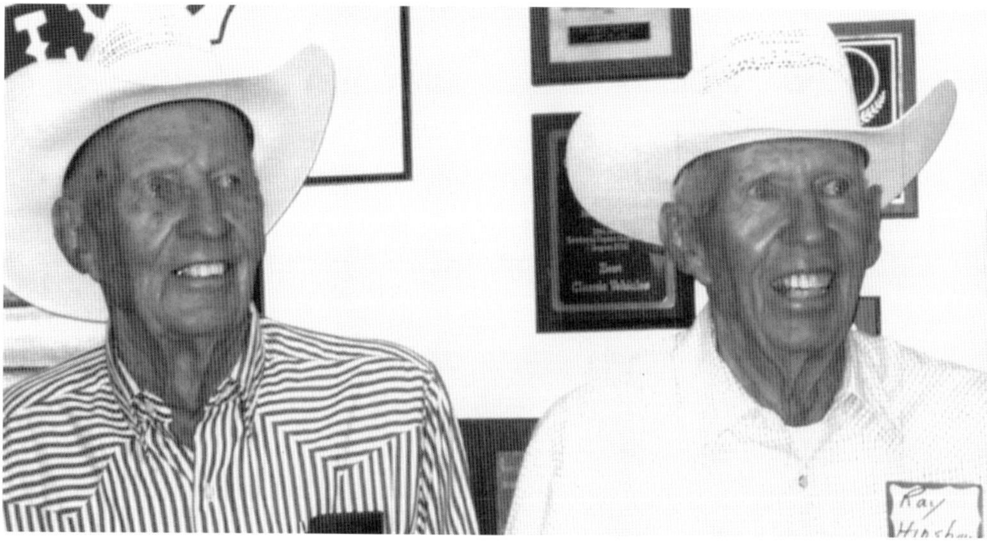

Rex Hinshaw, DVM, and Ray Hinshaw, DVM

Since they were children, the identical-twin Hinshaw brothers have been drawn irresistibly to horse and livery stables in Boulder, Colorado. Their identical features have made the Hinshaws a source of puzzlement for others. Dr. W.R. "Rex" Hinshaw (left) was a full-time veterinarian for the Arizona Racing Commission for 36 years (1952–1988), retiring around 1988. Dr. E.R. "Ray" Hinshaw (right) was a Buckeye veterinarian for 18 years. During his 18 years in Buckeye (1952–1970), Ray gave much to the community as a town councilman. He was also a member of the chamber of commerce, the zoning and planning board, and the Elks Club. He left Buckeye in 1972 and retired on October 24, 1992. Ray was very involved in helping to establish the Buckeye Hills Regional Park, dedicated on October 9, 1973. (All, courtesy of Ray Hinshaw.)

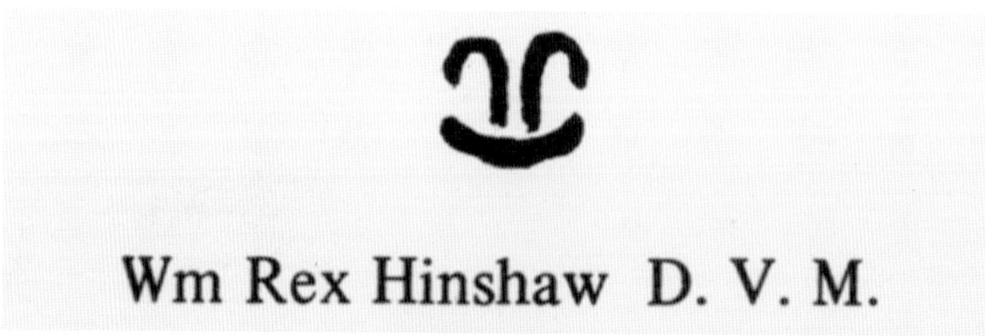

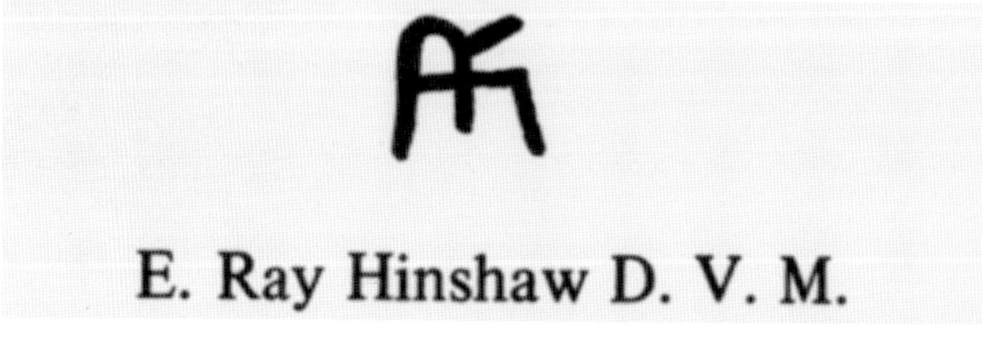

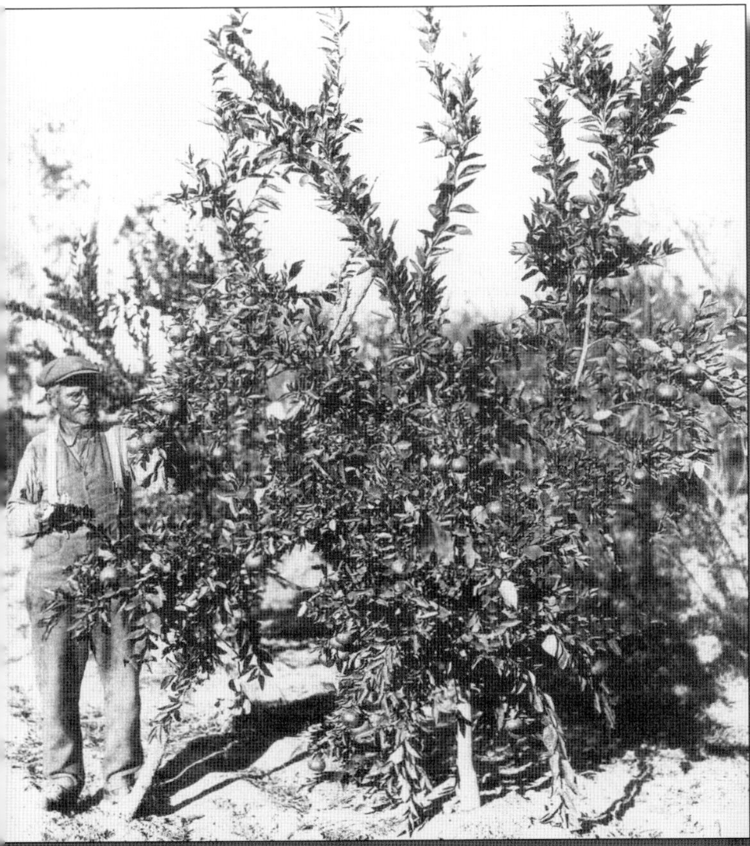

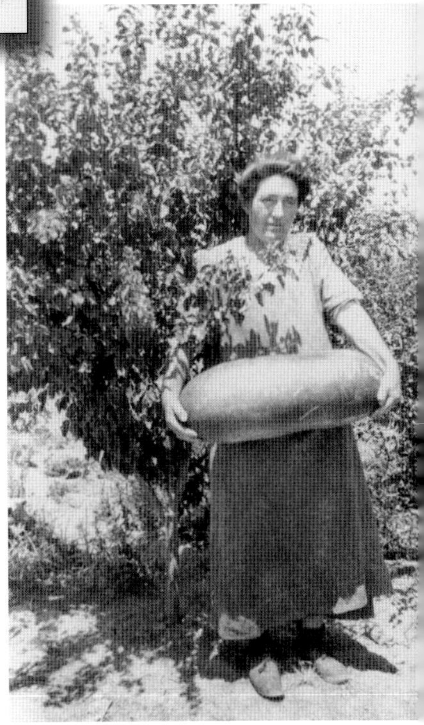

Robert Hegi

Robert Hegi immigrated to America from Switzerland with his wife, Fanny Carol, after he heard Horace Greeley's invitation to "Go West, young man." He became a naturalized citizen, settling near the small town of Buckeye. As Robert was skilled in many trades—carpentry, plumbing, winemaking, milling, and horticulture—he was determined to make the Hegi homestead an oasis in the Arizona desert. In 1917, on 160 acres, Robert and Fanny Carol began building a home west of Miller Road, north of Baseline Road. Cottonwood trees thrived with water transported by a horse-drawn water-tank wagon from the Buckeye Canal. Finally, a well was drilled, and the life-giving water flowed for irrigation as Fanny operated the enormous, noisy pump. Citrus, fruit trees, grapes, and fields of alfalfa and wheat (food for dairy cattle and poultry) flourished with irrigation and hard work. These photographs of Robert (above) and Fanny (right) show their citrus trees and watermelons. When the preliminary work of organizing the Roosevelt Irrigation District (RID) was undertaken, the Hegi ranch encouraged landowners to proceed with the project. In connection with the RID, Fanny Hegi was often referred to as the mother of the RID. She gave birth to the first surviving triplets in Arizona. (Both, courtesy of Margaruite Rains.)

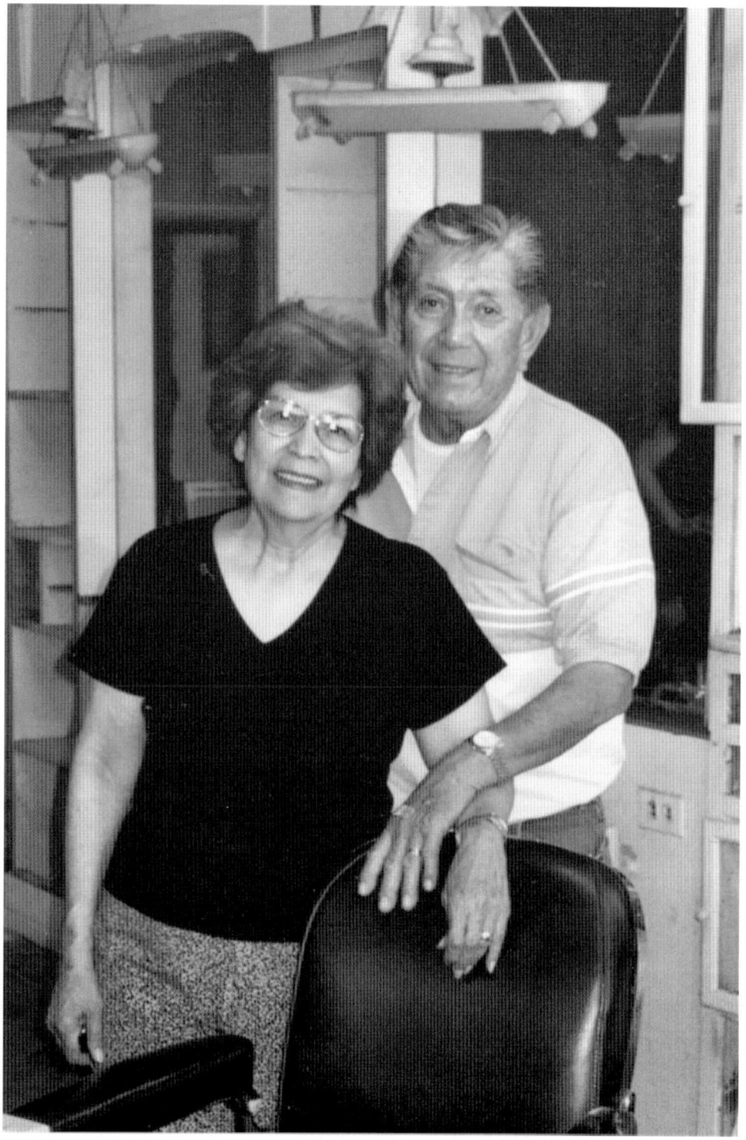

Fernando and Stella Carrera
Stella Fisher's life began on February 17, 1933, in Buckeye as the first child of Maria and Manuel Fisher. Fernando Carrera was born on July 8, 1932, in Buckeye at Long's Dairy. Fernando "Guero" Carrera and Stella married in June 1954 after Fernando returned from a tour of duty in Korea. Stella learned to fly an airplane when she was a junior in high school and had the distinction of being the youngest licensed female pilot in Arizona. She took her test at a very small Sky Harbor Airport in Phoenix, and her test flight was to Parker, Arizona. She began working at Buckeye Elementary School in 1970 as the principal's secretary and was there for 26 years. Music is a part of their lives. Since age 12, Stella has been a choir member at St. Henry's, and she was the organist for over 40 years. Fernando also sings in the choir, plays the guitar, and is often asked to be a soloist at weddings and funerals. After barber school graduation, Fernando began work for H.D. Williams in 1954. Beginning in 1956, he owned and operated Carrera's Barber Shop, retiring after 50 years in 2004. He has cut three generations of Buckeye residents' hair, and he loved being in the shop all day talking to people. (Courtesy of author.)

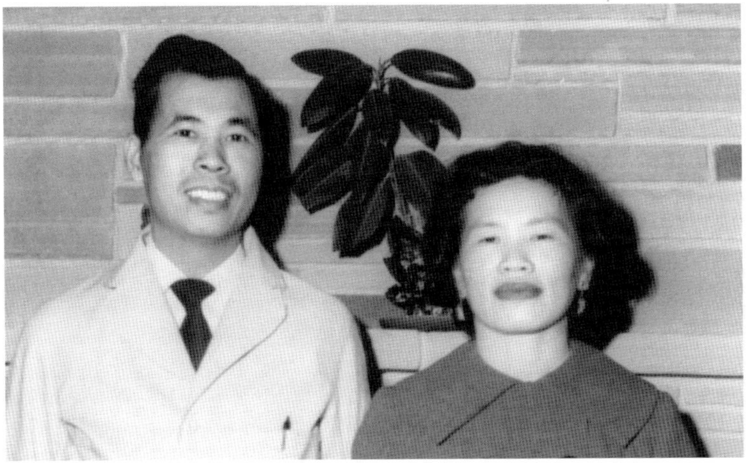

Larry and Jerfee Eng
Larry Eng was born in the village of Yen Peng, near Canton, China, on October 10, 1925. He came to New York City at the age of 12. When he was 18, he joined the Air Force, and he later became a pilot and instructor at Luke Air Force Base. Larry Eng became a US citizen in 1945. He was a member of the Kiwanis Club, American Legion, and Chinese Alliance Club. His hobbies were fishing, bowling, and hunting. Jerfee Ann Eng was born on January 22, 1920, in the village of Van Lang, near Canton. In 1923, she came to America and attended school in Flagstaff. In 1948, Larry and Jerfee were married in Flagstaff. After running a grocery store in Phoenix, they came to Buckeye in 1952 to start a grocery store, Payless Market. In 1964, they purchased the Buckeye Safeway store, which became Sav Mart. They raised a family of five children: Jacque, Edwin, Barbara, Carolyn, and Larry. Jerfee was a member of the American Legion Auxiliary, Business and Professional Woman's Club, and Buckeye Woman's Club, and she was treasurer of Our Lady's Sodality of St. Henry's Parish. Her hobbies included growing tropical plants, dress designing, painting, knitting, and preparing recipes from all over the world. In 15 years at the Woman's Club Flower Show, Jerfee took the grand prize 11 times. (Both, courtesy of Eng family.)

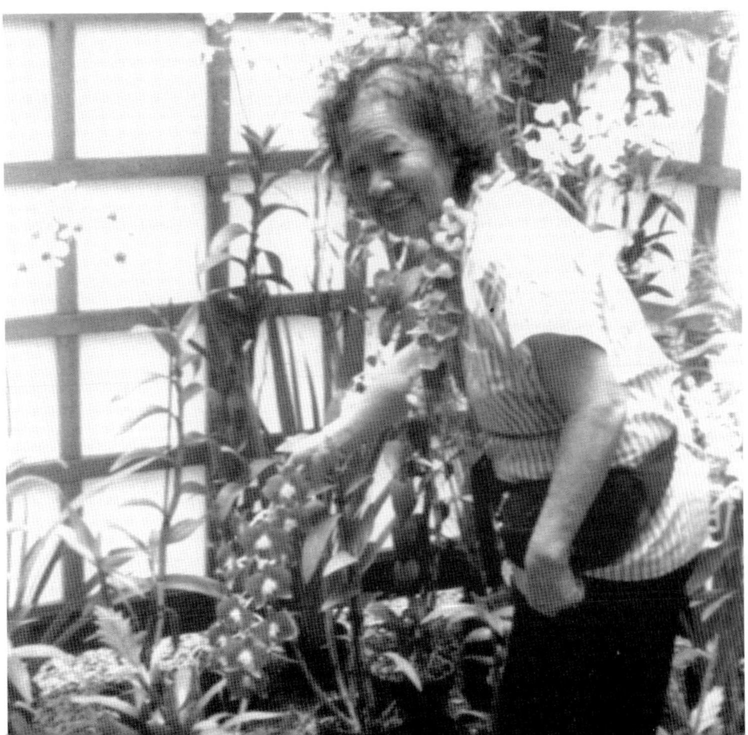

Luther Douglas McDonald

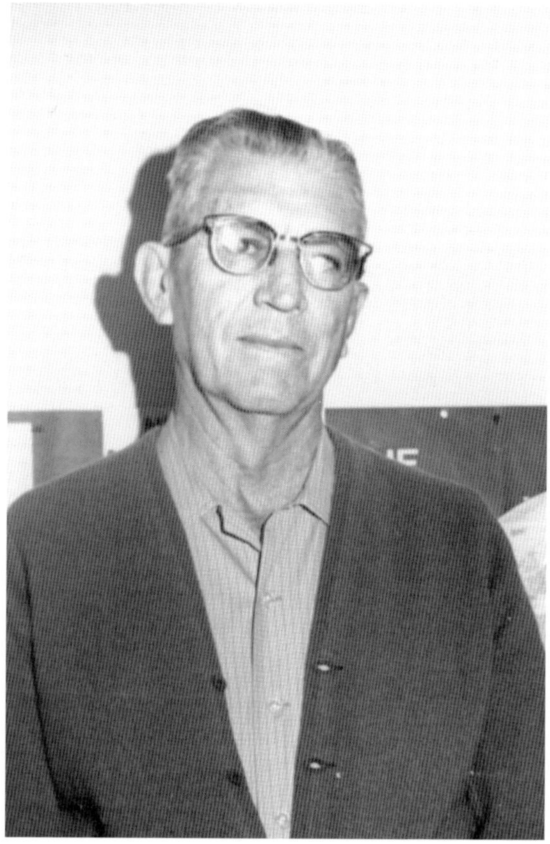

L.D. McDonald began the Shell Oil Company, a bulk plant, in 1931. The facility was built in 1929 and is shown below around 1940. Many years later, in 1968, the company was purchased by Lanier Calvert. Many memories of L.D. involve his giving attitude and dedication to others. He was mayor of Buckeye (1941–1943), Boy Scouts of America commissioner in the 1950s, and a strong Democrat in the 16th Arizona State Legislature. Frank M. Valenzuela, PhD, PMP, shared a story of L.D. "When he first started his business, he actually delivered gasoline to our house for my father. Since it was only 50 gallons at a time, I believe it was more as a favor, rather than one of his usual deliveries. We looked forward to his deliveries because he would always give my brother, sister and I at least a nickel. In those days, you could buy a meaningful treat for a nickel." In many citizens' minds, McDonald was a great man who did much for the community. He was always smiling and glad to see people. He was chosen Buckeye Valley Chamber of Commerce Man of the Year in 1967. (Both, courtesy of author.)

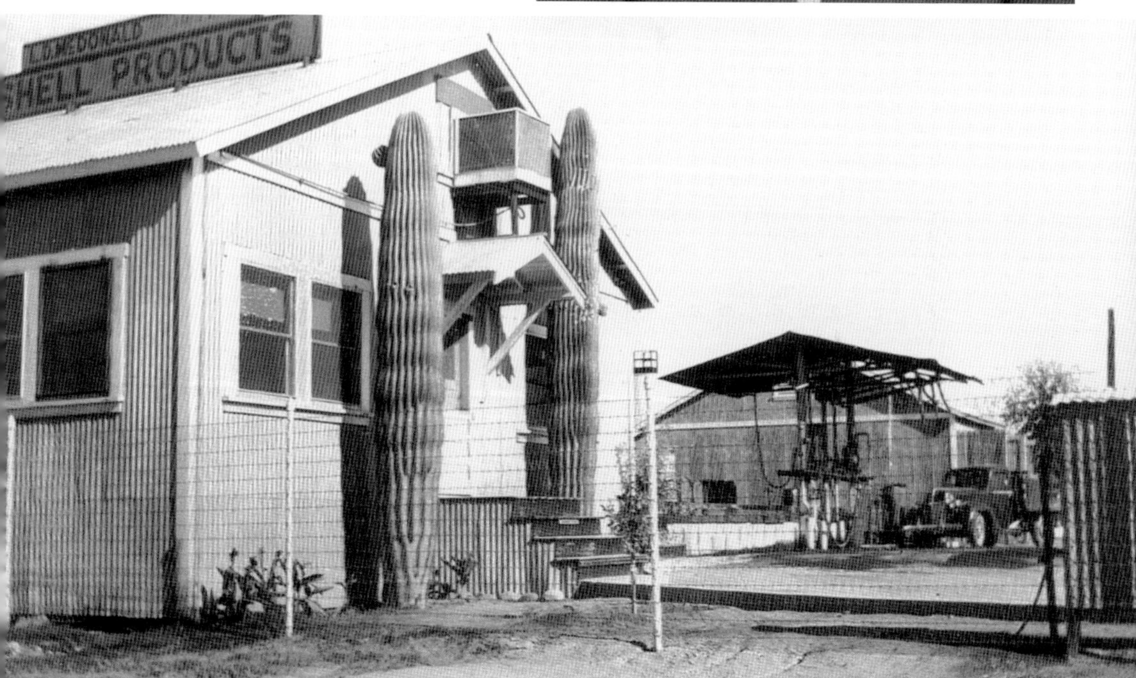

Sam Cambron

In 1936, Sam Cambron, with his parents, moved from Oklahoma to Arizona in a "forerunner of a Winnebago"—a Model T truck customized with a stove, bed, and table. According to Cambron, "They came because of their health as they were starving to death." The Harvey Cambron family spent its first two nights in Arizona camped under a tree until they located a tent. They found work in the cotton fields and fell in love with Buckeye, where Sam soon met his future wife, Bea Dunning, when they were both working in a cotton patch. Sam and Bea married in 1940, and Sam continued employment with the C.O. Vosburgh farm operation. He eventually was able to acquire some land of his own from Mr. Vosburgh. Sam Cambron has farmed everything from cotton to safflower, from alfalfa to grain. Cambron, at age 82, said, "I suppose I'm one of the few left from the days when we got $2.50 for 12 hours of work." He spent six years on the board of Grand Canyon University and 28 years on the BUHS governing board. He was chosen Buckeye Valley Chamber of Commerce Man of the Year in 1978. He said, "I wanted to be a part of a community when I was young, and I've been happy to serve my community." Friends have a special memory of Cambron in his older years. When asked, "How are you?" he replied that he was living in the hereafter—he would walk into a room and ask, "What did I come in here after?" Buckeye said "goodbye" to Sam Cambron in 2005. (Courtesy of author.)

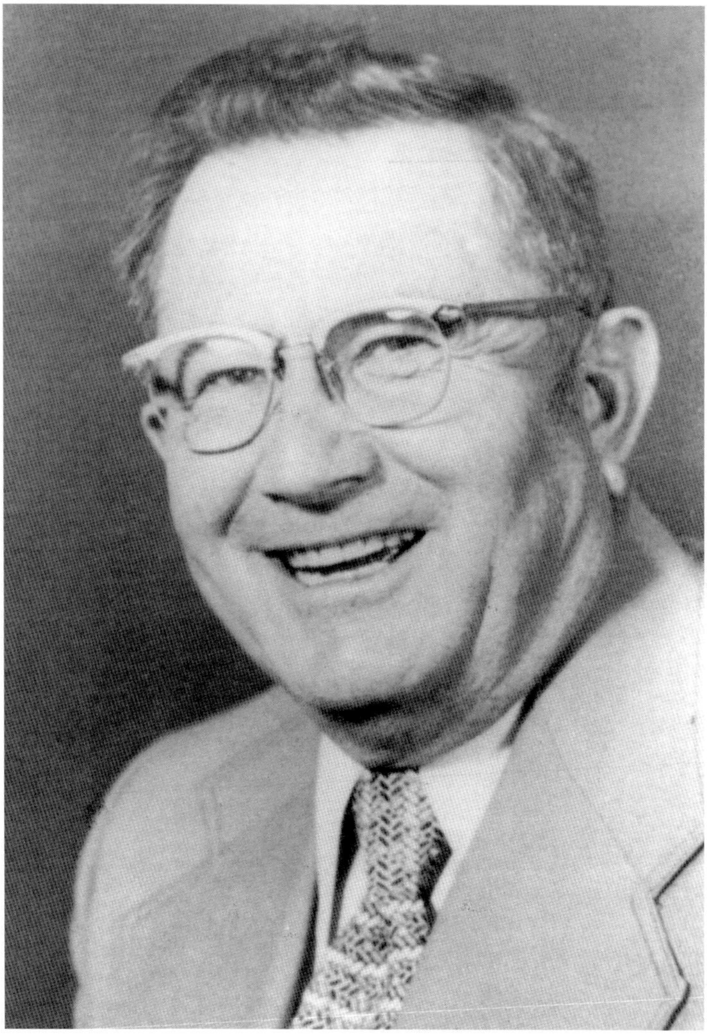

Clemie Arnold

Clemie O. Arnold tells his hometown story: "I was born in Buckeye, Arizona, February 23, 1936, and started working with my Dad, Otis Arnold, when just 10 years old. In the eighth grade, I made a lawn chair and that started me into wood working." At BUHS, he was busy with sports but still found time to build a 1,000-square-foot, three-bedroom, single-bath home. He sold it to Ross Simmons for $10,000. The year was 1953. Arnold, 17 years old, had his first home sale! After graduating high school, Arnold went to work for Steves Brothers, formerly of Buckeye, in Flagstaff as a bricklayer. When the snow started falling, he decided to come back to the valley. Clemie went to John F. Long, asking for a job laying block. Long told Arnold "to lay blocks for 30 minutes and see if you can keep up." After 15 minutes, Arnold was hired and was able to get his journeyman's license. Clemie Arnold then decided to get his own building contractor's license, which required taking a three-hour written test. Unfortunately, he did not pass it the first time. Arnold said, "I studied long and hard again, and passed the second time." In Buckeye, the Clemie Arnold Construction Company built the Garment Factory (Buckeye Industries), the Buckeye Public Library, apartments for Watkins Brothers, Buckeye Lumber & Supply, and many homes. (Both, courtesy of Gerre Arnold.)

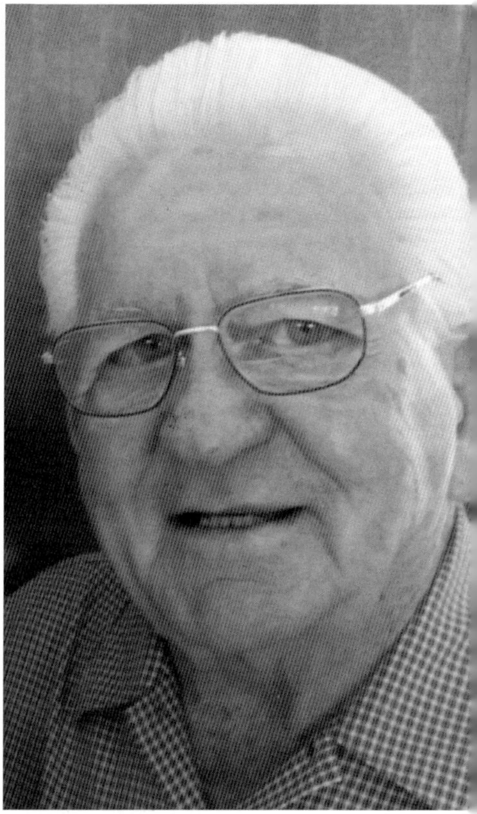

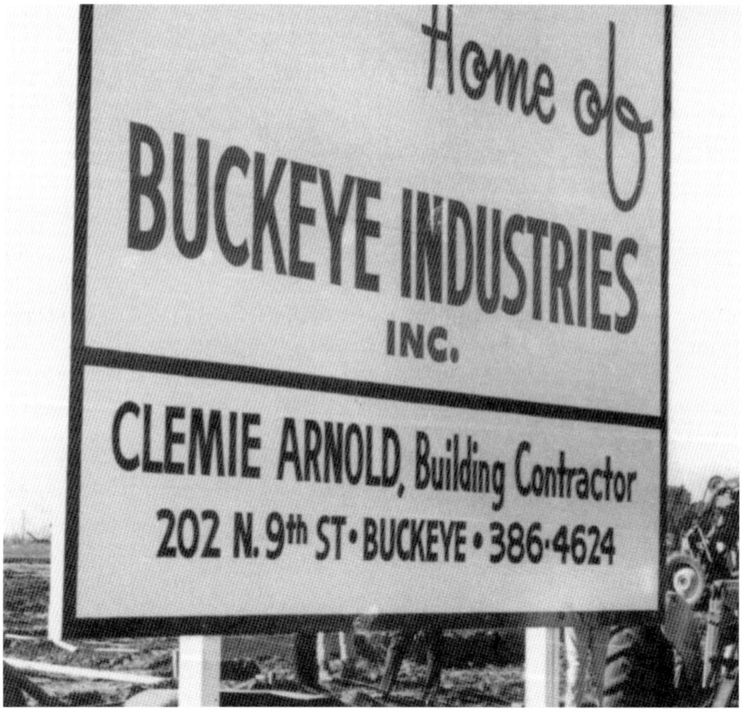

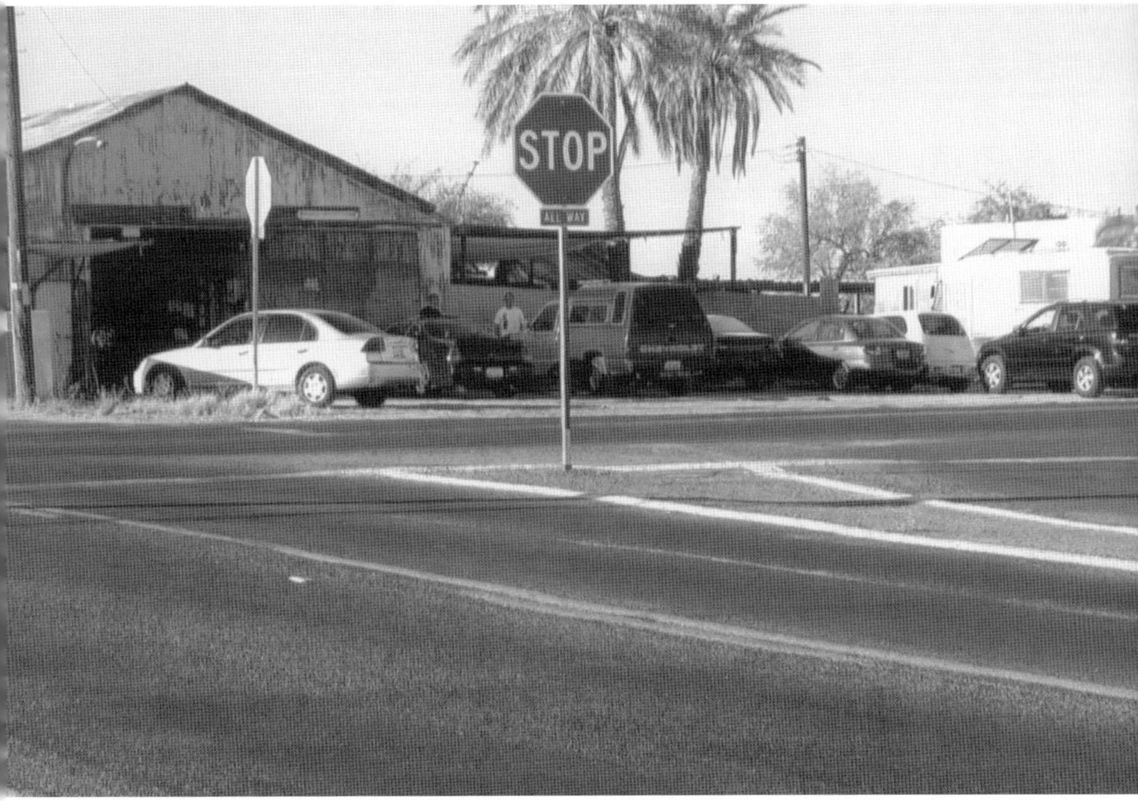

Perryville Citizens

Kay Jackson and Vangie McCulley roller-skated on the old, narrow Yuma Road that passed in front of the store/bar and turned south on Perryville Road toward Tamarack Corner (on Highway 80). They called it the "Perryville Roller Rink." In the 1930s, many people enjoyed the swimming pool located behind the pool hall. Other Perryville personalities and business owners included Cliff and Dimple Curtis and families such as the Sieges, Duncans, Woottons, Darnells, Dunlaps, and McCulleys. An incident of note took place in the Perryville Bar in the early 1950s, when two young men from Buckeye frequented the bar to play shuffleboard. After a few weeks went by, they noticed that, when closing time came around, the bartender was quick to leave after a long day of work. The two young men thought it would be great to get locked up one night in the bar and have it to themselves for several hours, drinks and all. One night, near closing time, they stepped into the restroom and did not come out. When they did emerge, the lights were out and everybody was gone. After an hour went by, things got pretty dull, and they decided to leave and lock the door behind them. Nobody would ever know the difference. But, when they tried to get out, the door had been locked from the outside. They looked up the phone number and called the café to see if they could get in touch with the bartender/owner. The bartender, eating in the café, could not believe what he was hearing. After much talking to the two intruders, the bartender decided it might be best for all concerned to just let them go. The 2014 photograph pictures a machine shop at the northeast corner of Yuma and Perryville Roads. (Courtesy of author.)

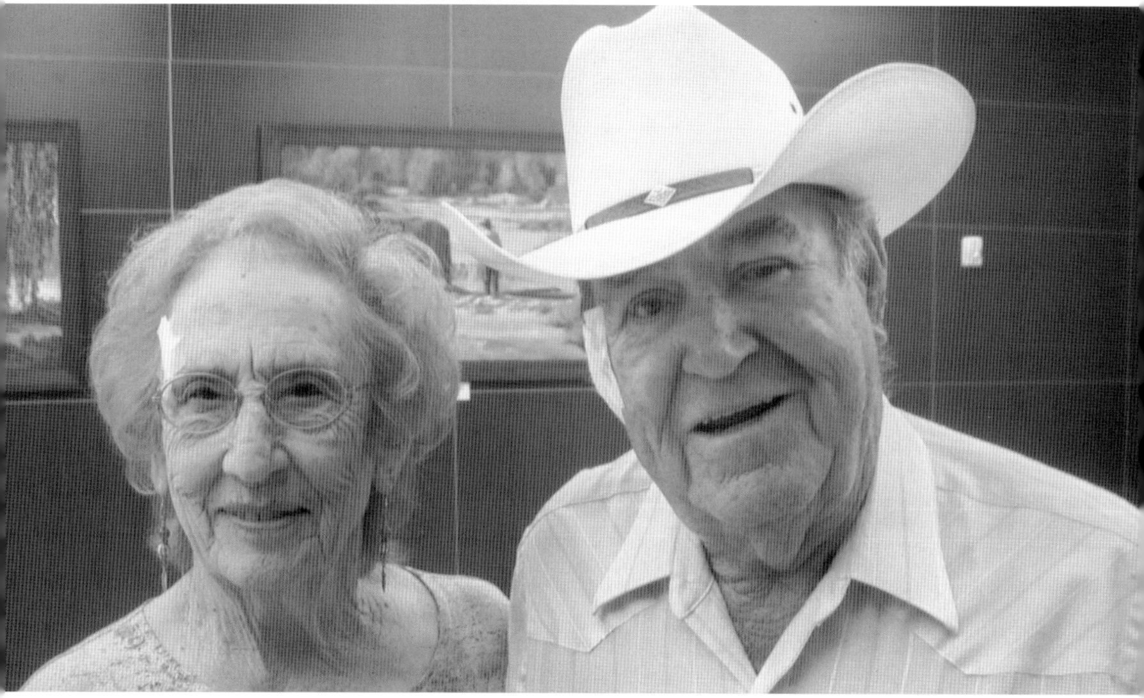

Bass and Irene Aja

Manuel Lavin Aja, father of Bass Aja, came to America in 1920 at the age of 17 from the Basque area of Spain. He worked his way by shoveling coal in a boiler on a ship. A family legend is told that when Manuel Lavin arrived in America and could not speak English, he heard a man say "ham and eggs." With only three words, Manuel traveled across the United States to Flagstaff, Arizona, around 1922. He then got involved in raising sheep. In 1934, he brought a flock of sheep to the Buckeye Valley. Basilio Aja was born in Seligman, Arizona, on October 27, 1929, to Manuel and Matilda Aja. He was delivered at home by a midwife. His family followed the sheep each winter down to the Valley of the Sun, where he graduated from Glendale High School. He was known as "Bass" by most folks, and as "Haytachi" by his family. He met the love of his life, Irene Echeverria, in Flagstaff at a Wool Growers Association meeting. They married on May 30, 1949, three days after Irene's high school graduation, and moved to Buckeye at the Aja sheep operation on Broadway Road. A lifelong sheep man, Bass spent most of his time out on the range or in the fields caring for his flock. He knew and, most importantly, respected hard work. He spent every day trying to instill the ethic of hard work into everyone, whether family or stranger. He said, "Don't talk about it—Do it!" He never really had employees, as he slept in the same camps as everyone who ever worked for him. Bass and Irene, in addition to being Buckeye Pioneer Days royalty in 2012, would have celebrated their 65th wedding anniversary in May 2014. Bass passed away on April 5, 2014. (Courtesy of Irene [Echeverria] Aja.)

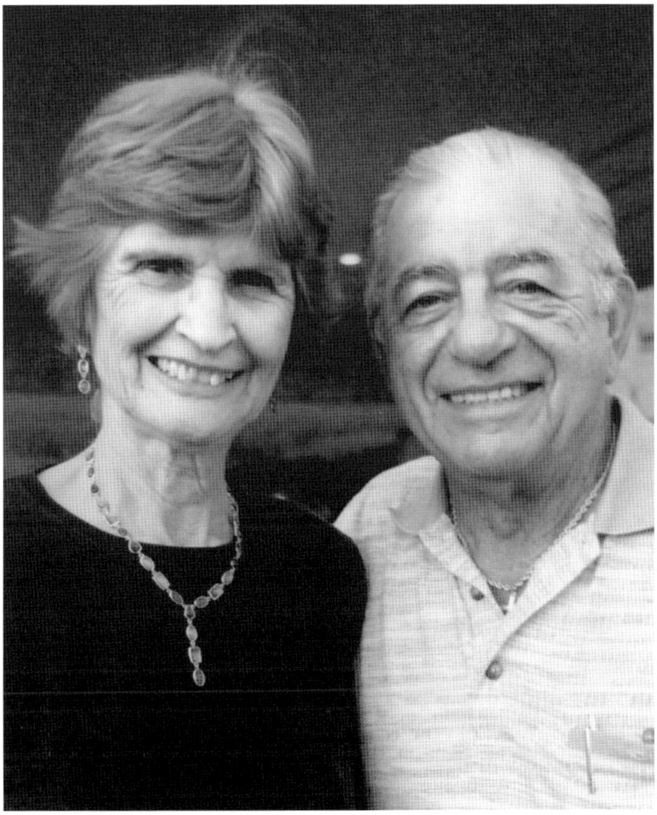

Dick and Annette Napolitano
It could be said that Dick Napolitano came into the world of agriculture through the back door. As a youngster growing up in Pittsburgh, Pennsylvania, making his living as a farmer never entered his mind. His passion was sports, and that love brought him to Arizona in 1953, when coach Clyde Smith recruited him to play football at Arizona State College (now Arizona State University). Many good things came Dick's way during his years at ASU. One of the most significant was meeting his future wife, Annette Marionneaux. They married in April 1958, and Dick went into military service that October. When Dick left the service and returned to Buckeye, teaching and coaching jobs were few and far between, so he and Annette joined her father, James Marionneaux, in his farming and ranching operation. The Marionneaux Ranch raised cattle and grew cotton, barley, and alfalfa on properties scattered throughout the West Valley. Dick did not know a disc from a plow, so his father-in-law taught him. The farm near Palo Verde was one of Dick's favorites. "We had about 350 cows there and my job was to ride through them and check on them and try to rope the little calves if I could, but I was never very good at it." He continued to run Dick Napolitano Ranches, Inc., until he "retired" in 2000 and turned the operation over to his son Rick. Throughout the years, sports continued to play a major role in his life. Dick Napolitano was a Little League baseball coach for over 10 years and spent several years coaching Pop Warner football. He worked with the BUHS football program for a total of 18 years, serving as varsity coach from 1993 to 1997. Throughout the years, Napolitano continued to give to his community. He served on the Acme Gin Co. Board for 35 years and the Soil Conservation Board for 36 years. He was on the governing board of Buckeye Elementary School for 20 years, serving as member, secretary, and president, and he was named Buckeye Valley Chamber of Commerce Man of the Year in 1979. In 1985, Annette made history as the first woman to be chosen Citizen of the Year (which replaced Man of the Year). Dick Napolitano was inducted into the 2014 Arizona Farming and Ranching Hall of Fame. Buckeye Lion's Club benefited from over 40 years of his service. (Courtesy of Annette [Marionneaux] Napolitano.)

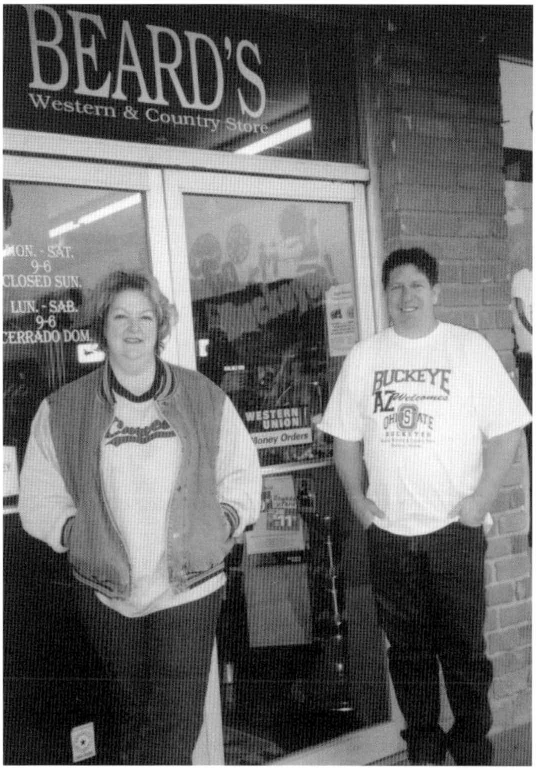

Levi and Judy Beard

Since April 1, 1998, Levi and Judy (Smalley) Beard (left) have owned the former Wolf's Department Store, complete with hardwood floors and the smell of leather. At Beard's Western & Country Store, a man once came in and said, "I'm here, make me a cowboy." Levi graduated from BUHS in 1974, and Judy graduated in 1976. Their Absolute Screen Printing business, managed by their son Curtis, is a city mainstay. With the Main Street Coalition, Levi and Judy weave in the past with the future, bringing in new business to help keep downtown one of Buckeye's financial hubs. The new Buckeye logo is proudly imprinted on Levi's cap (below). The store began in 1939 as Wolf & Nuttall, followed by Wolf's Department Store, then Wolf's Western Wear, then Beard's Western & Country Store. Today, it is Absolute Screen Printing, and the business continues to be a downtown staple. (Both, courtesy of author.)

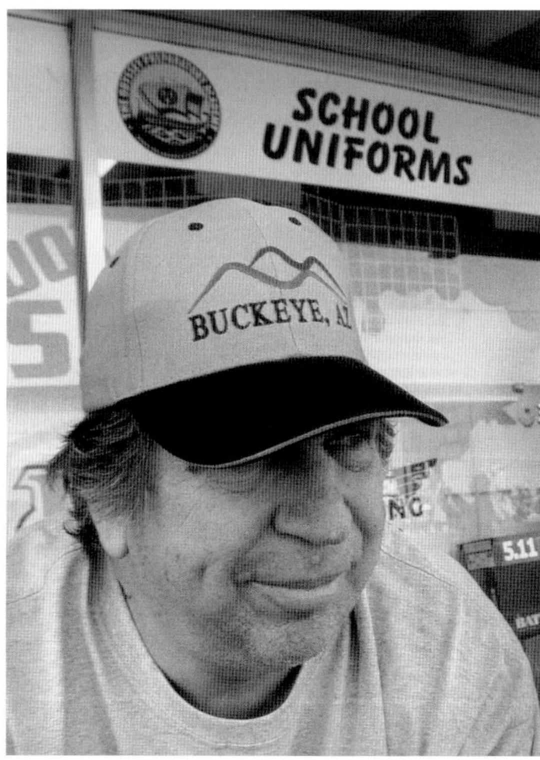

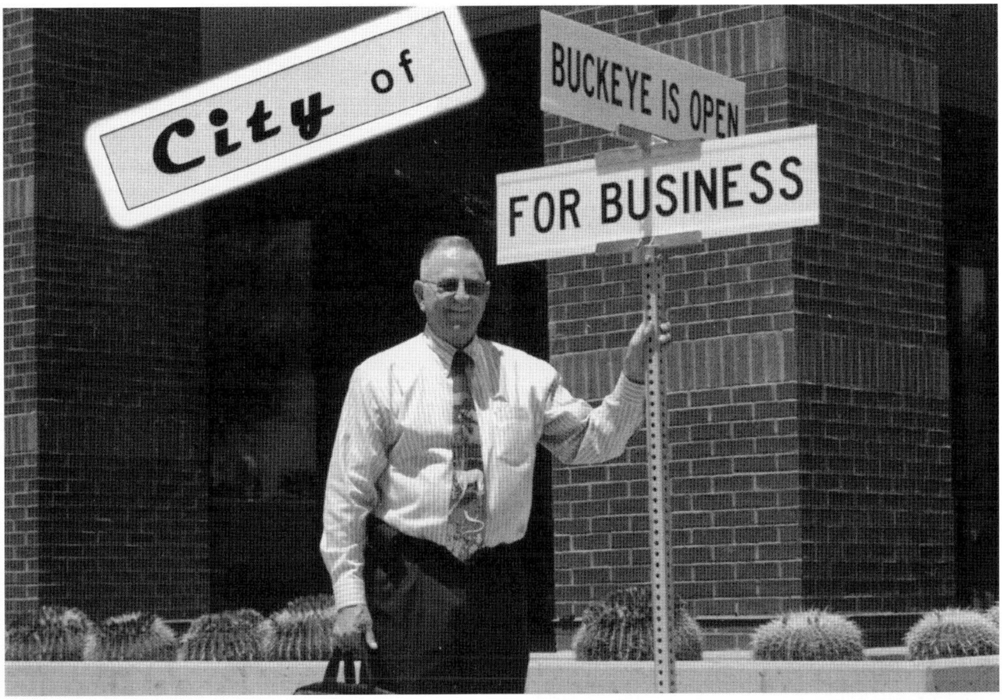

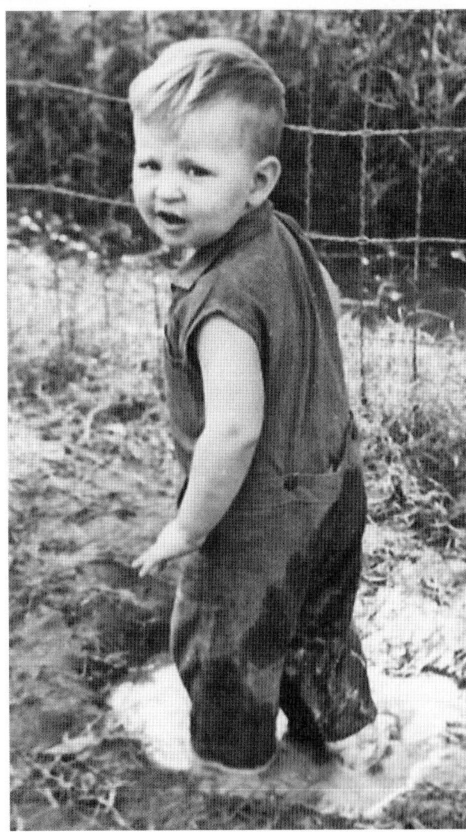

Jackie A. Meck
Meck's birth in 1941 took place directly across the street from the mayor's office in city hall. Meck holds the distinction of being Buckeye's youngest mayor, oldest mayor, and longest-serving mayor, with a gap of 33 years in between. In addition to being the current mayor, he is active in many organizations, including the Buckeye Valley Historical Society, Maricopa Association of Government, Luke AFB Fighter Country Partnership, El Rio Restoration Project–Gila River, and the Buckeye Valley Chamber of Commerce. He received the Buckeye Valley Chamber of Commercer Citizen of the Year Award in 2005. Meck has experience as a bank loan officer, seed salesman, crop appraiser, restaurant owner, accountant, farmer, feedlot manager, real estate agent, and football/baseball coach. He retired in 2007 after 10 years as general manager of the Buckeye Water Conservation and Drainage District. Even at an early age, with his boots on (pictured), he was deep in the water of Buckeye. "I was born here and I've never left. I love my community. I want to create a unity of community spirit throughout the entire Buckeye Valley." He is often heard saying, "Buckeye is open for business" and "Buckeye has water"—two keys to the future. (Both, courtesy of author.)

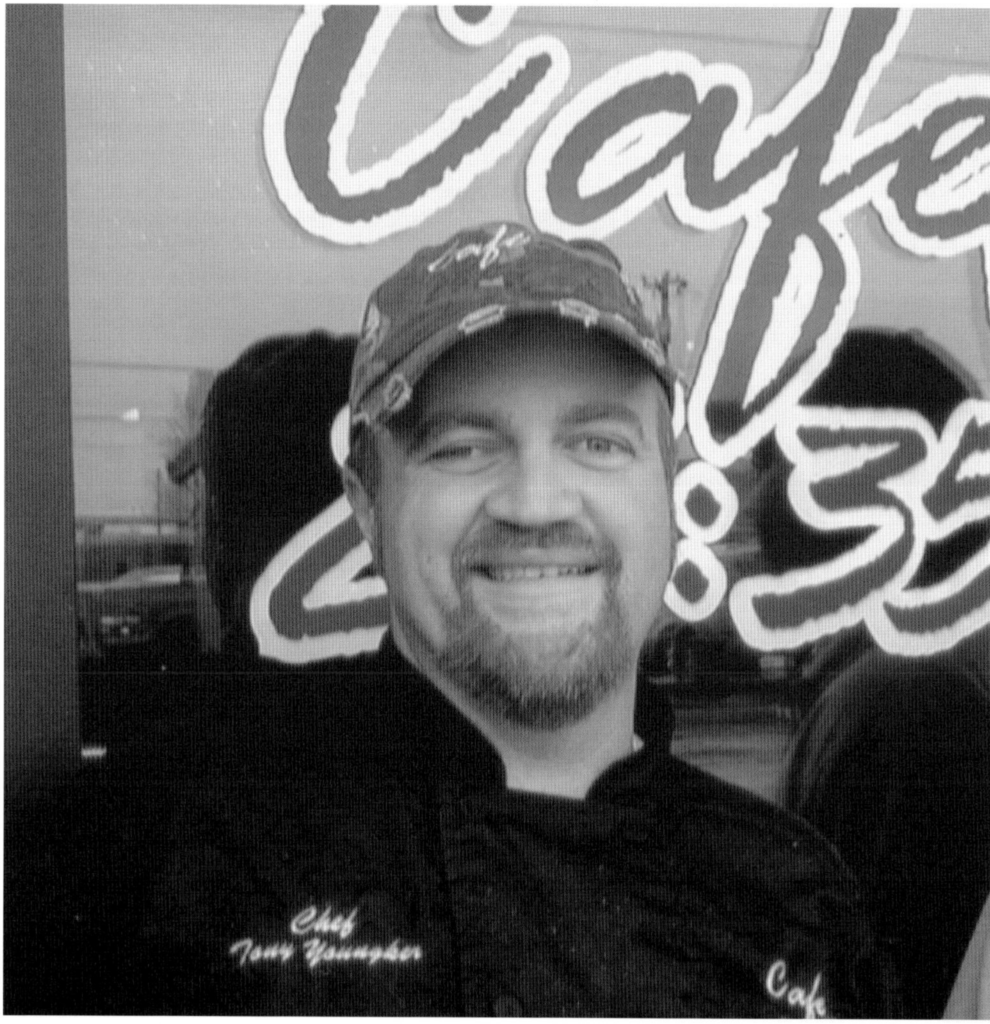

Tony Youngker

In 2012, a Buckeye native turned an 80-year-old downtown building known as the Palms Bar into a unique café, Café 25:35. Tony Youngker is the owner. The café dovetails nicely with the new Buckeye Benbow Veterans Memorial Park. The restaurant serves breakfast and lunch, and its menu includes the following items: the Buckeye Boy Breakfast, Downtown Burger, Tony's Garlic Burger, Arlington Burger, Rainbow Valley Burger, Palo Verde Burger, Liberty Burger, and the Buckeye Taco Salad. The building, vacant for 20 years, was stripped to its bare bones. Workers used pulverized walnut shells to blast more than an inch of plaster off the inside walls. Underneath were red bricks cast in 1930 at a company in Glendale. Youngker's childhood dream was planted by his grandparents. His mother's father, Carl Moore, was a chili cook-off champion who introduced Youngker to cooking. Moore taught him how to make chili, biscuits, and gravy. By the fifth grade, Tony Youngker knew he wanted to be a chef. After graduating high school in 1997, Youngker attended Scottsdale Culinary Institute. He opened the café with the help of his father, John Youngker, a retired cotton farmer. Tony Youngker plans to pass on his love of cooking to a community he says helped raise him. He wants Café 25:35 to be a community gathering place. The name comes from a Bible passage, Matthew 25:35, which emphasizes taking care of others. "For I was hungry and you gave me something to eat, I was thirsty and you gave me something to drink, I was a stranger and you invited me in." (Courtesy of author.)

CHAPTER FOUR

Educators, Creatives, and Athletes

This chapter presents people of various backgrounds, all of who contribute something special to life. Buckeye and its surrounding communities have created numerous artists, authors, entertainers, teachers, and athletes.

Forms of entertainment a century ago were described by Charles Mitten in *The Buckeye Printer Book*. He wrote: "Early summer always brought out the baseball teams of Buckeye, Palo Verde, Glendale and occasionally a team from the west side of Phoenix. Baseball games, ice cream socials, and watermelon feasts were the usual forms of entertainment in summer, while the dances in Joslin Hall were a year 'round custom." An interesting piece of news was written about new dances in the *Buckeye Valley News* on December 3, 1914:

> The good old waltz, two-step, and other popular steps aren't good enough for us anymore. The good old fashioned sociable dances we have been having in Buckeye for years have been the pride of the Valley and the admiration of our visiting friends. But the powers that be have decided that they must go. We have advanced to the stage where we must adopt the silly and vulgar in order to be in style. Our young men and women are learning to dance the Boll Weevil Wiggle, the Texas Tommy Tangle, the Bunny Hug, the Bear Dance, the Half Center, the Buzzard Flop, the Angle Worm Wiggle, and the Puppy Huddle. First thing we know someone will come along and endeavor to teach our women folks to adopt the shadow skirt, slit skirt, and transparent skirt.

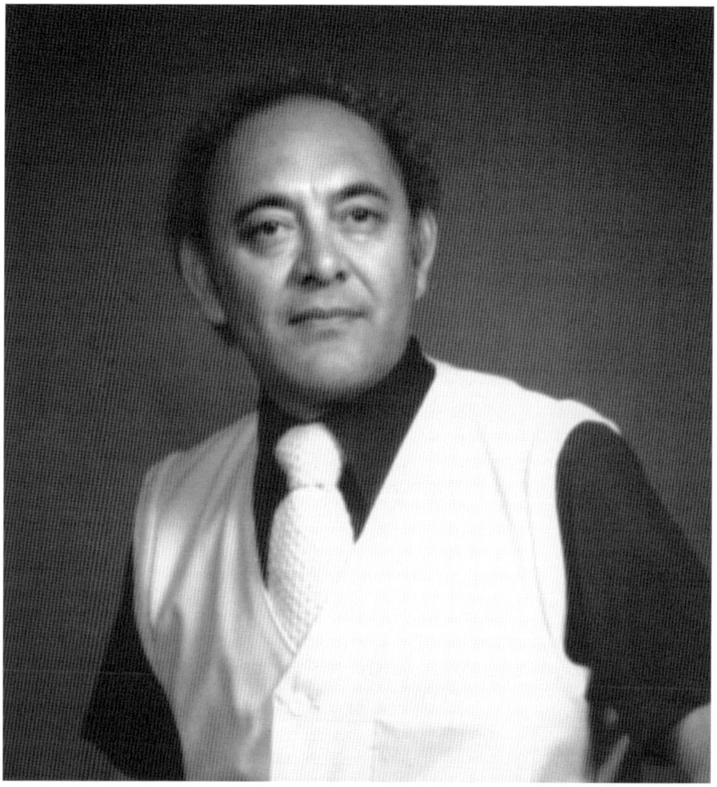

Eddie Amabisca
A Buckeye native, Amabisca became the BUHS art teacher (1960–1987). He made a lasting impression on hundreds of students, some of who remember the "must-do" paintings of lemons and limes and bowls of fruit. One of those students, Shawn (Wingfield) Cameron, is featured in this book. Amabisca preserved BUHS memories and history by being the *Falcon* yearbook advisor for 25 years. (Both, courtesy of BUHS Archives.)

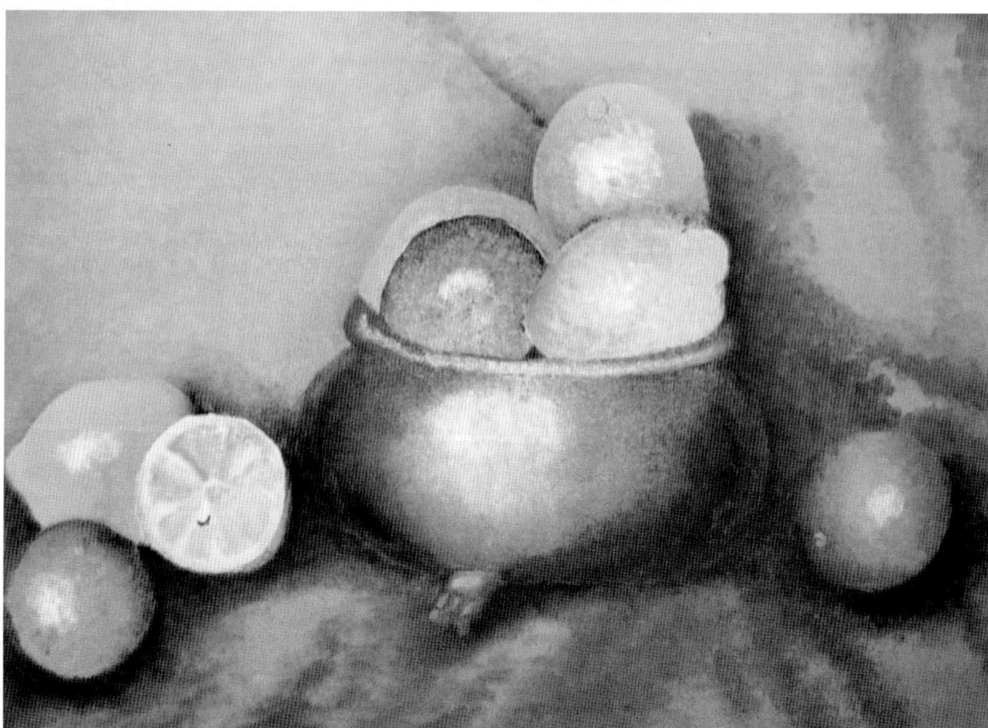

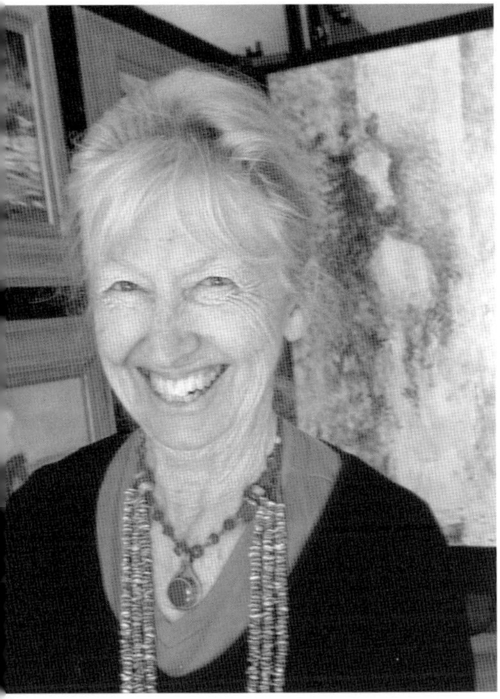

Loretta Musgrave

Loretta (Linn) Musgrave, who grew up on a ranch in south Phoenix, has spent her life capturing the ranching life and other natural scenes with oil and canvas. She is the resident artist at Buckeye's La Placita Café. Musgrave was born in Illinois, but, she says, "I think that was an accident." "My father, George Linn, had been looking, even before I was born, for a ranch out here," Musgrave said. They settled on a ranch at the foothills of South Mountain. Growing up on a ranch, she started drawing at age five and won her first prize at seven years old in a statewide contest. After earning a bachelor's degree in fine arts at ASU, Musgrave farmed cotton in Arlington for 12 years. Like many cotton farmers, she faced difficult times when the price of cotton plummeted. She also used her talents to teach art at Buckeye Union High School (1987–1995). Her artwork is on display in Buckeye City Hall. For many years, she served as vice president of Arizona Cowboy Artists. One of her favorite subjects to paint is donkeys. (Both, courtesy of author.)

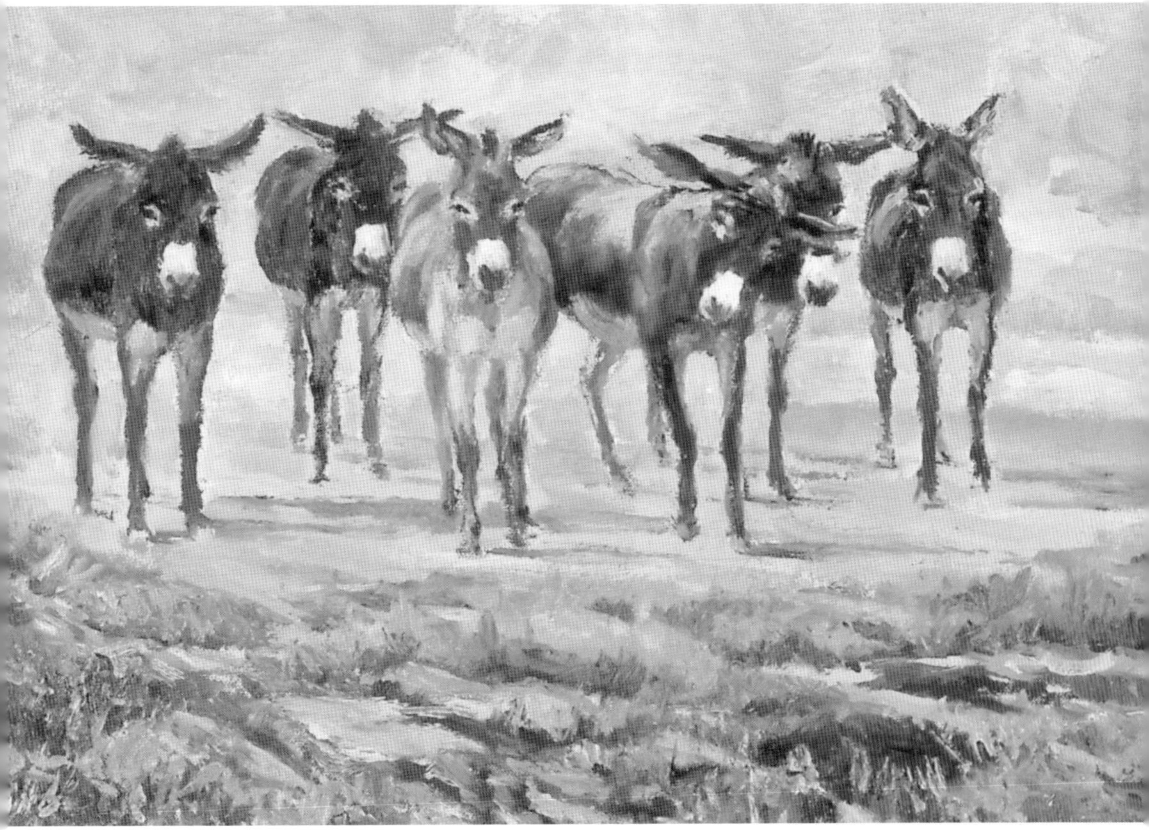

Maude Francis

Maude (Vickery) Francis was born on March 21, 1898, in Los Angeles, California. She was one of four children of her stepfather, Ted, and Molly (Vickery) Shoemaker. In April 1917, her family homesteaded south of the Gila River in the Buckeye Valley. The family moved to Third Street and Jackson Avenue in 1919, and Maude lived there until her death on July 28, 1983. During the Depression and the war years, she provided a home for and fed many young men. She also cared for elderly people and gave gallons of blood to the Red Cross. She raised four sons, Oscar, Jean, Don, and David, in a close-knit family atmosphere. At Christmas and rodeo seasons, Maude Francis literally painted the town with murals covering store windows. Her renderings were depicted on the 1988 Buckeye Centennial Commemorative Plate. Her true love was horses, which were reflected in her artwork. Asa Battles said of Maude in 1932: "Maude was called 'Cha Ma' by her Papago friends. She was a great Horse Woman, a superb Cowboy Artist and Painter. Maude helped and encouraged me to draw and paint more than anyone, when I was a young boy." (Both, courtesy of Ted Francis.)

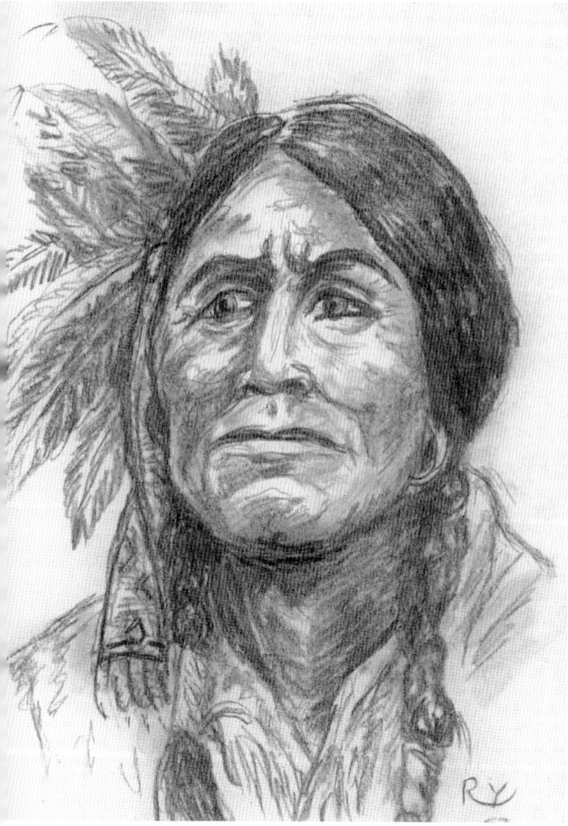

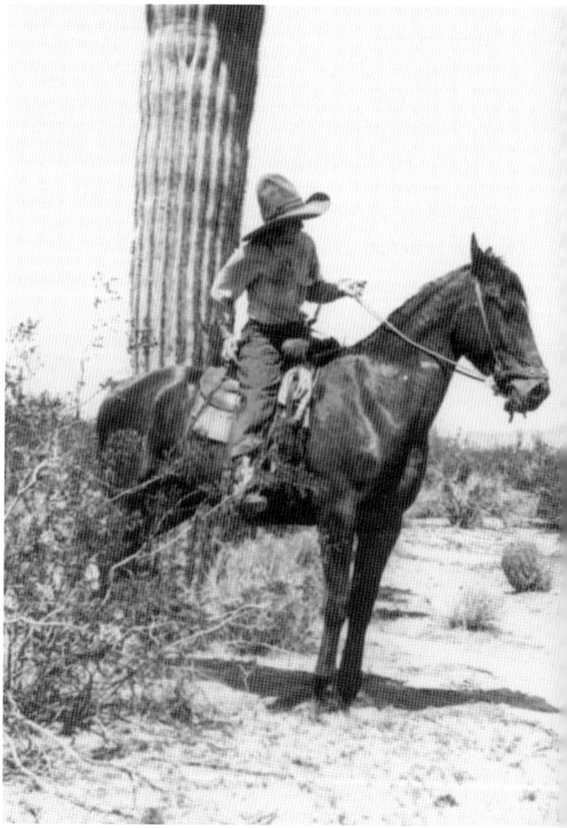

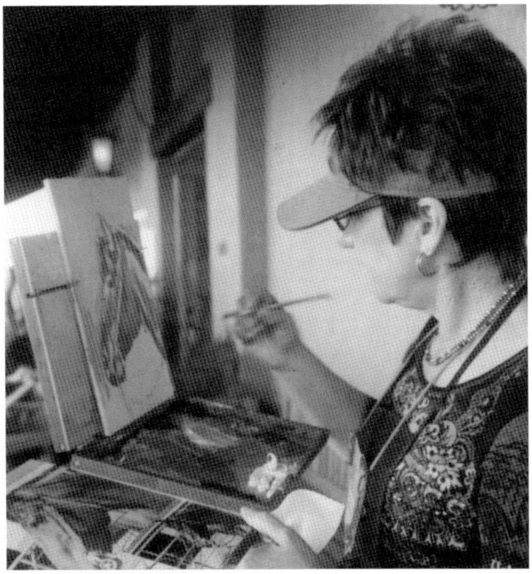

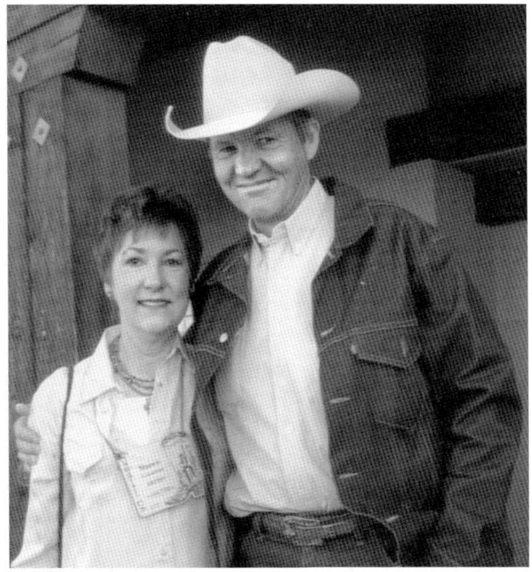

Shawn Cameron
Shawn (Wingfield) Cameron's roots go deep into Western life. She is the daughter of Louis and Billie (Osborne) Wingfield of the Arlington Cattle Company. Shawn (above, left) attended Arlington School and is a 1968 BUHS graduate. Her great-grandfather traveled west on the Oregon Trail in an ox-drawn covered wagon. He and his brother drove 200 head of cattle south into Arizona and began a ranching legacy around 1885 that continues today into the fifth generation. In 1970, Shawn and her "Buckeye Boy" husband, Dean Cameron (above, right), made their home on the Horseshoe Ranch in Bloody Basin and raised three children. She received a degree in education and written expression, but Dean encouraged her pursuit of art. A quote from Shawn tells her story: "I paint contemporary cowboys and cattle ranching scenes I have personally known. My passionate desire is to accurately share the people, animals, and way of life that has been my families' for well over a century in Arizona. My inspiration is the nobility of men on horseback." She was a cofeatured artist at the C.M. Russell Show in 2008. In 2007, she received the Artist Choice Award at the Cowgirl Up Show in Wickenburg, Arizona. (Both above, courtesy of author; below, courtesy of Shawn [Wingfield] Cameron.)

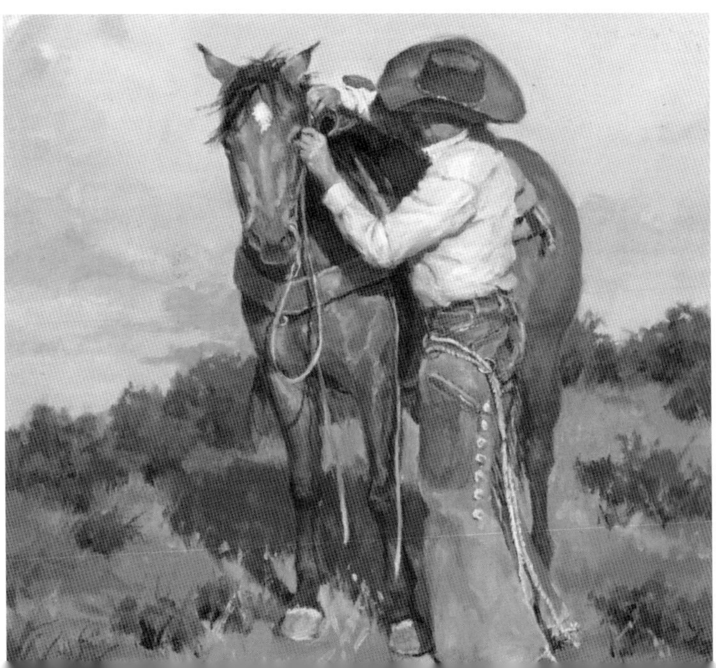

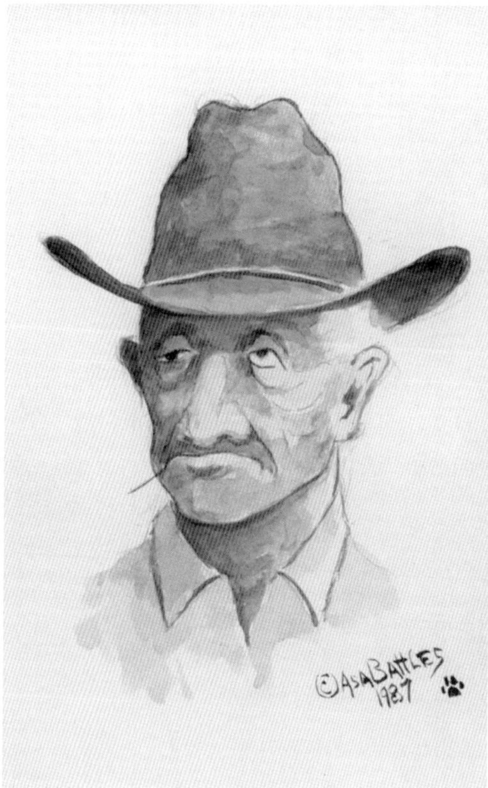

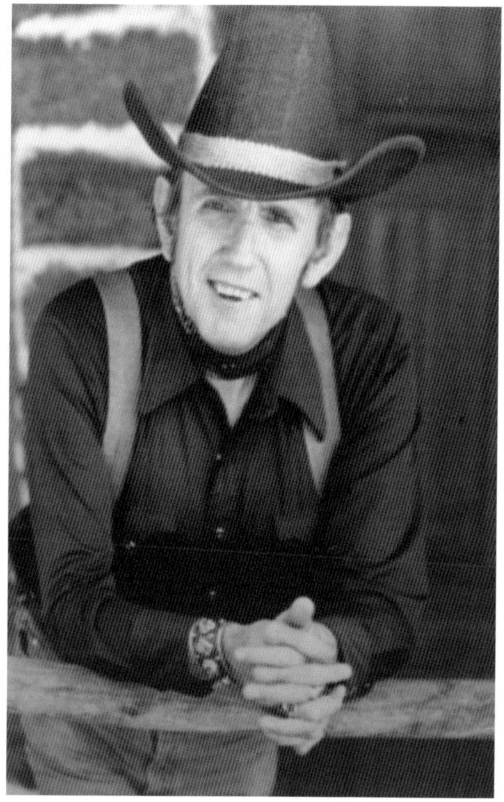

Asa Battles

At six feet, four inches, Asa Battles, born in Buckeye on August 12, 1923, was truly a big "Man of the West." Asa's story is that of the self-made man. His father left the six-year-old boy and his mother to find their own way. Asa helped provide for his mother and himself by working at a local grocery store. He worked hard on several ranches in the area and was fascinated by tales of settlement. Pride in his Cree heritage took hold in those early days and produced an ever-strengthening bond with all things Indian that powered his world for the rest of his life. He fought in the Battle of the Bulge and ended his two-year military stint in 1946. A brief return to Buckeye in 1948 revealed little opportunity for employment. Battles moved to Denver, where he was a warehouse supervisor for 32 years. Asa Battles married Marge Montgomery, who promoted his art. After winning the Most Popular Artist Award at the first George Pippin Art Show in Denver (1976), demand for his talent increased. Battles worked in scratchboard, oils, and sketches, and he lectured, juried, and taught those styles in Colorado and Wyoming from 1980 to 1987. Asa Battles died in 2005. The Buckeye Museum has his artwork on display. (Both, courtesy of Kathleen Rowe.)

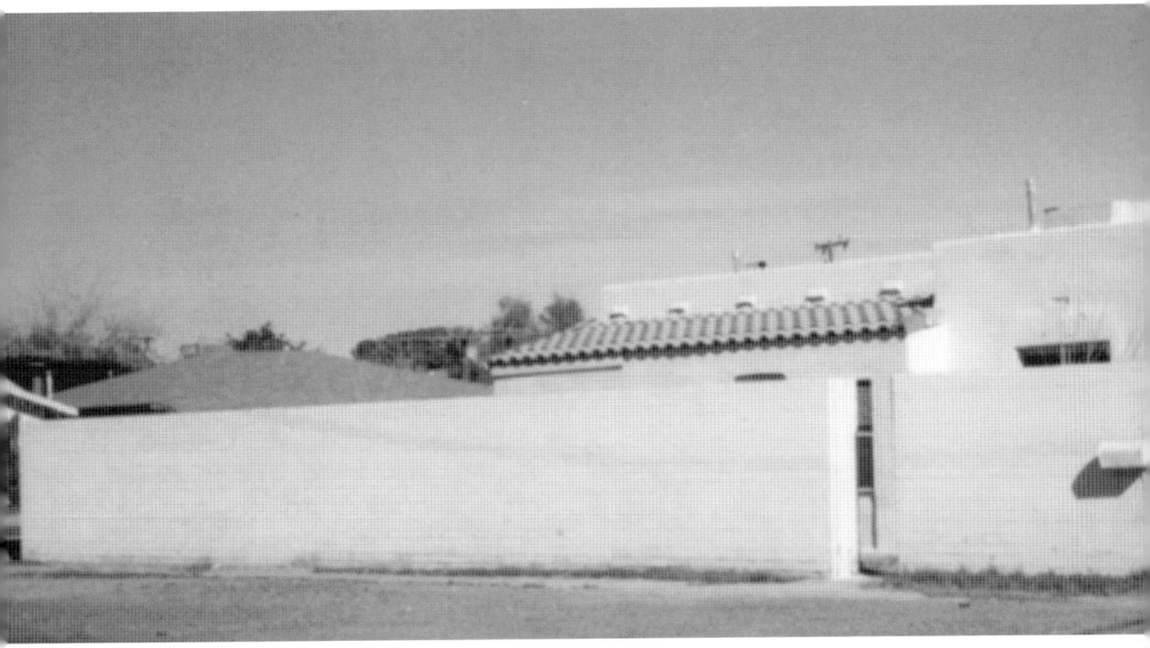

Upton Sinclair

Sinclair (1878–1968) had a significant impact on American culture. He was a novelist, essayist, playwright, and short-story writer whose works reflected socialist views. Sinclair's most famous book, *The Jungle* (1906), launched a government investigation of meatpacking plants in Chicago and led to a change in food laws in America. Recollections of his life in Buckeye are shared by Nancy (Curry) Brainard. The Travis Curry family lived at Seventh Street and Edison Avenue, one block north of where Upton and his wife, Mary Craig Kimbrough Sinclair, lived from 1952 to 1954. The political climate in the United States in the 1950s was such that there was a lot of talk about the communist threat and the Soviet Union. People were anxious when Sinclair chose to move to Buckeye. Local residents were concerned when he built a wall around his property (pictured), thinking he had something to hide. In reality, he had moved to Arizona because of his wife's health. Nancy Curry used to walk past their house almost daily and rarely saw the Sinclairs outside, probably due to Mary Craig's failing health. But this did not stop the neighborhood kids from looking over the wall surrounding the property. The only visible things were numerous sheds built to house Sinclair's many manuscripts. Hunter Kimbrough, brother of Mary Craig, lived in Phoenix and would come to Buckeye every Sunday to check on the Sinclairs. After tending to their needs, he would stop by the Curry home for several hours, where he and Nancy's father, Travis, would have lively political, conservative, discussions. Nancy recalls that Travis met Upton Sinclair on several occasions, having been introduced by Hunter, probably at the Curry Texaco Station. Travis found the famous author to be a quiet and very private person. (Courtesy of author.)

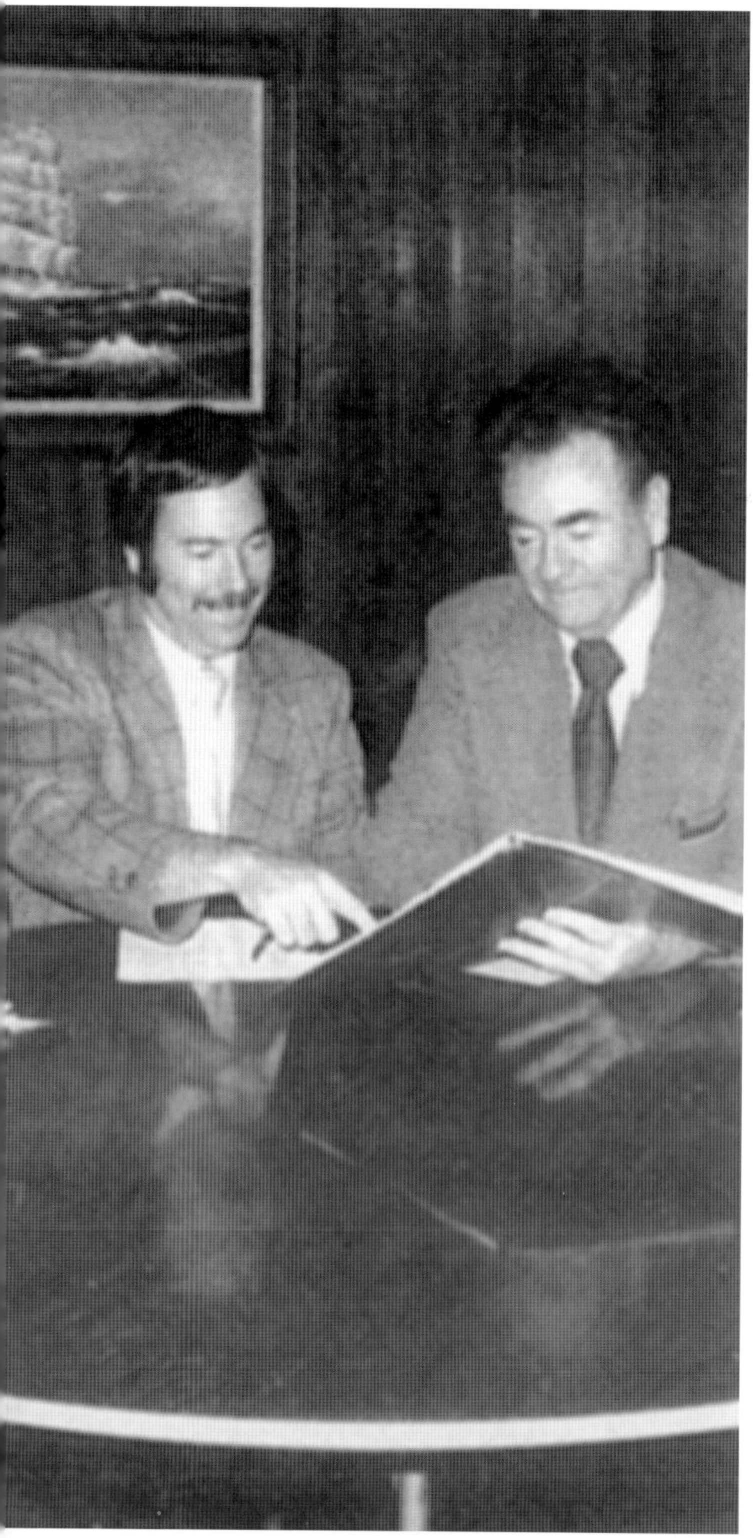

Clyde and Bruce Narramore
The Edward Lawrence and Emma Narramore family joined the community of Palo Verde in 1913. From that family came two outstanding authors in the field of psychology. Edward's youngest son, Clyde, who will be 99 in 2015, is a BUHS graduate. After high school, he earned a bachelor of arts degree and a master's degree at Tempe Normal School (now ASU). He then earned a second master's degree and a doctorate in education at Columbia University. After serving for 12 years as a psychologist for the Los Angeles County Schools, he founded the Narramore Christian Foundation (NCF). Dr. Narramore was the first Christian psychologist to host a national radio program, *Psychology for Living*. He had a bestselling book, *Psychology of Counseling* (1960). In addition, Clyde and his wife, Ruth, were accomplished musicians. For many years, they led Easter sunrise services at the Rose Bowl in Pasadena. Clyde's nephew, S. Bruce Narramore, PhD, was born in 1941, the son of Lawrence and Jennie Belle Narramore. He attended Palo Verde Elementary School and graduated from BUHS in 1959. Bruce (left) and his uncle Clyde (right) cofounded the Rosemead School of Psychology, now a part of Biola University in California. Bruce was president of the Narramore Foundation for 15 years, retiring in 2014. He has authored 10 books, three of which were best sellers: *Help! I'm a Parent* (1972), *You're Someone Special* (1978), and *Freedom from Guilt* (1976). (Courtesy of Bruce Narramore.)

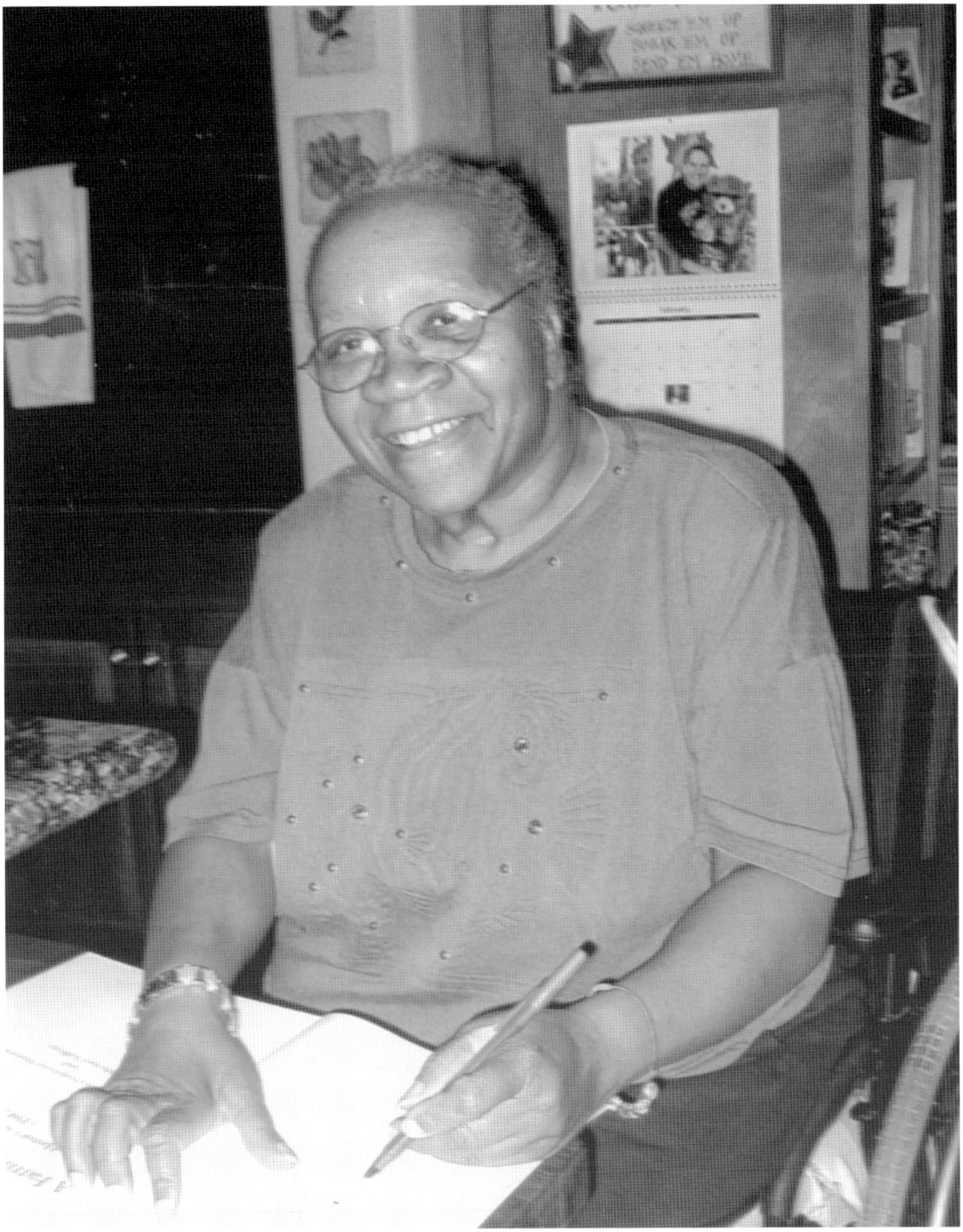

JoAnn Shoemaker

JoAnn (Anderson) Shoemaker was born in Allenville on November 29, 1955, to LeeRoy and Lovie Mae Anderson. She is a 1973 BUHS graduate. In 1989, a devastating car wreck left her with severe injuries and the loss of six-year-old twin boys. Her disabilities made her even stronger, as she planned local Juneteenth homecoming celebrations. She was never a quitter, beginning an Allenville book in 1999. She completed it 13 years later, in March 2012, with assistance from Michael Sullivan. *A Family within a Family* shares the Allenville story from 1945 to 1981. Shoemaker is pictured signing the newly released book in February 2013. (Courtesy of author.)

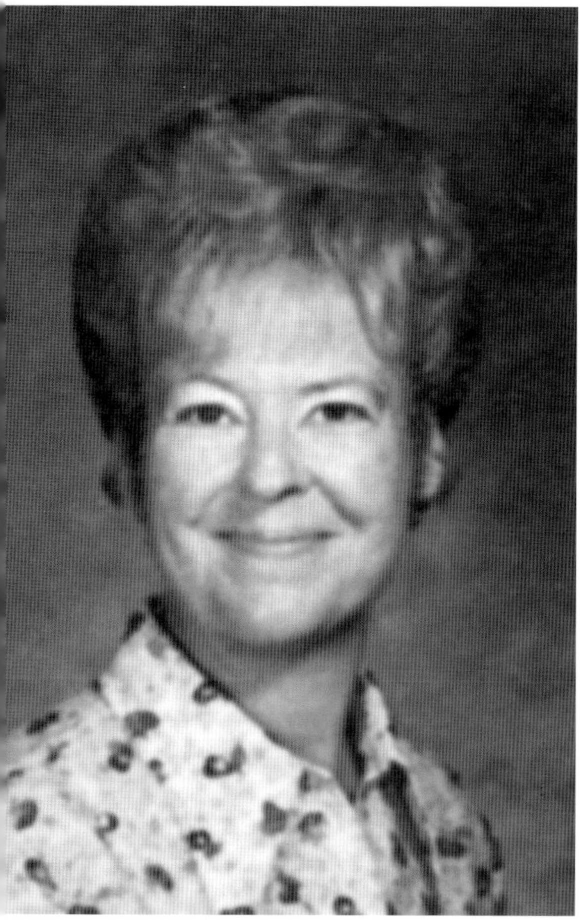

Martha Gayle

Martha (McElhannon) Kauffroath Gayle (left), an only child, was born in 1932 to William and Grace McElhannon. Because they lived in Rainbow Valley, Martha's mother, Grace, had Dr. George Rubel give her a bottle of chloroform in case Waterman's Wash was running and impassable. In that case, she would need to give birth at home. But they were able to ford the wash and get to Phoenix, where Martha was born in Good Samaritan Hospital. Martha lived by Waterman's Wash for the first three years of her life (below). In 1935, the family moved to Tempe. Martha returned to the Buckeye Valley (Arlington) in 1943 and attended BUHS (1946–1950). She married Frank Kauffroath in 1952, and the couple moved to California. She moved back to Buckeye in 1991 and helped celebrate the BUHS 75th anniversary (1995–1996). Martha wrote many articles for the *Buckeye Valley News* about former BUHS students. The first one was an interview with Velma (Couch) Benbow. Her last interview was for 2012 Pioneer Days royalty Les and Joan Meredith. She wrote a total of 86 interview stories. Martha also researched and wrote articles about local POW camps during World War II. Martha and Frank had four children: Loren Kauffroath, Carol Down, Elizabeth Bates, and Cynthia Hendrick. (Both, courtesy of Martha Gayle.)

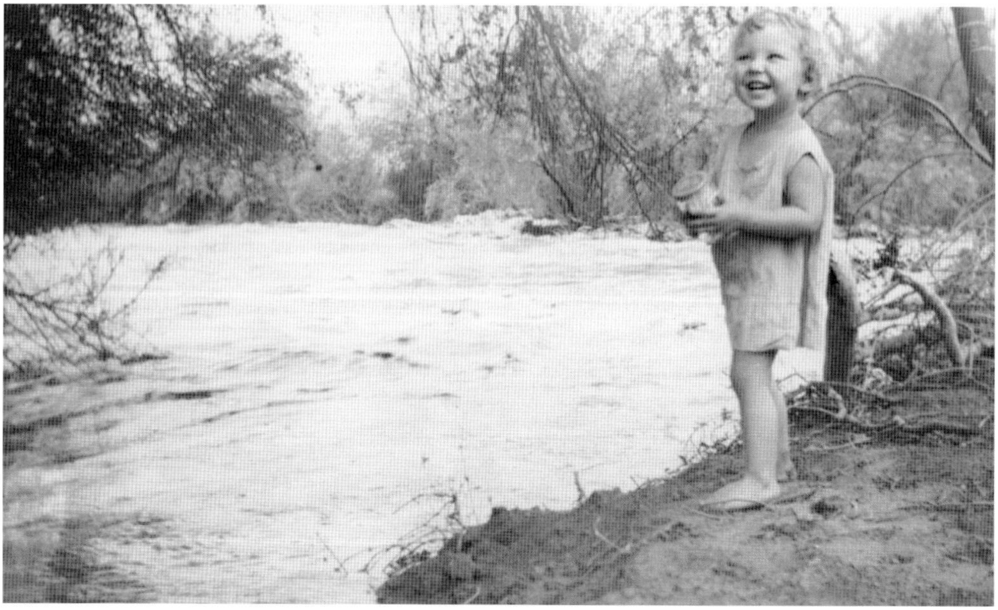

Dan Narramore

Born in Phoenix in 1937 to Othel and Eliza (Walton) Narramore, Dan Narramore (right) lived in "downtown" Palo Verde, next door to a home his Walton grandparents built in 1910. He still lives in Palo Verde as the unofficial "mayor." As a boy, he crossed the road to Palo Verde School and later to BUHS (1950–1954). He then graduated from ASU in 1959. Narramore's hobby for a long time has been roping. He participated in his first roping contest at age eight, making this a nearly 70-year hobby. He says, "the addiction takes over and you don't have a choice." In the spring of 2014, World Series roper "Cowboy Dan" was 75 and still roping strong. He states, "One of the reasons that it was like that, is because when I was a kid, I wanted a bicycle and the folks wouldn't get me one because a youngster, on his bicycle in Buckeye, had gotten hit by a car and was killed. So, they told me, If you want to go somewhere, you saddle up a horse and go and that's what I did." In 2014, Narramore said the best horse he has ridden is the one he has now, a 14-year-old horse named Rooster (pictured). (Both, courtesy of Alois Kutnar.)

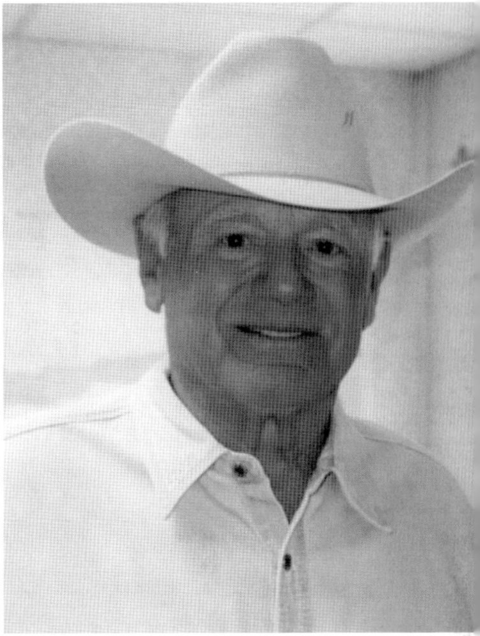

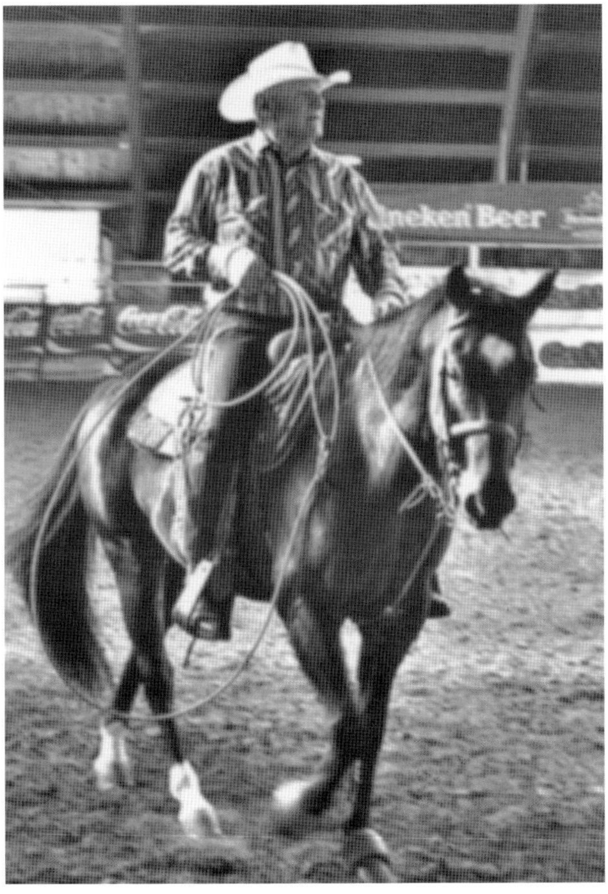

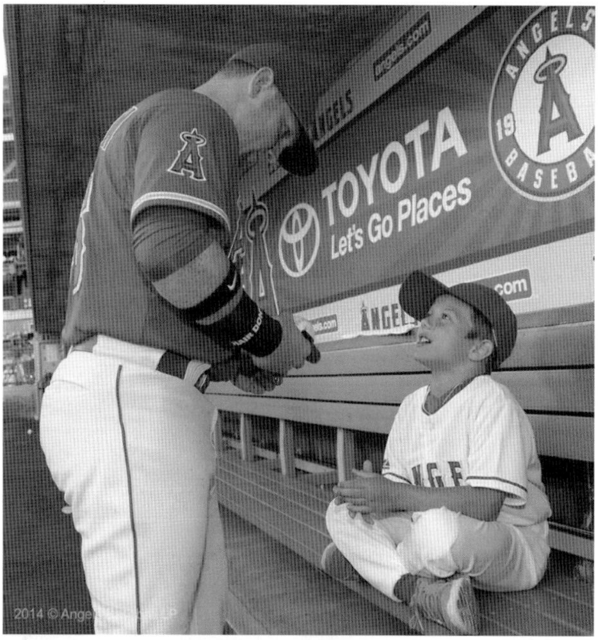

Kole Calhoun

Kole Alan Calhoun, a 2006 BUHS graduate, is a professional baseball outfielder for the Los Angeles Angels of Anaheim. He was drafted in 2010 by the Angels and made his major-league debut on May 22. On July 15, 2014, the *Arizona Republic* reported that Calhoun (left), the Angel's leadoff hitter, had scored more runs than any player in the major leagues since May 29, 2014. (Courtesy of Mary Nunez.)

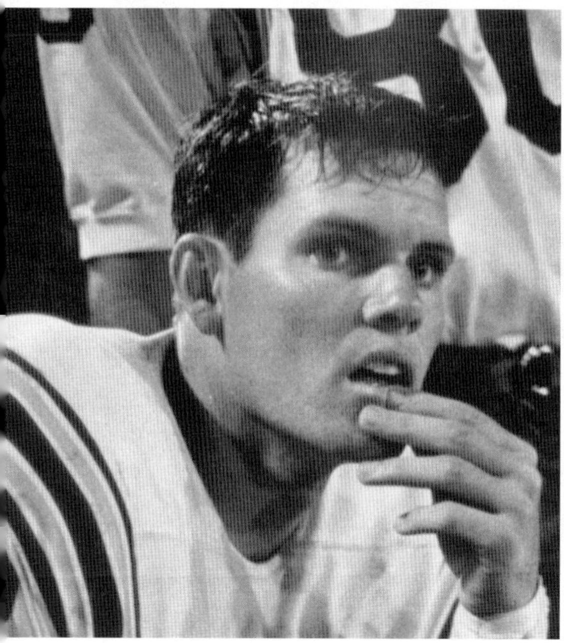

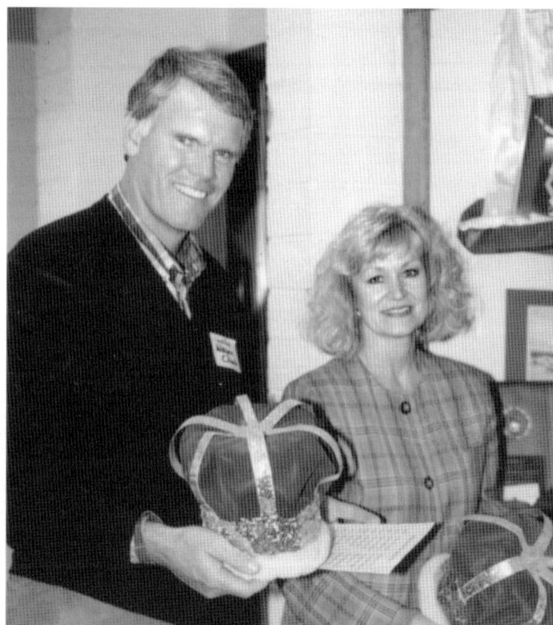

Wayne Clark

In 1973, the *Buckeye Valley News* reported that Wayne Clark (above, left), a 1965 BUHS graduate, had been quarterbacking for the San Diego Chargers a great deal that season and had done well. He was drafted by the Chargers in 1970 and was with the team until 1974. Clark's last year with the NFL was in 1975, playing for the Kansas City Chiefs. He offers these words for others: "Football, as wonderful of a sport as it is, isn't so important. The most important thing isn't if we win or lose, it's about the player." At the BUHS 75th reunion in 1995, Wayne and Susan (Youngker) Truax (above, right) checked out the crowns they wore as 1964 homecoming royalty. (Both, courtesy of BUHS Archives.)

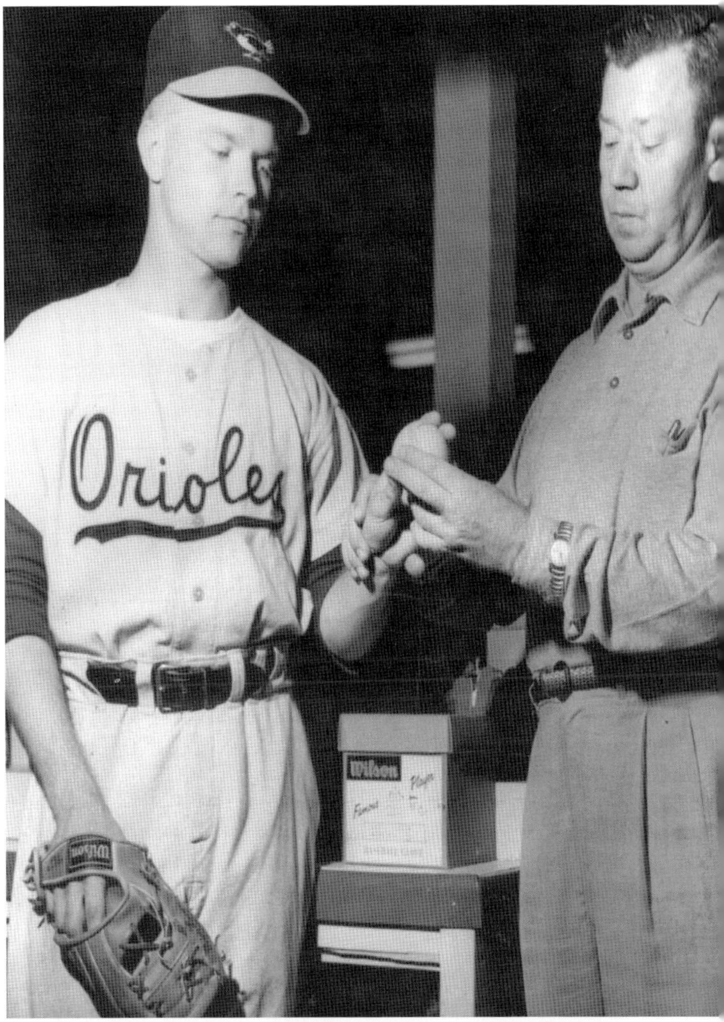

Buzz Bartylla

Bartylla, a 1955 BUHS graduate, was a left-handed pitcher for the school's 1955 state champions. It was the first, and only, state title for BUHS. The photograph at right of Buzz Bartylla and his dad, Ed (owner of Western Auto Store), was taken during 1958 spring training with the Baltimore Orioles in Scottsdale, Arizona.

The following year, Buzz Bartylla went to Knoxville, Tennessee, and played with a Class A minor-league team for one year. After that, he played in Canada for two years. That completed his professional baseball career. Bartylla was probably the first BUHS baseball player to play for a major-league or minor-league team. On February 27, 2009, he pitched at the first BUHS Baseball Alumni Game. Other alumni players that day are shown in the below photograph. They are, from left to right, Ronnie Henry, George Miller, Buzz Bartylla, Bruce Heiden, Robert Edgar, and Earl Wooley. (Right, courtesy of Buzz Bartylla; below, courtesy of BUHS Archives.)

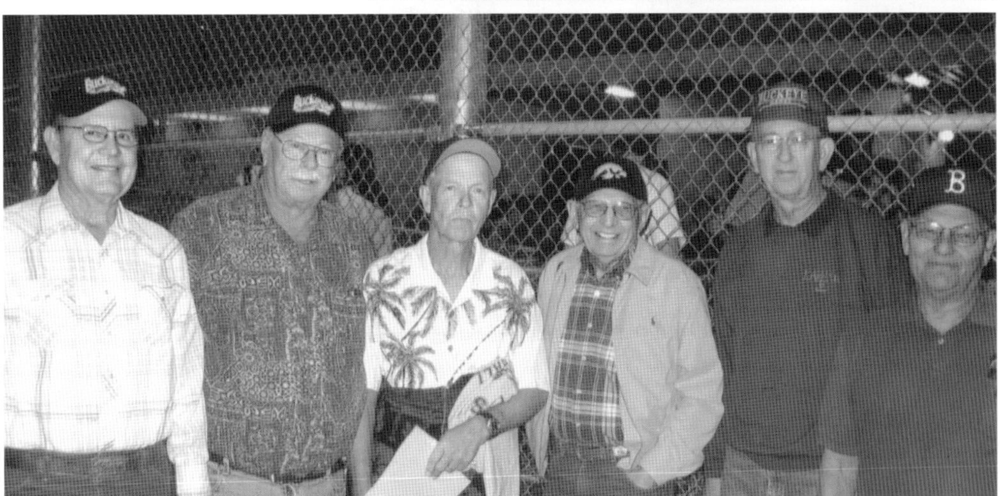

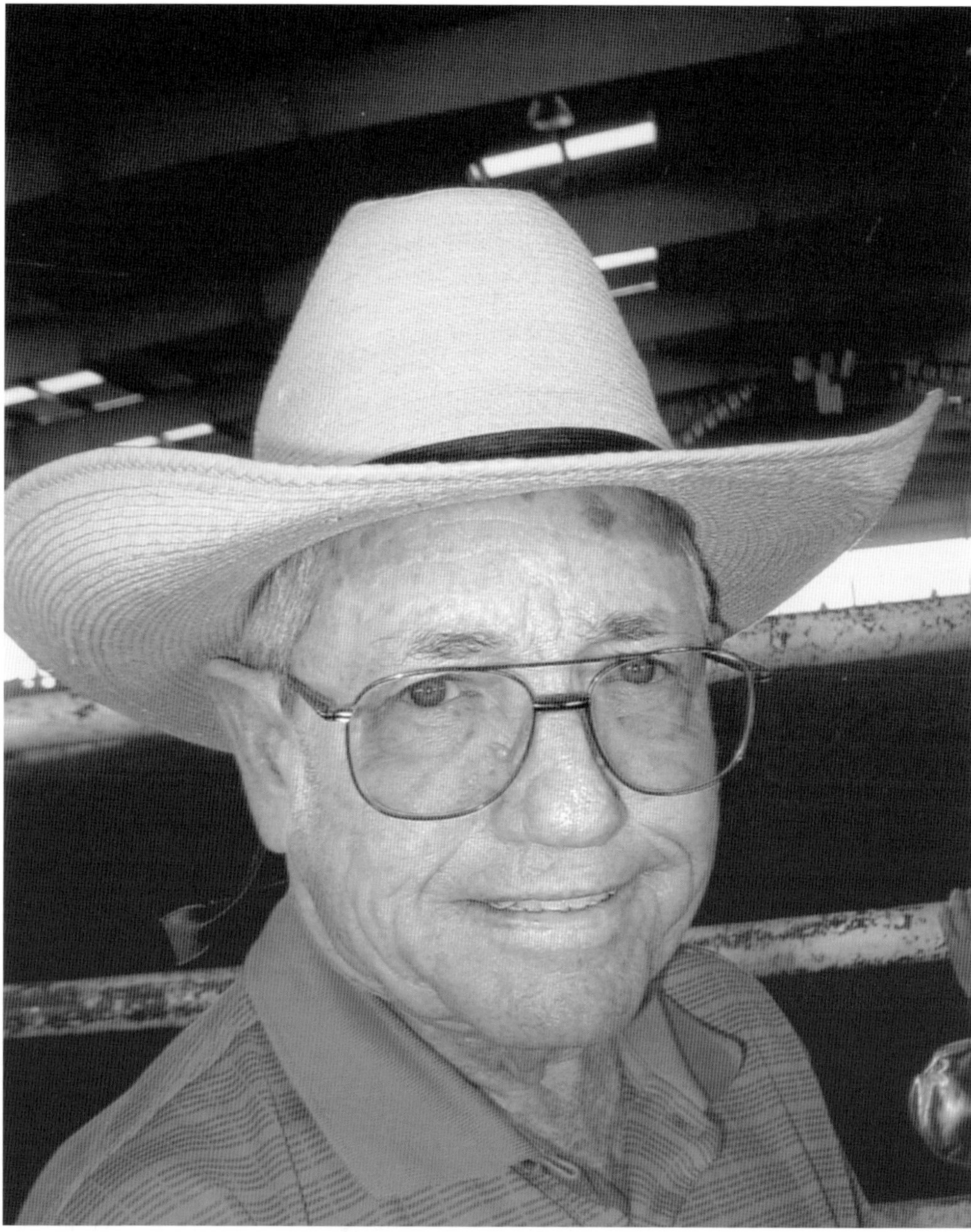

Art Arnold

Art Arnold is truly a cowboy's cowboy. Born and raised on the ranch of his father, Carl Arnold, on Hazen Road, Art continued the cowboy lifestyle, raising cattle, competing in rodeos, and providing livestock for local rodeos. His event of choice was team tying/team roping. The team-tying event requires the header of the team to dismount and tie the steer's hind legs. With his skill, speed, and desire to compete, Arnold made team tying, a difficult event, look easy. He qualified for his first National Finals Rodeo (NFR) in 1959, just one year after graduating from Buckeye Union High School. Not only was it Arnold's first NFR win, 1959 was the first year of NFR team roping! He ultimately qualified for 13 NFRs and became the 1968 PRCA (Professional Rodeo Cowboy Association) world champion team roper. (Courtesy of author.)

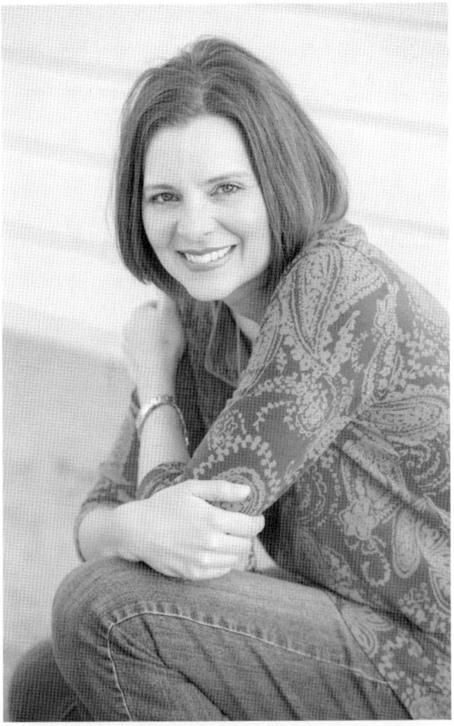

Amy Gerak

Amy (Saylor) Gerak has shared her gift of music since she began singing for others at age seven. Her mother, Sherry Saylor, says Amy began singing into a hairbrush at age three. Amy shared a favorite memory: "When I was growing up, I remember walking out on my parents' farm and singing to the mountains all around me. Though the mountains weren't very near, they encircled me. It was just me, Jesus, mountains and I was worshipping. That was a beautiful start to my lifelong love of music and how music so powerfully connects us to God individually and corporately. I so enjoy connecting with God and people through His music in me." Her favorite songs are "Amazing Grace" and "The Old Rugged Cross." She has produced two CDs, each with eight original songs. The second CD (below) is titled *Asaph's Daughter*. Amy is a Buckeye native, a 1994 BUHS graduate, a wife (to husband Ed Gerak), a mother of twins, born in 2006 (Moses and Lancey), a worship leader at Grace Fellowship, and a singer extraordinaire. She also was a high school tennis player on four state championship teams (1991, 1992, 1993, and 1994). (Both, courtesy of author.)

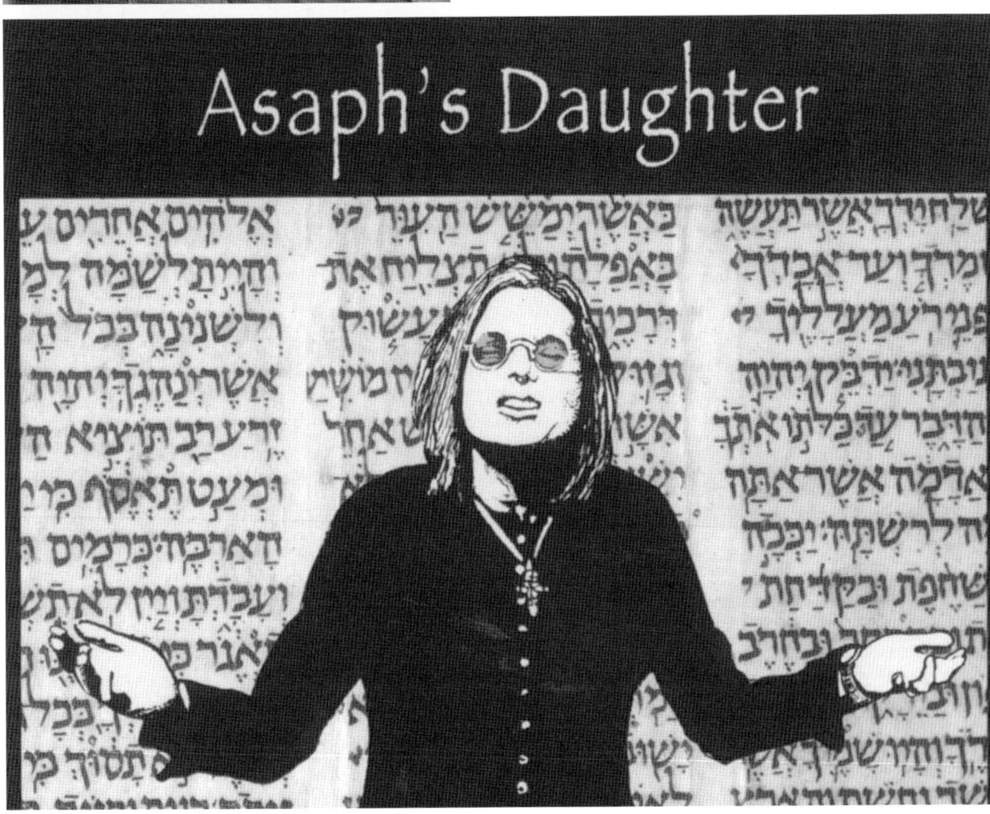

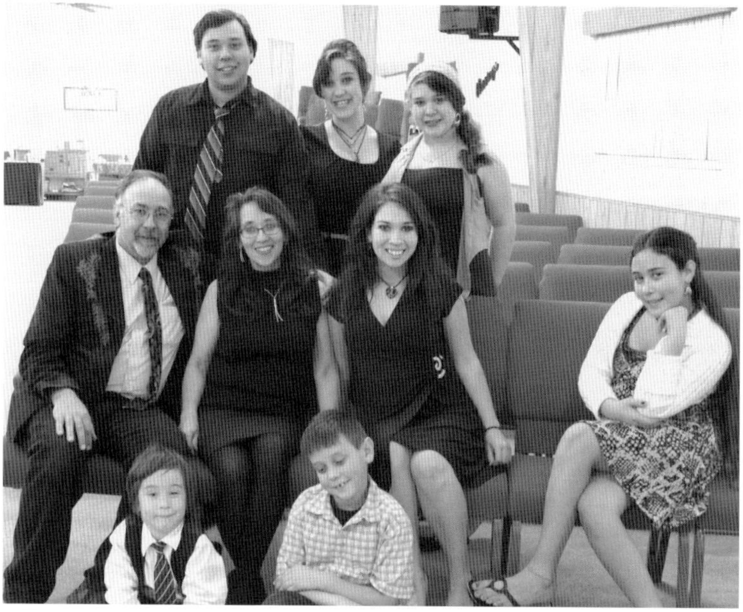

Bost Family Traditions
Jeff Bost graduated from BUHS in 1982 and was assigned to West Point. Pamela Dennis graduated from BUHS in 1984. The couple started "going steady" in 1979 and married on May 30, 1986. Jeff was assigned to Armored Cavalry at Fort Knox, Kentucky. He chose Kentucky because of the great bluegrass music scene. Pamela finished her undergraduate work at the University of Kentucky. Jeff left the Army in 1995, and the couple settled in Bisbee, Arizona. Their children are Brooklyn (born in 1989), Micah (1991), Faith (1993), Liberty (1996), Felicity (1999), Charity (2002), Will (2005), and Jon (2008). From 1995 to 2002, Jeff worked for Iron Horse Guest Ranch as a staff entertainer. Bost Family Traditions began in 2002 and won fourth place at a contest. The family went on the road to play music beginning in 2006. From 2006 to 2013, the group played about 150 concerts per year at churches, festivals, and resorts. (Both, courtesy of Pam [Dennis] Bost.)

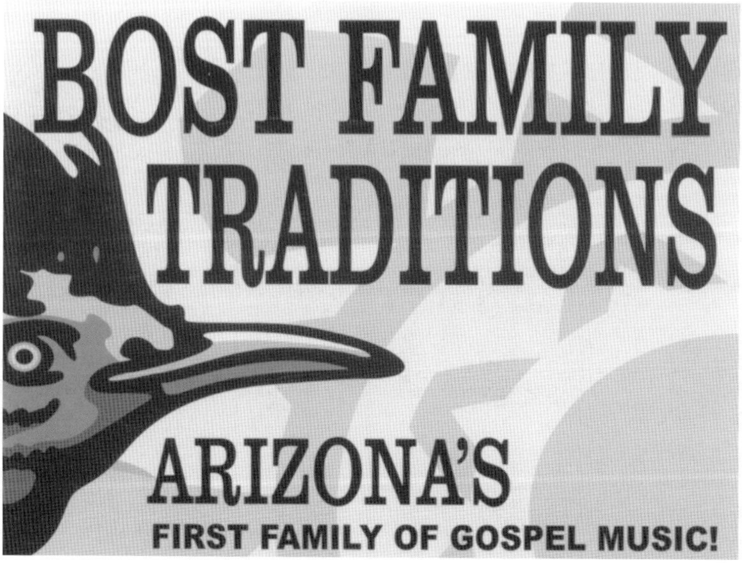

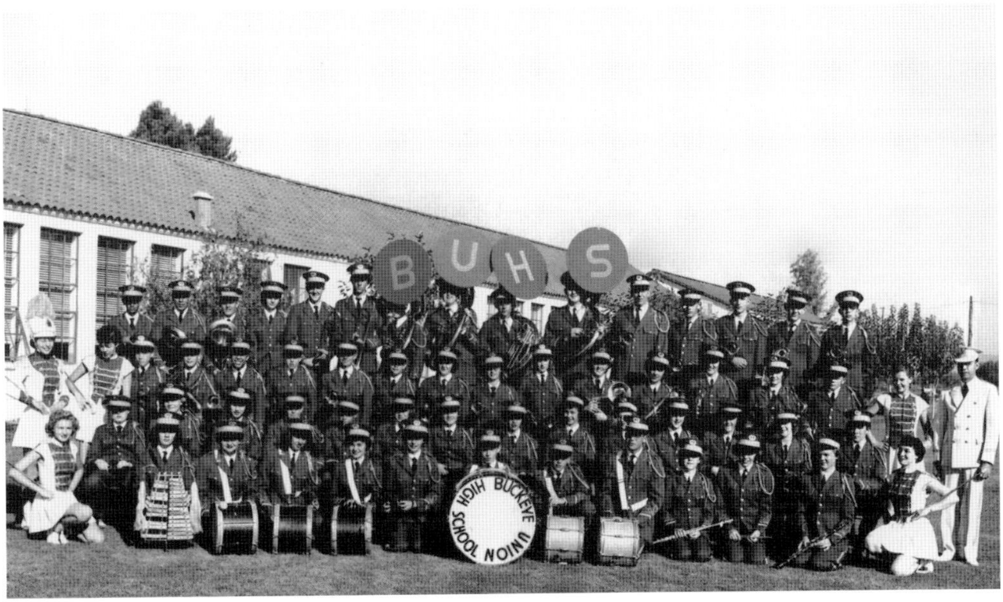

John McConnell

Music at Buckeye Union High School from 1945 to 1962 was under the direction of John McConnell. His music legacy began in the basement under the stage in the BUHS auditorium, erected in 1930. Former students have never forgotten the "stand at attention" discipline provided by McConnell, as displayed in the above photograph of the 1955–1956 marching band. He directed the BUHS band in 1996 for the school's 75th-anniversary pageant (below). McConnell then presented the baton he used to the BUHS archives. It is on display in the BUHS Verlyne Meck Library. (Both, courtesy of BUHS Archives.)

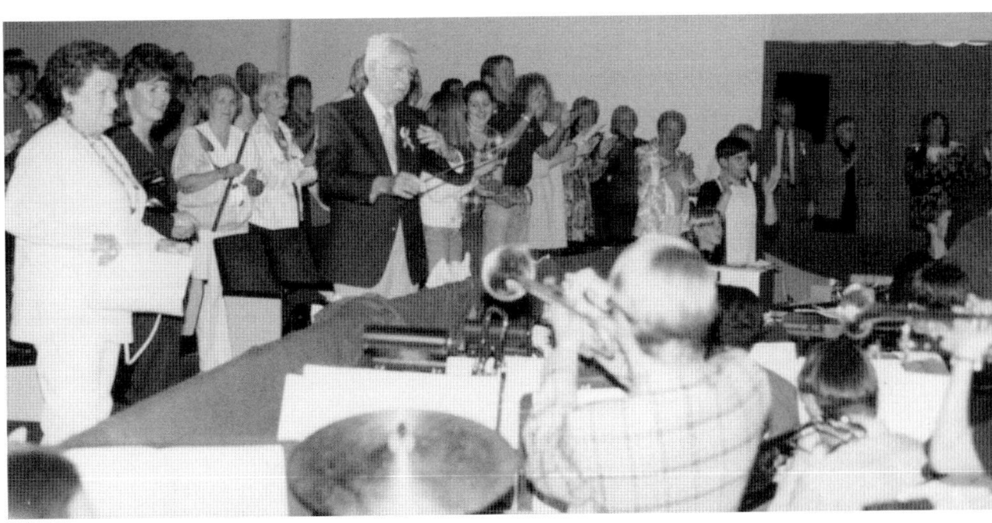

William "Bill" Olsen

"Ole" Olsen was born in Bogalusa, Louisiana, on April 26, 1912. He came to Tempe in 1919 and graduated from Tempe Union High School in 1930. He was captain of the all-state basketball team and a four-year baseball letterman. He had been offered a professional baseball contract. In his spare time, Olsen was also a high school state tennis champion. In 1934, he graduated from Arizona State Teachers College (now ASU) as an all-conference guard on the basketball team, the third baseman on the baseball team, and president of his college fraternity. He graduated during the Depression, a time when jobs were hard to find. He was hired as a football and basketball coach at Ajo High School in 1936. In 1940, BUHS principal Herschel Hooper convinced him to move to Buckeye to become the basketball and baseball coach. During the next 29 years, he coached football, basketball, baseball, and tennis, and he served as vice principal, principal, and athletic director. Olsen's greatest loves were supervising student activities and being a senior class advisor, athletic director, and men's and women's tennis coach. In 1969, when he died, the longtime senior student/athlete award, as well as the football stadium, were named in his honor. (Both, courtesy of BUHS Archives.)

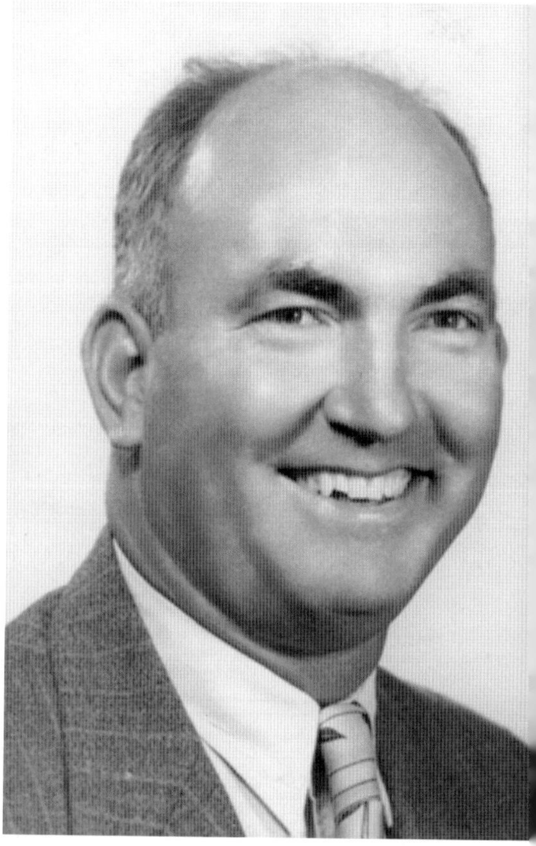

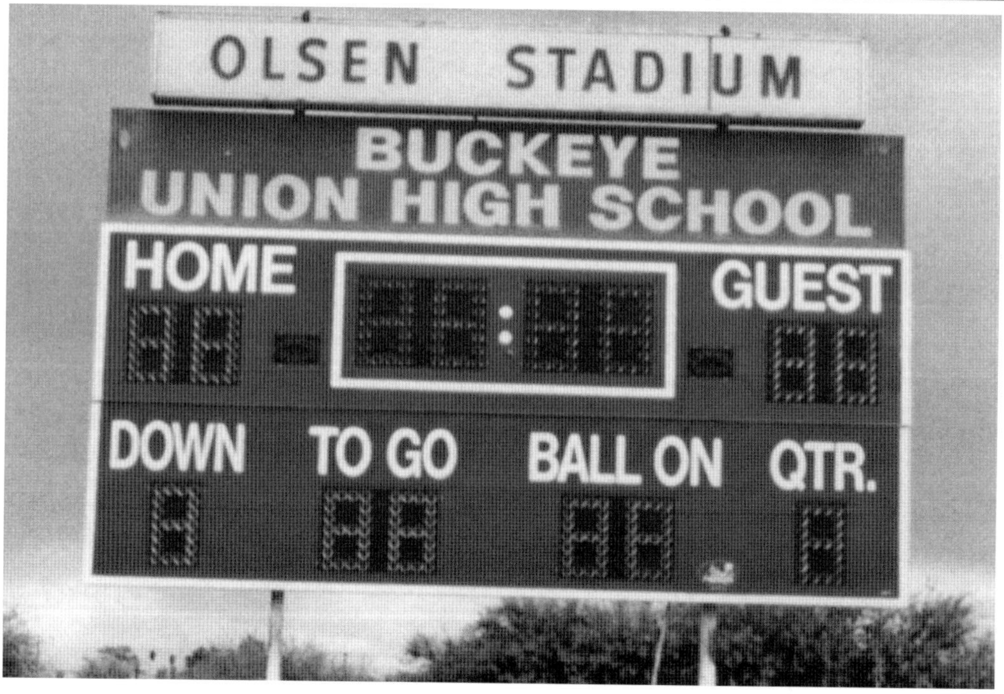

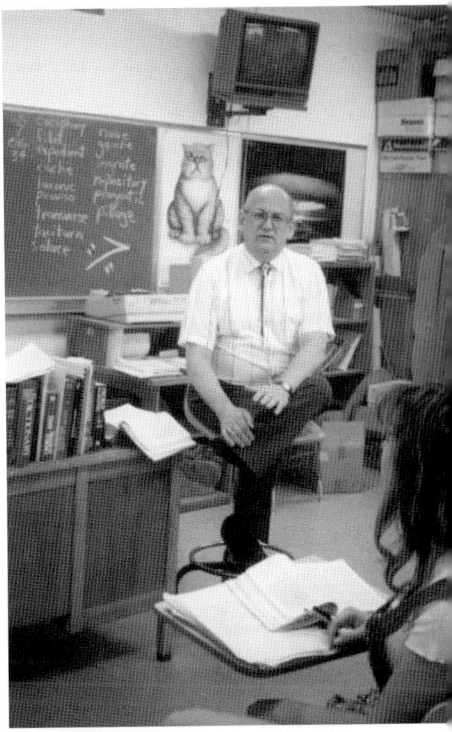

James D. Grosbach

James Douglas "Jim" Grosbach was born in New Albany, Indiana, in 1939. His family in 1952 moved to Phoenix, Arizona, where he attended high school. He graduated with a bachelor's degree in English from Grand Canyon College in Phoenix, married Gloria Norris in 1962, and spent two years in the US Army. After the military stint, the Grosbachs returned to Arizona and settled in Buckeye, where they both pursued teaching careers. During this time, they both earned master's degrees. Jim taught English at BUHS for 32 years, retiring in 1996 and setting the school's record for years in the classroom. He read theology, philosophy, science fiction, popular fiction, and *Batman* comic books. When assignments were due, he sat in a lawn chair in front of his 710 Eason Avenue home and received last-minute term papers. Because he taught *Julius Caesar*, students commemorated Caesar's assassination on March 15, 44 BC, with a toilet-paper ritual at Grosbach's house every year on the Ides of March. Grosbach used a unique shorthand to announce classroom activities on the chalk board: GST (Grosbach Story Time), GTPE (Grosbach True Personal Experience), GVTT (Grosbach Video Tape Time), GFQ (Grosbach Famous Quotes), and TAG (Thanks a Lot Grosbach)! (Right, courtesy of BUHS Archives; below, courtesy of Jim Grosbach.)

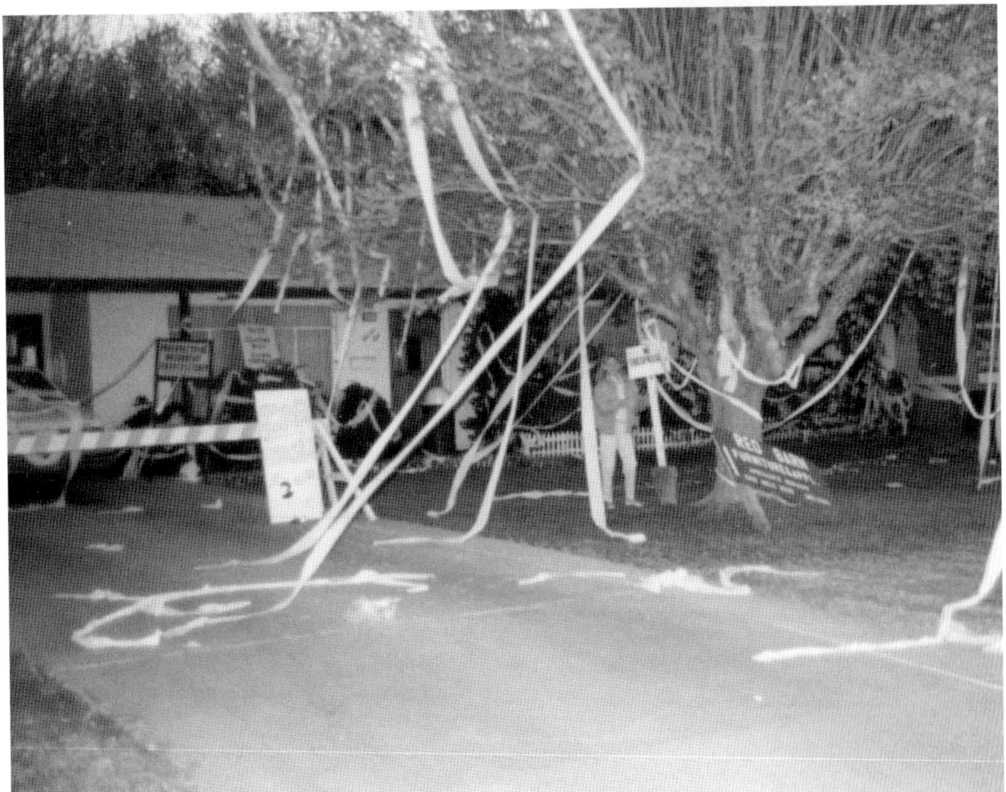

Dr. Clifton Frederick Newberry Jr.

Hank Newberry was born on March 31, 1935, in Wheeler, Texas. His preschool education consisted of being the first child and grandchild on a farm. In 1953, he graduated from Canyon High School in Canyon, Texas. From 1954 to 1958, the US Air Force was his life. He became a member of Strategic Air Command and was the special weapons mechanic on B-36 bombers. On July 22, 1958, Hank Newberry's enlistment ended. From 1958 to 1961, he was involved with teacher education and industrial and vocational education. Degrees in this profession, including a doctor of philosophy, led him to Buckeye in May 1966 with his wife, Dorie, and their four children. During his first year at BUHS, he coached football and wrestling and taught world history and woodworking. Starting in the fall of 1968, Dr. Newberry coached cross country for eight years and also taught driver's training. In the early 1970s, Newberry taught a construction class that built a chamber of commerce building and sidewalk along Ninth Street from Monroe Avenue to Eason Avenue. Other projects included a concession stand and an elevated press box on the east side of the football stadium. In May 1987, Supt. Dr. Everett E. Myers Jr. asked Newberry if he wanted to be assistant principal for the next school year. Hank Newberry took the job and remained in the position for the next 10 years. After more than 50 years, Newberry retired from teaching and became a permanent substitute teacher. He summarized his life in this way: "In essence, I have traveled nearly three quarters of the way around the world. All of it south of the Arctic Circle and north of the Equator and west of the Prime Meridian at Greenwich, England, passing through the International Date Line to Naha, Okinawa Island. Of all the places that I've been, my favorite place is: Buckeye, Arizona." (Courtesy of author.)

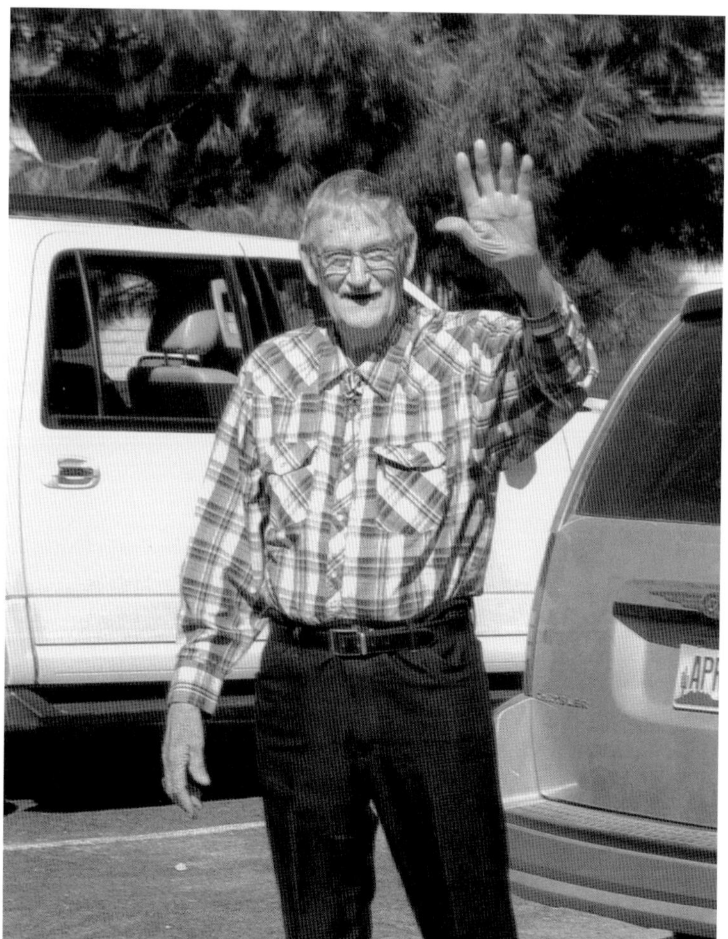

CHAPTER FIVE

Personalities Plus

During the Depression, several favorite schoolteachers lost their jobs. School-board rules stipulated that only one parent in the household could work, so many female teachers were fired. Among those who lost their jobs were Vera Olsen and Dessie Miller. Esther Narramore kept her marriage a secret until the rule was changed in the mid-1930s. The people of Buckeye were fortunate to have unique personalities that cared and made life fun and wonderful. It was exciting to go to the rodeo, the Halloween Carnival, staged shows at BUHS, softball games, and the Fourth of July celebration. Among the "different" personalities in the Buckeye Valley included in this chapter are the following: Dessie Miller, first town librarian; Earl Edgar, "Mr. Baseball"; Irene Makin, who knew everything at BUHS; Lester Way, "Clown Man"; Lola Johnson, Buckeye pageant director; Louis Joslin, a man who did it all, but forgot some things; and Robert A. Saide, MD, doctor on the sidelines.

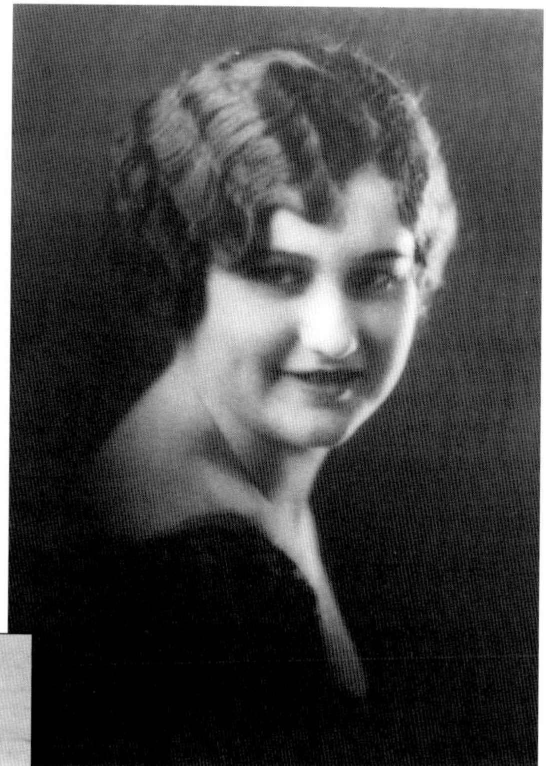

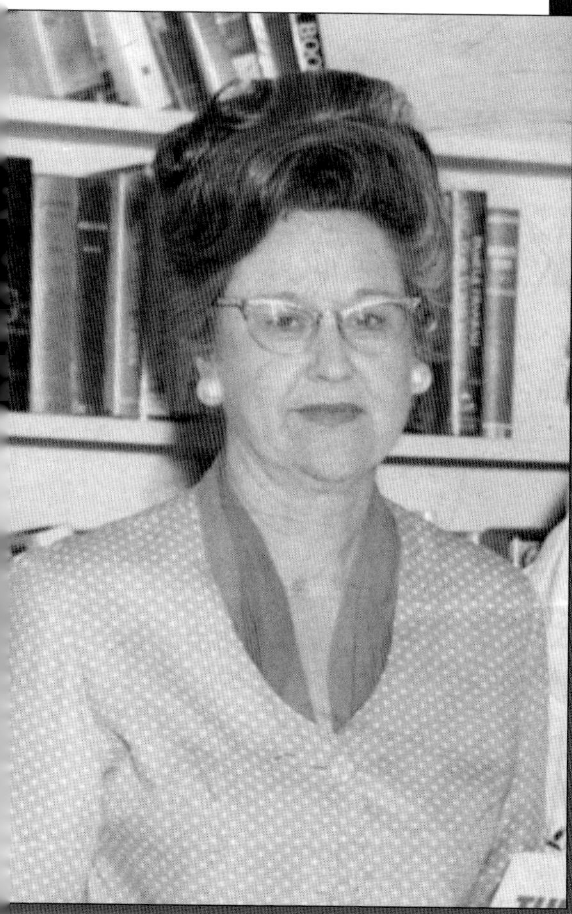

Dessie Miller

Dessie (Hardesty) Miller was born in Palo Verde at the home of her parents, George and Maud Hardesty, on March 12, 1907. She was one of six children. After graduating from BUHS, Dessie furthered her education at Arizona State Teachers College (now ASU). She returned to Buckeye in 1927, where she taught third and fourth grades until 1933. Dessie Hardesty married Harold Miller in April 1935. Their family grew to three in 1938, when their son George was born. Dessie stayed at home to care for George until the outbreak of World War II in 1941, when she was called back to teach fifth grade at BES. In 1948, Dessie became the town librarian. Later, she took on the job as manager of the Buckeye Valley Chamber of Commerce, serving for 16 years. She held down both jobs for many years. Dessie is remembered for her hard work on chamber luncheons and with the Halloween Carnival. Many people remember her friendly afternoon chats at the chamber office. (Both, courtesy of Ellen [Hardesty] Bolen and Belinda [Bolen] Dykstra.)

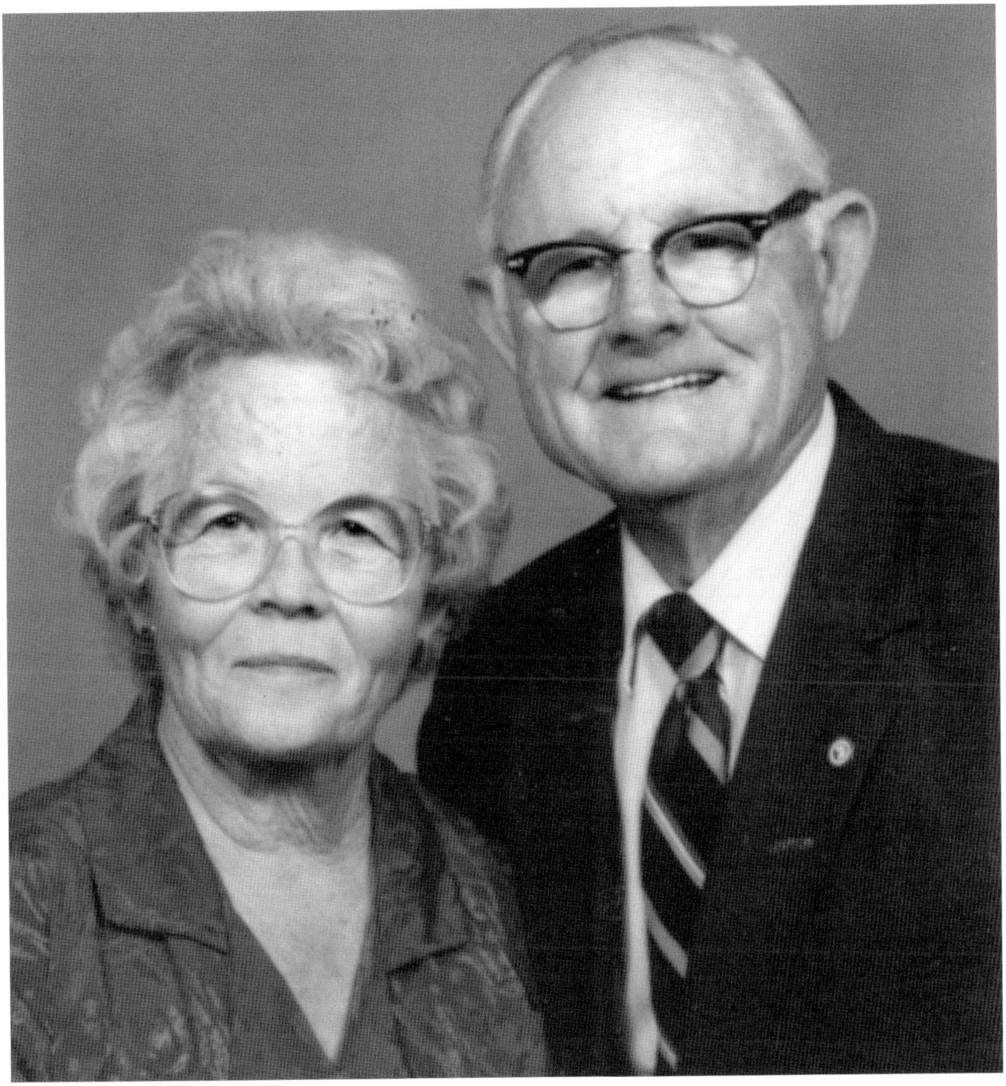

Thomas and Melba Townzen
Tommy Townzen's mother, Grace, ran the Buckeye Maternity Home for many years. Tommy said, "She worked for all the doctors here in Buckeye. I was raised in a maternity home." He is a 1942 graduate of BUHS. Melba's father, Delbert Wood, was a dairyman in Palo Verde. "He had bees plus the dairy and farm," she recalls. From 1942 to 1946, Tommy served in the Navy, returning to work for the Roosevelt Irrigation District as its tax, land, and legal secretary. Wanting to be involved in the educational system, he went back to school to get his teaching credentials. He taught at Palo Verde School for two years, then left to take a position with the Scottsdale School District, where he spent the next 20 years. After Scottsdale, he returned in 1977 to Palo Verde, where he took over the duties of principal from the retiring Louis Joslin. Tommy Townzen retired from Palo Verde in 1988. It was through their mutual interest in teaching that Tommy and Melba met. They were married at the Palo Verde Church in 1955. Tommy was active in the Old Settlers Union, which meets every May at Palo Verde School. Melba stated that her favorite activity over the years has been to help with programs at church, sewing costumes for plays and presentations, painting backdrops, and lending a hand where needed. Tommy and Melba (Wood) Townzen led the Pioneer Days Parade as grand marshals in 2002. Tommy died in 2012. (Courtesy of author.)

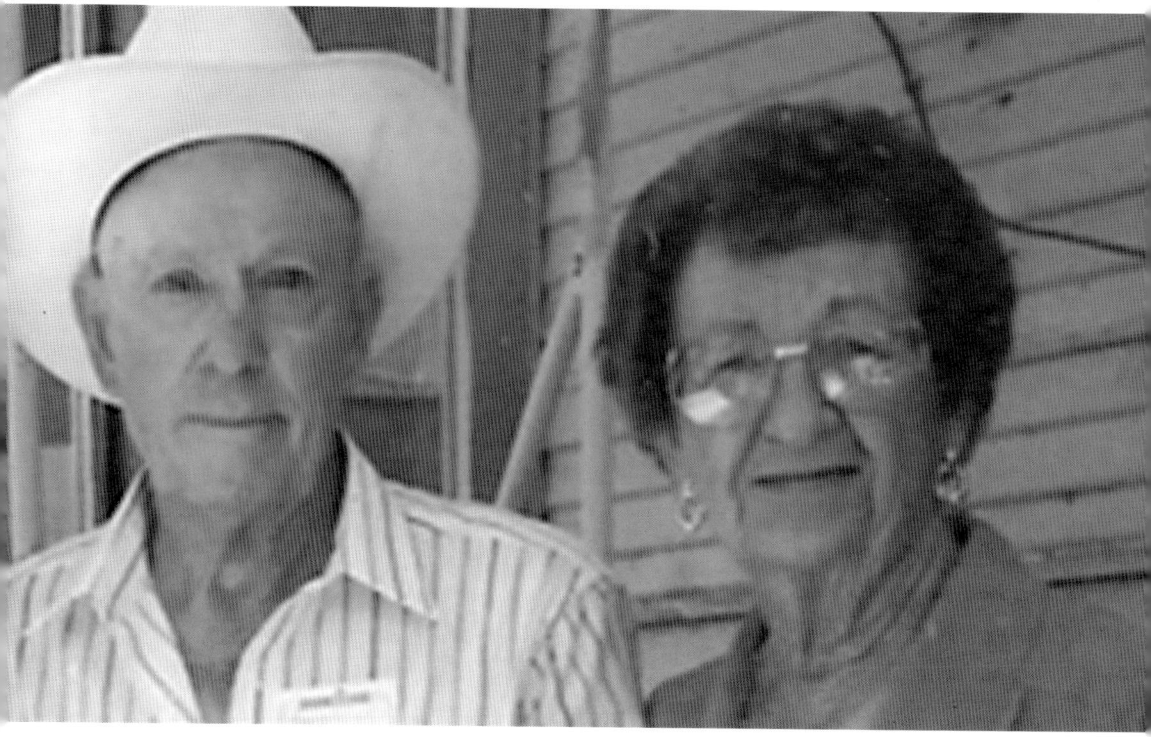

Earl Edgar

Alice Makin married Earl Edgar on June 2, 1936. Together, they owned and operated Edgar's Garage for 52 years. They were married for 63 years. The photograph pictures Earl and Alice at their 60th wedding anniversary. In 1956, Earl and Alice (Makin) Edgar started and supervised a summer Little League program. With the support of the Hazelton-Butler American Legion Post No. 53, they operated it for 11 years. One of Earl's favorite sayings was, "Everyone plays every night." He made sure the kids learned the fundamentals of the sport and had fun. Among his lessons were the following: wait on a pitch in the strike zone; watch the pitcher for just the right moment to steal; and know where to throw the ball in the event a batter hits the ball to you. Earl Edgar taught every detail of the game of baseball. In the Buckeye 1988 Centennial Old Timer's Game, pitting the 1950s BUHS players against the 1960s players, Edgar threw out the first pitch. In the end, the 1960s team won. On November 11, 2006, Buckeye's recreation and sports complex was named the Earl Edgar Recreational Facility. (Courtesy of Doug Edgar.)

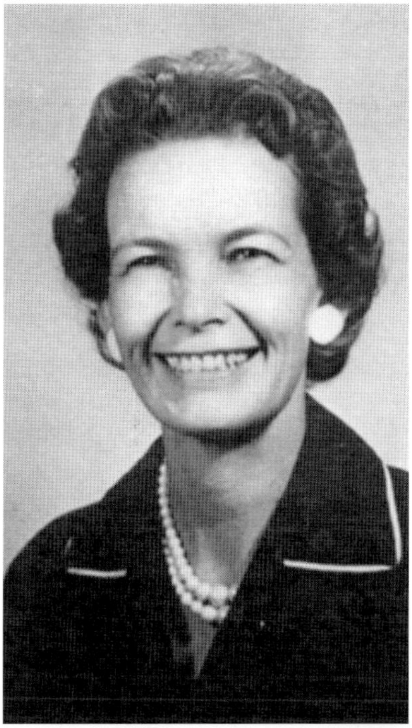

Irene Makin

Irene (Hunter) Makin was born in Liberty, Arizona, on February 23, 1920, to Curg and Mable (Hollenbeck) Hunter. Makin was a gentle giant at BUHS for 38 years. She began in 1944 as the secretary to principal Herschel Hooper. In addition, she ran the bookstore between classes, served as the school nurse when there were injuries, and substituted in the classroom if a teacher was absent or called away. Students would come to her with their troubles because they were not comfortable talking to anyone else. She sold tickets at every home ball game and at the school plays, and she ordered the supplies for Halloween Carnivals. Her daughter, Diane (Makin) Dearmore, says, "She loved her job." Principals and superintendents following Hooper included Alvin E. Ellis, Chester D. McNabb, and Dr. Everett Myers Jr. Administrators come and go, but Irene stayed and served until 1982. She was preceded in death by her husband, Mark, her son Allen, her brothers Ralph and Willard "Til", and her sister Norma (Mickey). Irene died on October 3, 2013. A 1950s BUHS student, Sharon (Balmes) Sapp, said of Makin: "How she put up with all of us, I'm really not sure. She was always smiling." (Both, courtesy of BUHS Archives.)

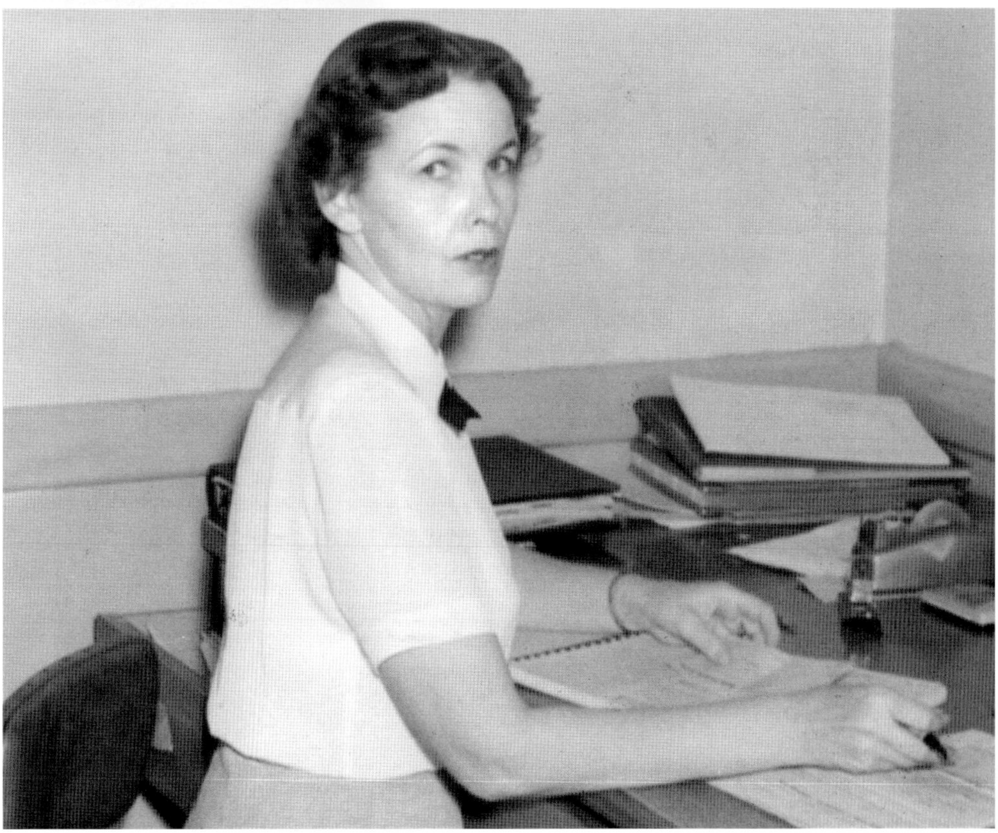

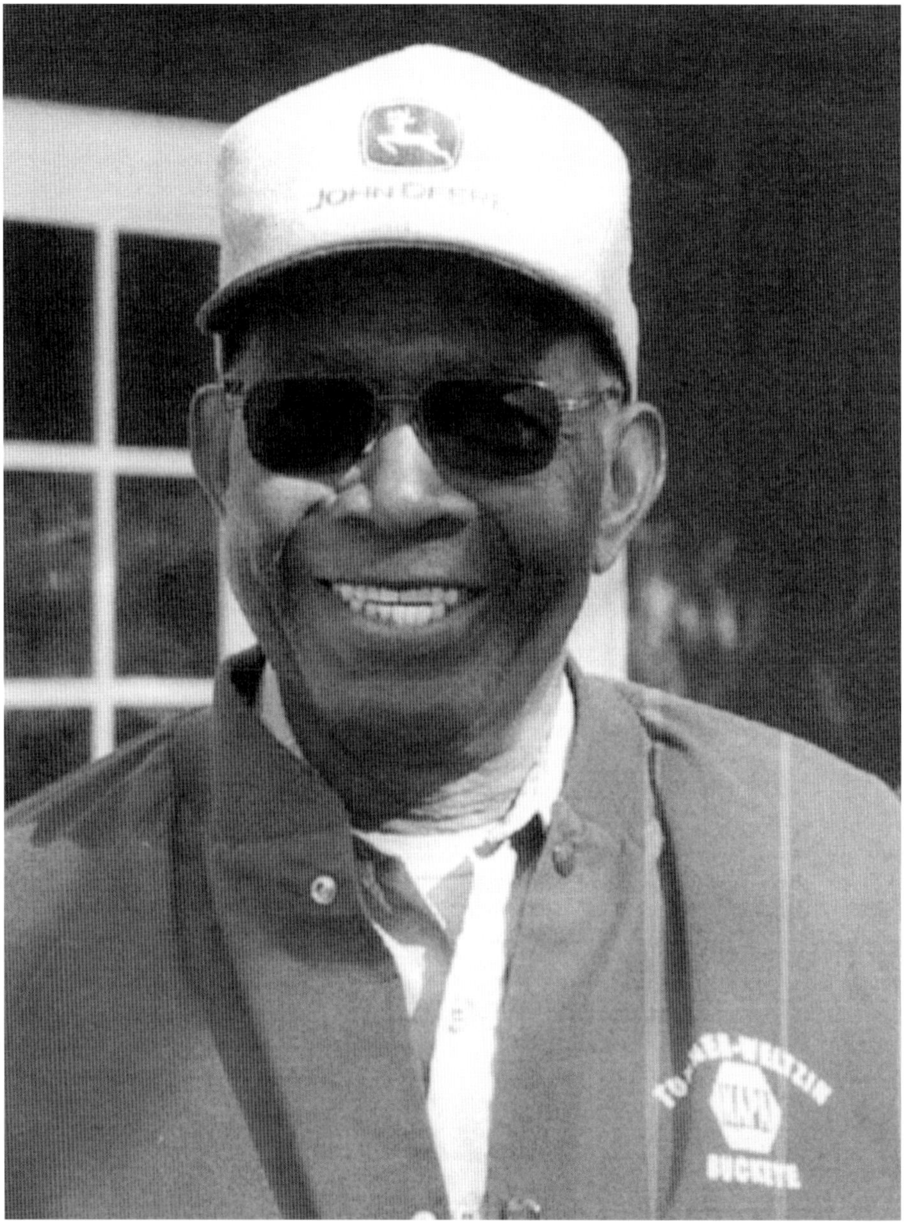

Clyde Cobbin

The name Clyde Cobbin brings to mind a man dedicated to others. His only flaw may be that he was born in Texas, but he has been in Buckeye since the late 1940s. Cobbin began at BUHS in 1976 as a bus driver. He was then the attendance office assistant and a maintenance department expert. Cobbin retired in 1998 after 22 years. He kept Buckeye Union High School in good working order and was always ready to lend a hand. His personality attracted many friends. Due to three Gila River floods, the community of Allenville had to relocate. Cobbin, Abe Harris, James Brown, and others became involved with the planning and relocation to a new community, called Hopeville. It was not an easy task; many meetings were held and many opinions were given. Allenville, now Hopeville, exists on Palo Verde Road, just south of I-10. (Courtesy of author.)

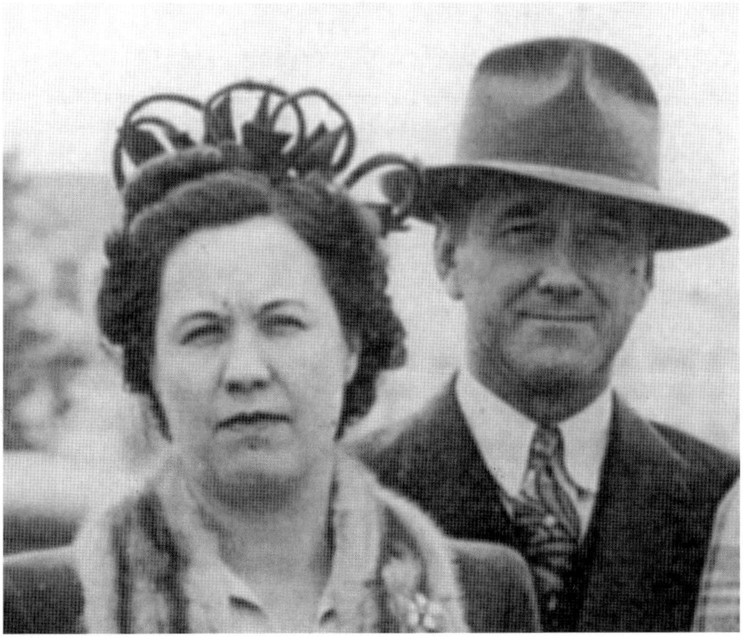

H.C. and Ethel Gable

On May 24, 1922, H.C. "Jack" Gable and Ethel Peterson eloped to Florence, Arizona. Their first son, Jack "Jackie" Charles, was born on October 29, 1923. Then, 20 months later, on June 28, 1925, Warren Carter was born to complete this happy family. Jack and Ethel (above) moved to Arlington in 1926, where they, with Ethel's father, Warren Peterson, managed the Arlington Store and Post Office. The Gable boys (below) shared in the work. Among the items on stock to encourage regular trade were metal washtubs, scrub boards, and ready-to-wear clothing. The establishment also had a meat counter, vegetable bins, and the blank glass stares of the post office cubicle. In the land of lizards, mesquite beans, and locusts, life would have been difficult without a general store. Jack and Ethel sold the business in 1940 and moved into Buckeye. Ethel managed George's Market for almost 25 years. Jack and Ethel both served as school board members and were active in community affairs. Jack was the mayor of Buckeye (1952–1954). Jackie and Carter have always been passionate about flying and the cowboy life. Jackie also developed a love for petroglyphs. For eight decades, he has been a "rock artist." His work is on display at the Buckeye Museum. (Both, courtesy of Jackie Gable.)

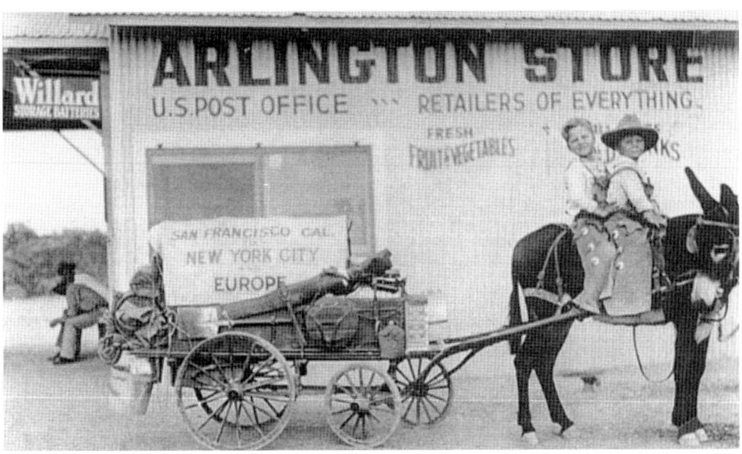

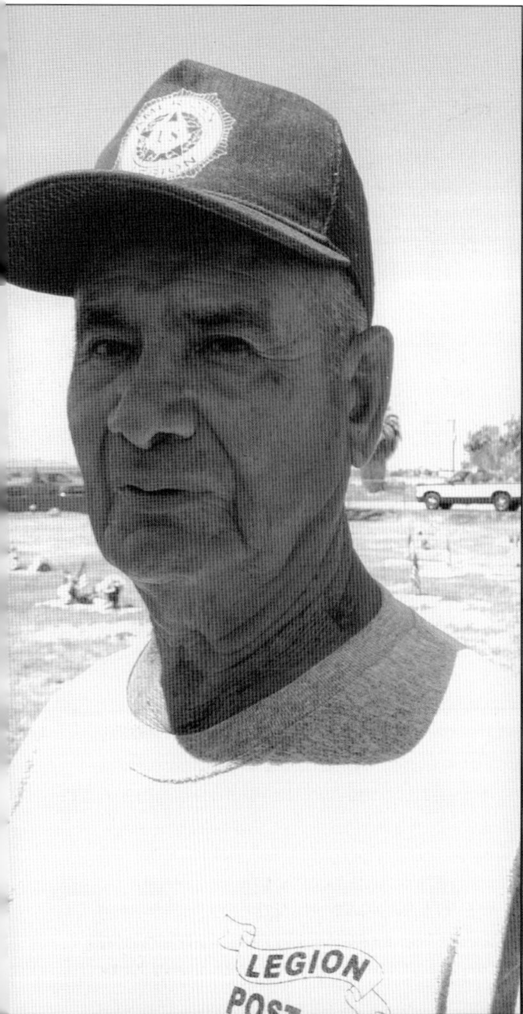

Alex Villa

Alex Villa (left) and his native-born Buckeye brothers Frank and Steve Villa "inherited" the American Legion Little League from Earl Edgar in the 1970s. Alex, along with his brothers, their wives, and all their family, provided this community service for 27 years. The Fourth of July barbecue celebrations, with ice-cold watermelon busts, were major fundraisers for the league. Alex Villa said that all the barbecue meat was donated by local cattlemen. One year, six cows were donated by Wallace Bales, Murray Johnson, John Beloat, Robert Aja, Ray Parker, and Robert Parker. American Legion members cut up and cooked the meat for the feast. Below, Villa throws out the first pitch for the 2009 Little League season. (Both, courtesy of author.)

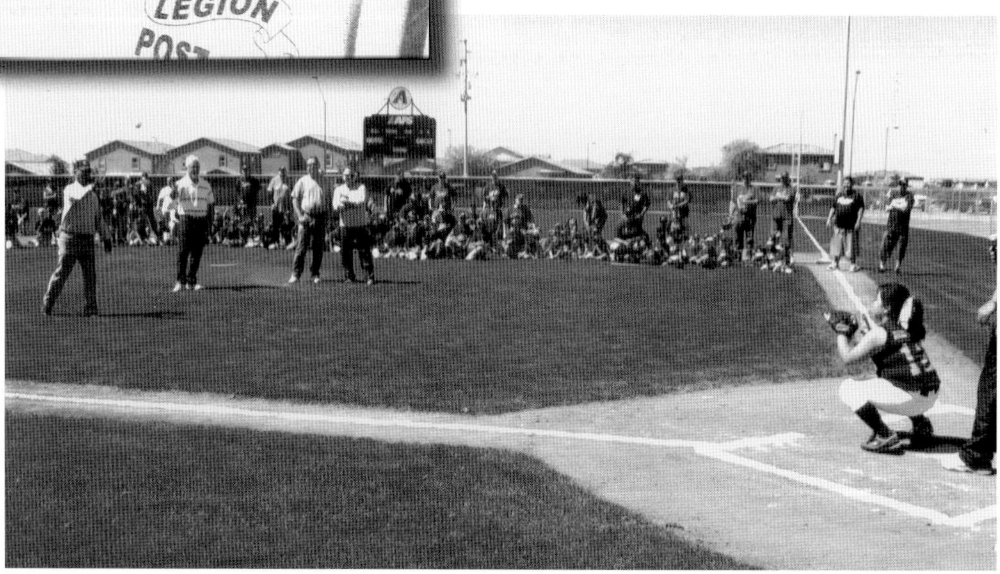

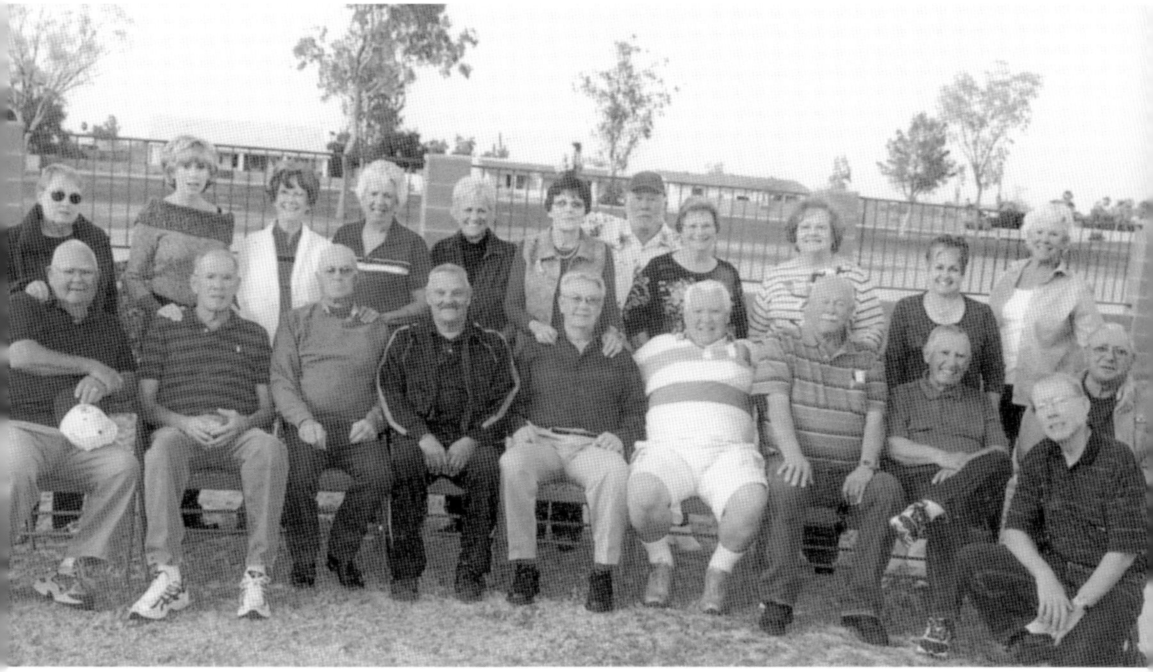

Jack Rowland

In 2004, Jack Rowland held a golf party at his house in Arizona City and invited friends from the BUHS class of 1957. The party was such a success that the group has been meeting three times a year since then. The meetings rotate between Rowland's home, the Bruehl home in Payson, and the Lemons home in Pinetop. They called themselves the 57 Golf Group. But classmates from other years have been acquired, and the "Golf Group" extends to a couple of golfers and all the rest, so the group's name is now the 57 Plus, Golfers and Hackers. Seen here on March 5, 2011, are, from left to right, (first row) Joe Smothers, Corky Hendrick, Benny Aja, Earl Wooley, Gloyes Lemons, Frank Zellner, George Miller, Jack Rowland, Paul Bruner, and Gary Bruehl; (second row) Carolyn Smothers, Evie Hendrick, Herbie Aja, Judy Bruner, Willie Wooley, Jane Lemons, Tom Roberts, Edna Roberts, Carolyn Miller, Connie Jackson, and Katy Bruehl. (Courtesy of Katy [Karstetter] Bruehl.)

Jose Yanez Sr.

Jose Yanez Sr., father of the Buckeye Yanez family, was born in Chihuahua, Mexico, in 1890. He and his sister Maria moved north to El Paso in 1906, then on to Arizona, where he worked the mines in Globe/Miami before settling in the Buckeye Valley in 1909. Yanez married Manuela Amparano on September 5, 1911. It was the first wedding at the "new" adobe St. Henry's Catholic Church on South Sixth Street. While living in Palo Verde, Jose sold vegetables from his farm. When he moved his family to Buckeye, he entered into a partnership with Long's Dairy & Farm, selling vegetables from about 1930 to 1940. Jose and Manuela parented 10 children, two of who died at an early age. Manuela died on March 28, 1942, and Jose died on September 29, 1955. Their eight sons and daughters gave Buckeye many legends. Mike Yanez married Odessa Pesqueira, operated a lawn maintenance service, and worked for Duncan & Sons. Carmen married Ramon Amarillas and was the operator of Carmen's Beauty Salon for more than 30 years. She was the first Mexican American woman elected to the Buckeye Town Council, serving from 1960 to 1964. Frank married Marie Rangel and worked for Long's Dairy. Joe Jr. married Mary Sernas and also worked at Long's Dairy. Antonia "Toni" married Luis Estrada and worked at Buckeye Home Supply, Buckeye Bakery, and Buckeye Industries. Jessie and her husband, Henry Estrada, both retired in 1987 from teaching at BES after 31 and 28 years, respectively. Alex, married to Erma Perez, worked at Long's Dairy and O'Malley's Lumber Co. Ruth married Ted Cope and taught school in both Buckeye and El Cajon, California. A story is remembered by Frank Yanez about the first BUHS school bus. The bus was purchased by the Longs around 1938. The top part was removed (seen here with Joe Jr.), and the bus was then used to feed pigs at Long's Hog Farm from about 1939 until the 1970s. It was a Model A bus, painted yellow with six tandem wheels. (Courtesy of author.)

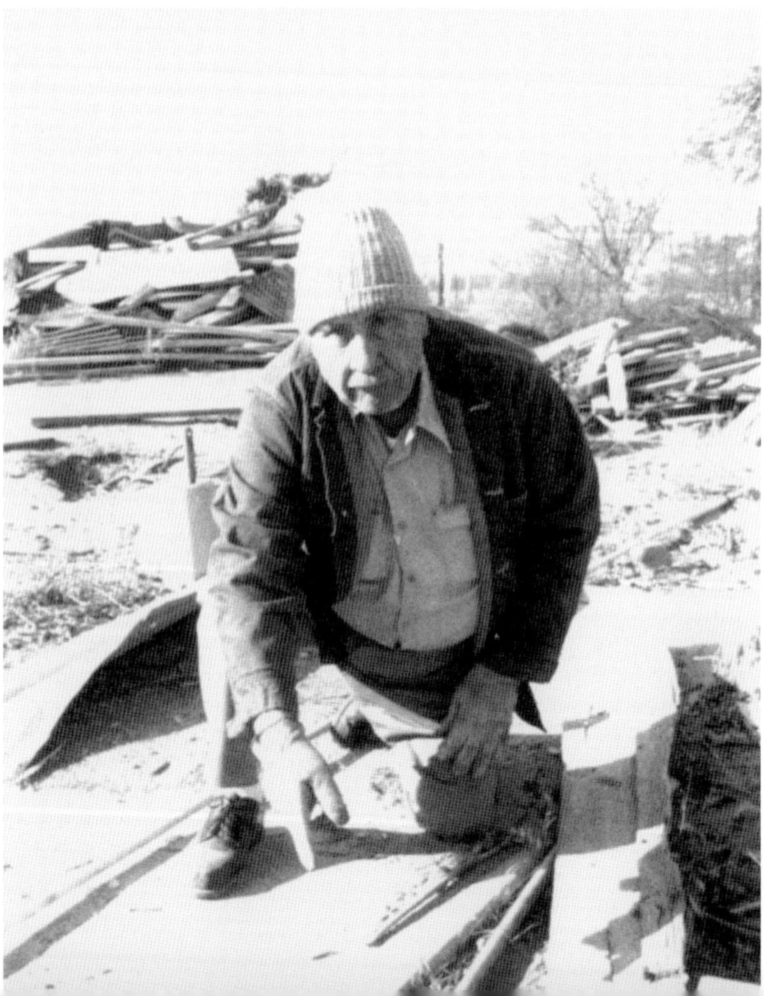

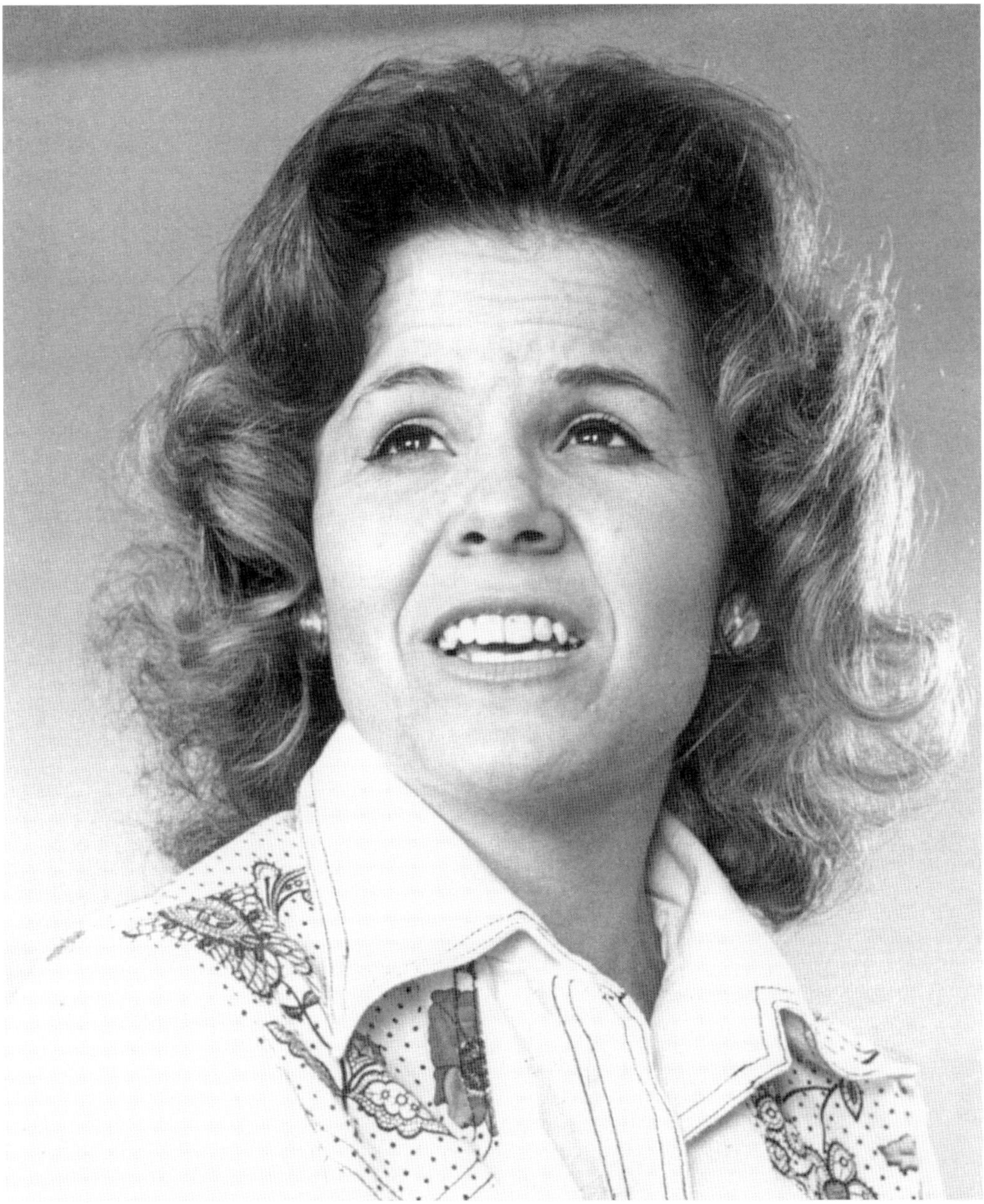

Shirleyan Johnson

A Buckeye native born in 1945, Shirleyan (Cambron) Johnson is the daughter of Sam and Bea Cambron. One of her first singing performances was at a BUHS Y-Teens Talent Show around 1955—she won! Her well-remembered performance was singing "The Angels Are Lighting God's Little Candles." After marrying Gary Johnson in 1965 and becoming the mom of two sons, Shirleyan began a concert and speaking ministry in 1968, traveling nationally and internationally. She says, "Music became a passion as a very small child and praise God I have learned I can serve Him through the passion He placed in my heart." She retired as a church worship leader in 2012. Shirleyan Johnson cut two record albums, *This Is My Story* and *And He Loves Me*. She was the 1963 Safflower Queen at Buckeye's first and only Safflower Festival. (Courtesy of author.)

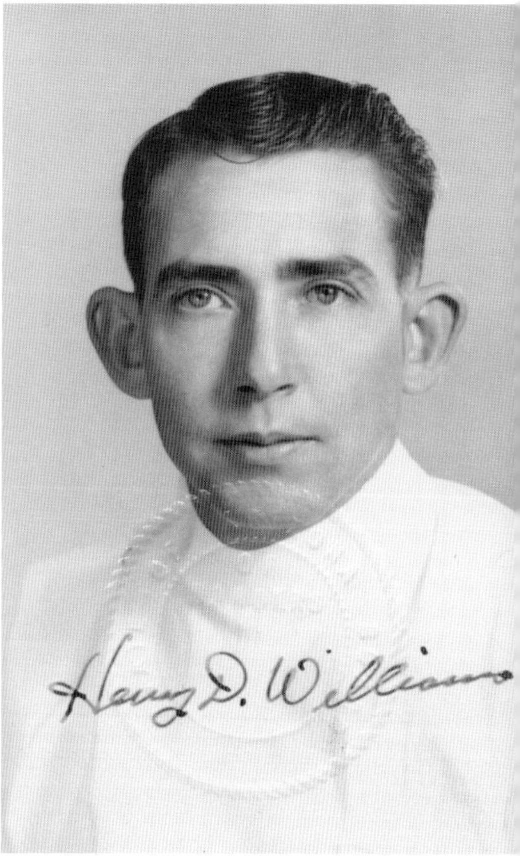

Henry Darrel Williams

H.D., or "Hook", was born on December 3, 1921, to Viola and E.T. Williams in Konowa, Oklahoma. The family with six children left Oklahoma in 1933 in a 1928 Ford Model A sedan. Mattresses and a box of clothes were loaded onto the car, and in 1936, the family arrived in Buckeye. Hook Williams attended Palo Verde School and graduated from BUHS in 1942. Following graduation, he was drafted into the Army and was part of the 16th Signal Battalion. During World War II, he served as a cryptographic technician in the Pacific theater. H.D. and Royleen "Chickie" Balmes were married on March 1, 1947. He attended Arizona Barber College (1949–1950) and operated Williams Barber Shop for 47 years, retiring in 1998. He was a lifetime member of the Buckeye Masonic Lodge and served as master in 1964 and 1975. In 1953, he was commander of the Hazelton-Butler Post No. 53. Williams was elected to the Buckeye Town Council (1972–1973). He and Chickie were active in the annual Masonic Barbecue, Helzapoppin Rodeo, and Little League. In his 1989 memoir, he stated, "I love our Buckeye Valley or I wouldn't still be living here after all these years." Hook Williams, the left-handed barber who gave awesome flattops, died on June 5, 2007. (Both, courtesy of Karen [Williams] Goins.)

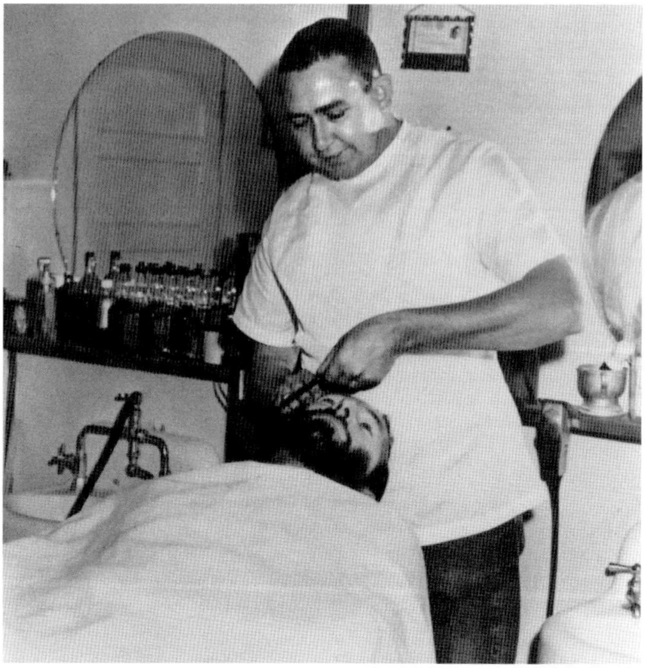

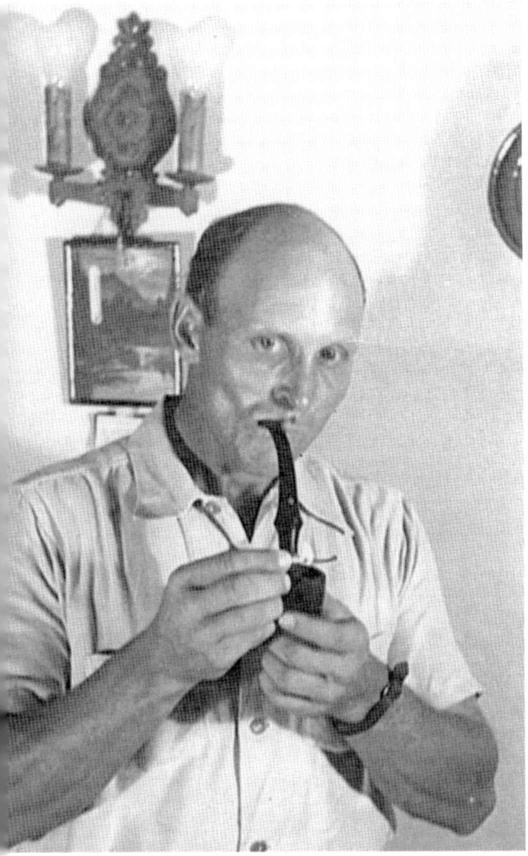

Lester Way

Lester Pearl Way was born on December 20, 1904, in Exline, Iowa, the oldest of 12 siblings. He began his journey to Arizona in 1930 with many bad roads and flat tires on his flivver. His sweetheart, Mildred Hutton, remained behind. He was going to be working for C.O. Vosburgh in Buckeye, working with irrigation for cotton, alfalfa, grain, and citrus trees. Lester Way suffered a terrible blow when the tent he was living in burned down. He wrote to Mildred and cancelled their plans. Vosburgh bought some more shacks, and Lester fixed one up and saved $100. He then wrote to Mildred to come on out, and they were married on June 13, 1931. Lester could buy 10 acres if he stayed for five years and 12 days. He bought land and built a home (below) in 1939 on Broadway Road, where he lived until his death in 1960. He had farmed for 30 years. Lester Way had a love for Palomino horses, which he and his daughters Joan and Jane rode in Helzapoppin Parades. At Halloween Carnivals, Way dressed up as a clown with boots made into webbed duck feet. He was a member of the Palomino and Quarter Horse Association, County Farm Bureau, Cotton Growers Association, Zoning Commission, Roosevelt Irrigation District Board, and BUHS Board. (Both, courtesy of Jane [Way] Thomas Miller.)

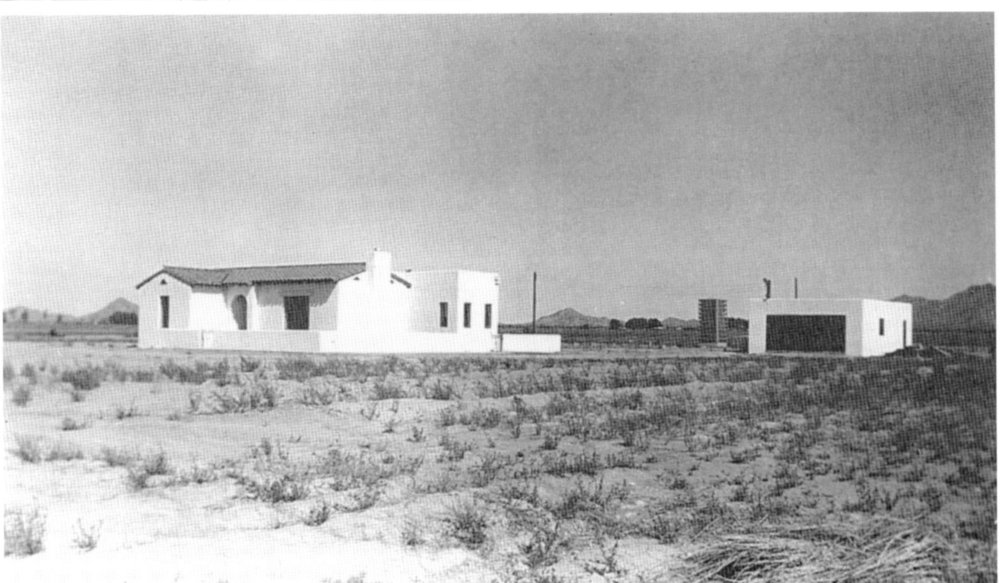

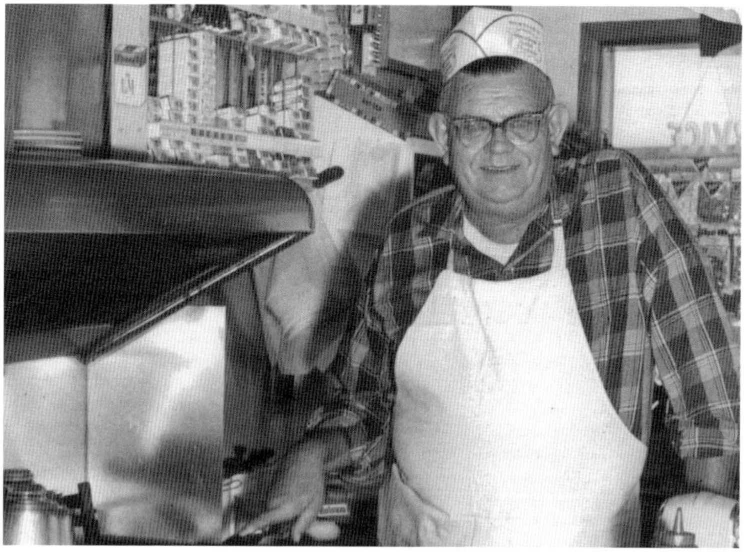

Joe Marshall

Not too much is known about Joe Marshall and his wife, Edith. They were married when Joe was in his late 40s or early 50s. Edith worked at the Boston Store in Phoenix. Soon after their wedding, they built a home on the northwest corner of Eighth Street and Eason Avenue, which is still standing. Joe Marshall was not the most outgoing guy, but he knew how to cook hamburgers, including grinding his own meat. The menu was limited: hamburgers with or without cheese, along with stew and chili. Joe served breakfast as well. Marshall drove to Blaine Duncan's to get water in order to brew coffee. A neighbor boy, Kemp Biddulph, said that Marshall let him sort through red beans in his garage to make sure there were no stones. Joe also introduced the first Baby Ruth and Butterfinger candy bars to downtown Buckeye. Another remembrance of this little eatery comes from Diane (Makin) Dearmore. "In 1945, the war in the Pacific Ocean continued. My uncle, Ralph Hunter, was stationed on a destroyer that left San Diego, heading west. Because of censorship, sailors were not allowed to disclose their destination. Ralph knew how concerned and worried his family was about him. He sent a letter home stating they were heading to 'Joe's Place.' In our small community of Buckeye that meant Joe Marshall. The family then figured out his ship was headed to the Marshall Islands." Elaine (Perry) McKee said her dad, Jim Perry, purchased the well-used grill from Joe's Café. The grill is still in their family. (Both, courtesy of author.)

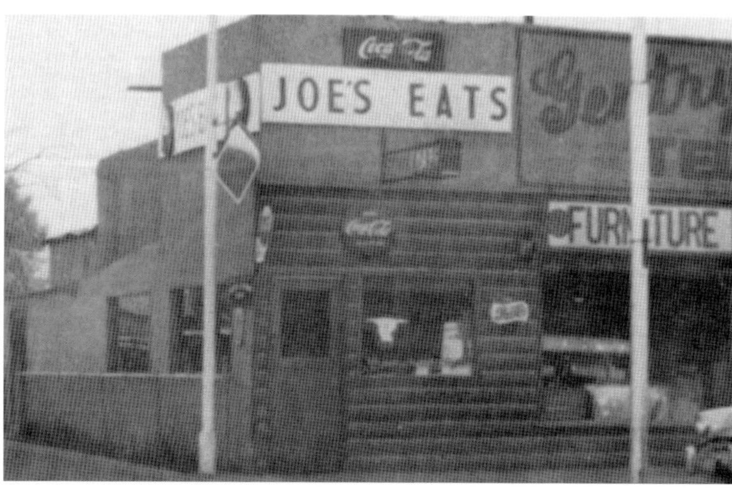

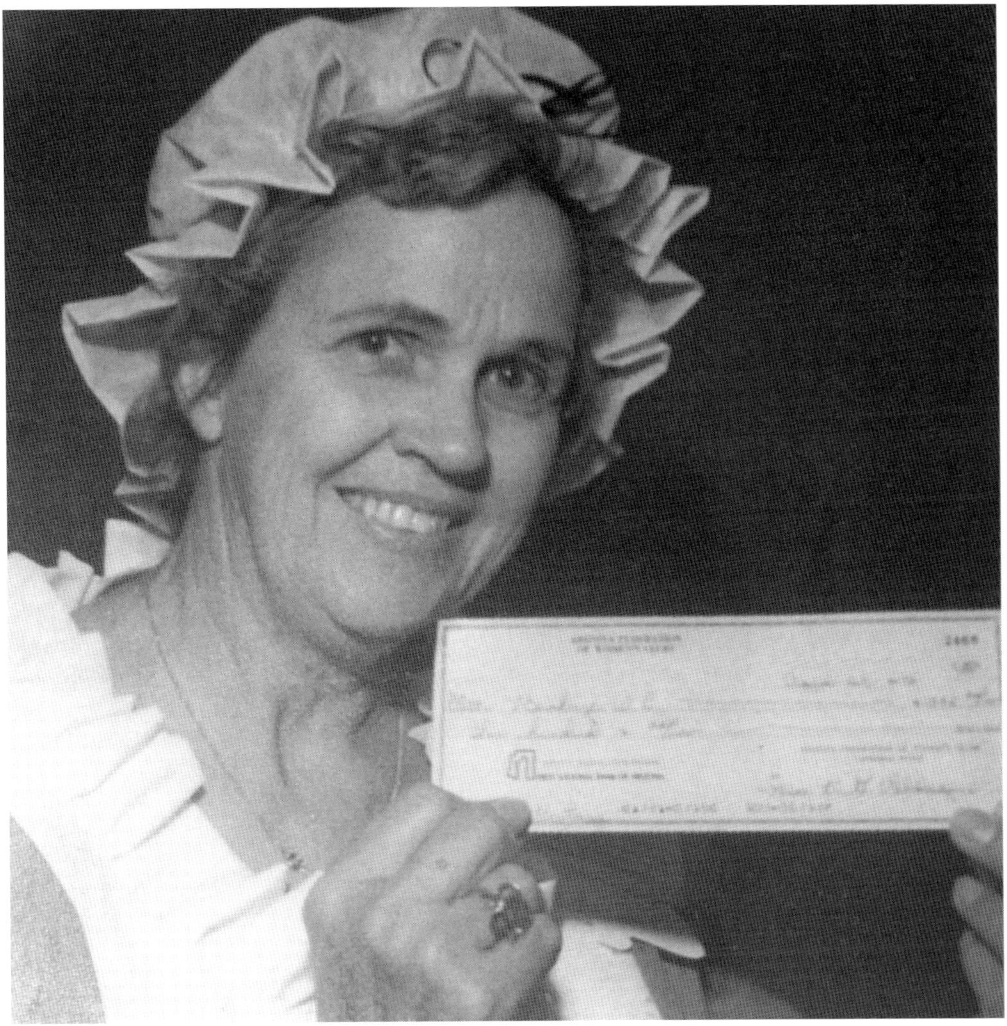

Lola Johnson

Lola (Buckelew) Johnson was born on February 14, 1922, in Chandler, Arizona. Her close-knit family consisted of seven sisters and three brothers. Lola graduated from BUHS in 1940. After being crowned Cotton Queen that year, Lola Buckelew spent three weeks in New York City as the guest of vaudeville performers Ole Olsen and Chic Johnson. One of her New York City memories is receiving a surprise kiss from Flash Gordon. During high school, Lola had met Murray Alden Johnson. After some courting, they fell in love and married in 1942. Lola became a fixture at Buckeye's community events. She composed scripts, arranged music, and directed Buckeye pageants. She headed the first historical pageant during Pioneer Days in 1967, which raised funds for the Buckeye Library. Winning third place in a state contest brought $100 to the club for a community building. During America's bicentennial, on July 4, 1976, Lola and Mary Joslin directed *Land of Our Fathers*, a pageant depicting America's first 200 years. There was only one rehearsal for the production, which had 300 actors, as well as lights and props, to coordinate. Mary and Lola made it happen, and this production received state and national recognition. Lola Johnson rewrote *Tales of the Buckeye Valley*, a historical pageant, for the 1988 centennial celebration. At age 91, on June 23, 2013, she passed away. (Courtesy of author.)

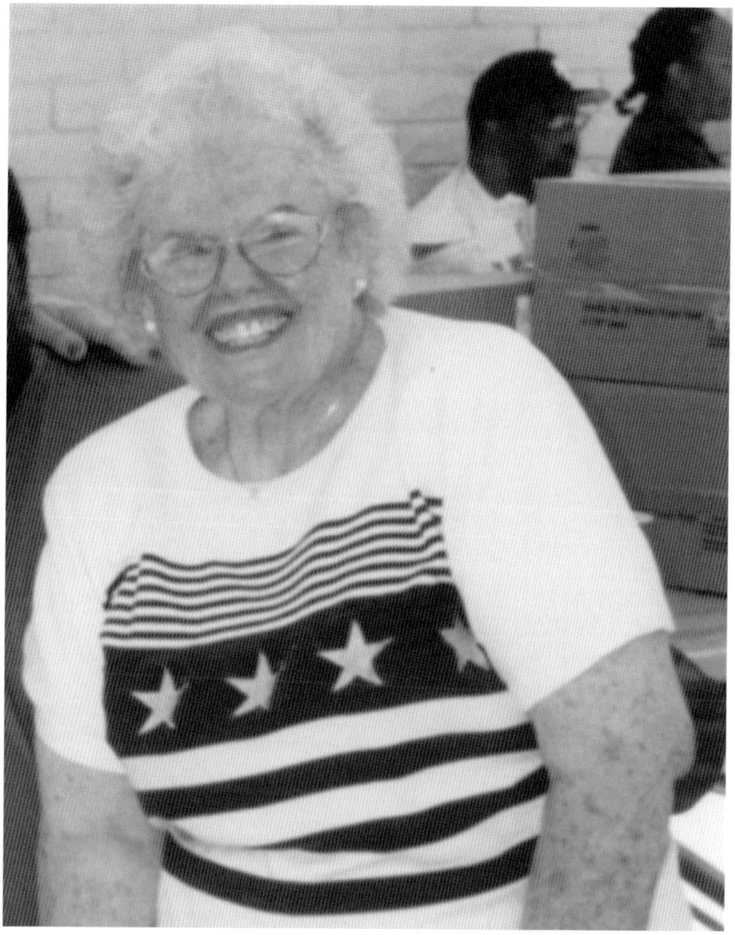

Mary Joslin

Mary (Marsh) Joslin was born in Fullerton, California, on November 26, 1916. After her father's death in World War I, Mary's mother moved her family to Monrovia. While at Monrovia High School, Mary was a cheerleader, president of Girls League, and a yearbook staff member. She participated in school plays and played violin in the school orchestra. In 1937, she went to summer school at USC, where she met Supt. Charles Fillerup from Buckeye Elementary School. He talked her into coming to Buckeye to teach music. Mary Marsh bought a secondhand car and drove alone to Buckeye. When she got to town, she thought it was the hottest place on earth. After completing her state requirements at age 20, she began teaching fourth grade and music. That is when she met a tall, red-headed teacher named Louis Foster Joslin, who asked her for a date. They were married on August 23, 1939. In 1942, they moved to the campus of Palo Verde School and taught there for 37 years. For more than 24 years, Mary was chair of numerous melodramas and olios during Pioneer Days. Mary and Louis were queen and king of the 1968 Pioneer Day Parade. For 19 years, Mary was chair of the Buckeye Food Bank, which began in 1984. She joined a retired teacher's group called Saguaro and became the president. She was chosen the Buckeye Valley Chamber of Commerce Citizen of the Year in 1999. One of her greatest honors took place in 1987, when she received the Twelve Who Care Award for being an outstanding volunteer in Arizona, sponsored by KPNX-TV Channel 12. When people asked Mary why she stayed in Buckeye after Louie died in 1984, she said, "there are such wonderful people here and always something to do." She wore many hats: daughter, sister, student, teacher, wife, mother, friend, director, leader, and servant to all. Mary Joslin passed away on August 13, 2010. (Courtesy of author.)

Louis Joslin

Louis "Louie" Foster Joslin was born on June 17, 1912, south of Palo Verde, across the Gila River, where his parents, Wallace and Ada Joslin, lived on their homestead. The river was flooded at the time, and the midwife, a Mrs. Campbell, had to ride in a boat to cross the river to attend the birth and deliver the 12.5-pound baby. Ada was very sick with a high fever and had no milk for her baby. The family had a dog that had just given birth to a litter of puppies, so they had baby Louis nurse with the mother dog. In a few days, Ada recovered, and her milk "came in," as the old saying goes. Baby Louis thrived. This story of the mother dog saving his life was told by Louie's wife, Mary. Louie's father, Wallace Joslin, built the Joslin Building, also known as 3H Mercantile, on South Fourth Street and Monroe Avenue. Louie grew up in the Buckeye area, attending Phoenix Union High School and Tempe Teacher's College (now ASU). After graduating in 1936, he taught school in Buckeye. He later became principal of Palo Verde Elementary School, holding that position for 35 years, until his retirement in 1977. He and Mary had three children, Bob, Jane, and Bill. They all graduated from both Palo Verde School and Buckeye Union High School. Louie was the first Buckeye Valley Chamber of Commerce Man of the Year (1951) and was the first president of the Buckeye Valley Coordinating Council and Buckeye Parks Board at the time the present city park was established. Louie is remembered for his use of war surplus rations. When former teacher Teresa (Meck) Kennedy received a filing cabinet in the 1980s, she found a 1940 rations request that Louie had forgotten to mail. As a result, Joslin had to go around the school district, begging for flour and sugar. Louie Joslin died in 1984 at the age of 72. (Courtesy of author.)

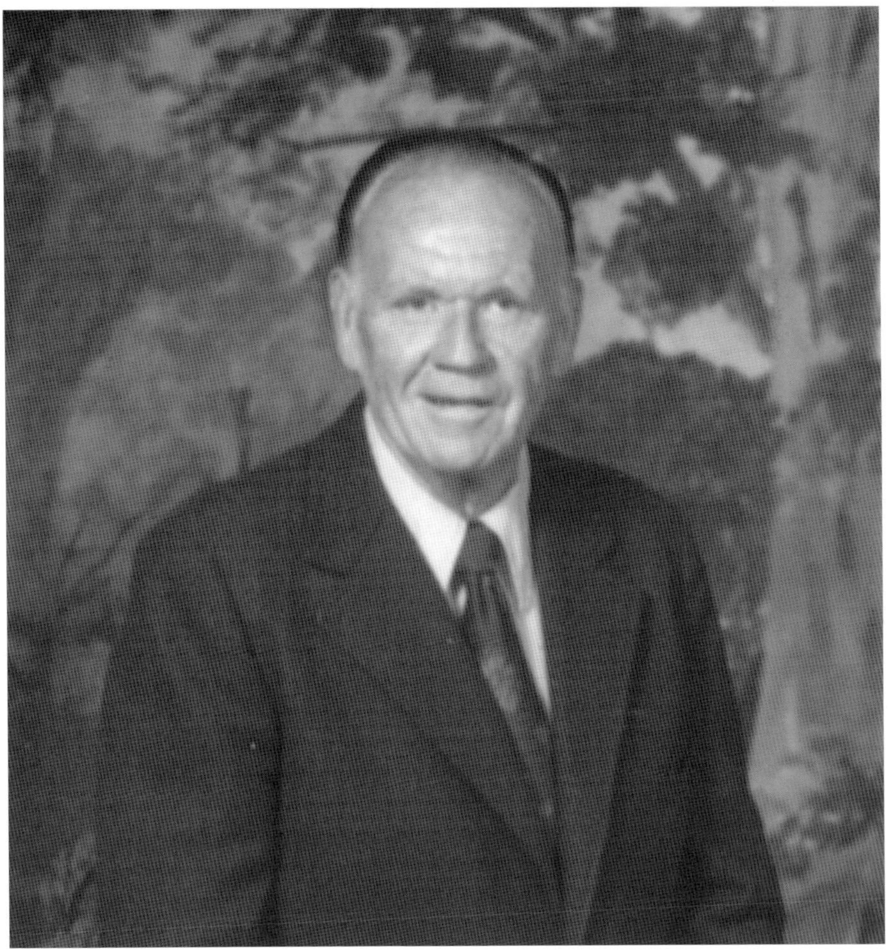

Noel E. Scott

Noel Scott was born on June 14, 1919. At the age of 13, by hitchhiking and riding freight trains, he moved himself from West Texas to Arizona. He quickly settled in the Buckeye Valley, working at various farms in the area to support himself. Maude Francis provided room and board. When he was 18, he worked for the CCC (Civilian Conservation Corps), improving campgrounds in Northern Arizona. Following this, he went to work for O'Malley's Lumber Co. in Buckeye and also joined the Arizona National Guard. On September 21, 1941, he and Dorothy Elms of Palo Verde were married. Following the outbreak of World War II, Noel Scott joined the Army, returning to Buckeye after serving in the Pacific. He was doing custom farm work when Arizona Central Power & Light, the predecessor of Arizona Public Service (APS), approached him with a job offer as meter reader for its western division. He held that position until his retirement in 1982, after 33 years of service. Scott, an avid outdoorsman, scouted, hunted, hiked, and flew over every corner of Arizona. For several years, he enjoyed working as a desert bighorn sheep guide. He knew the name of every mountain range in the state. The landscape at his home in the Sunora residential area was a work of Southwest art. It even housed a 1928 streetlight that once illuminated the Valencia community. After his retirement from APS, Scott volunteered at the Buckeye Public Library and was in his 20th year in that capacity when he died on August 10, 2007. (Courtesy of author.)

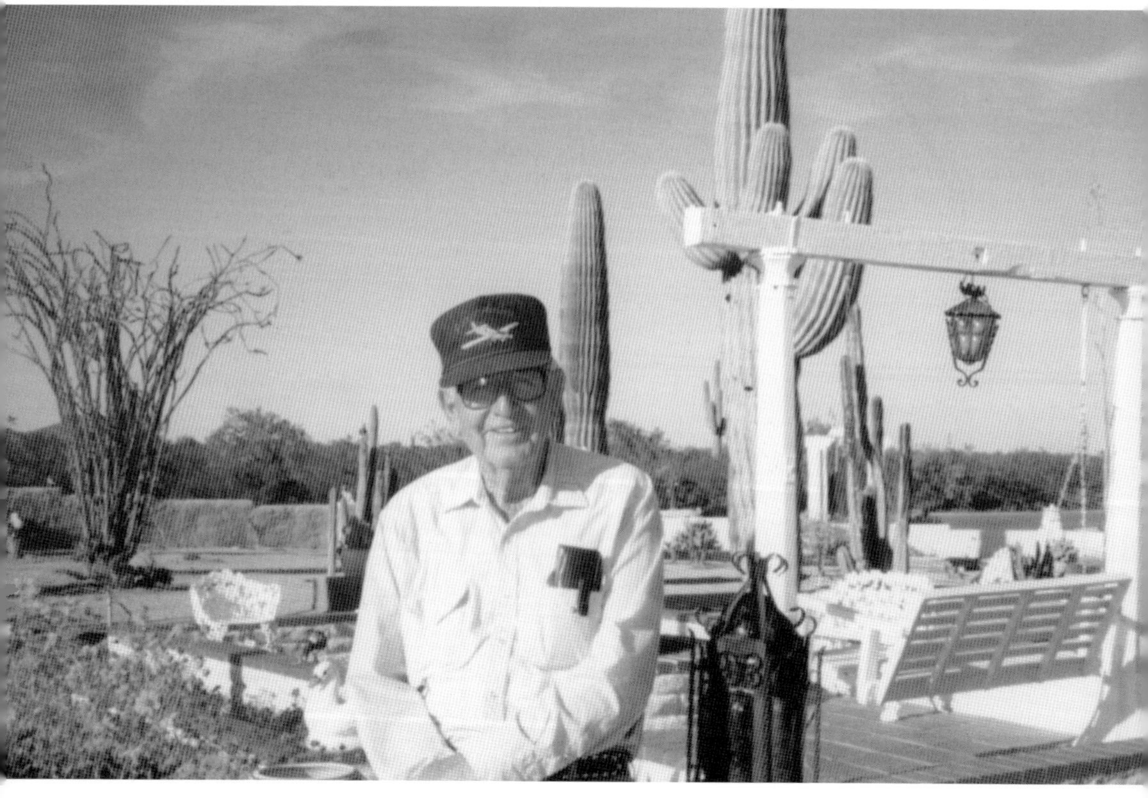

Vera Hollaway

The family of David and Hazel (Pirtle) Swaim moved to Rainbow Valley from Scotia, California, in 1929 with a three-year-old daughter, Vera. Today, Vera (Swaim) Hollaway continues to be a Rainbow Valley icon. She has fond memories of attending Underwood School, located five miles from the Swaim home. Vera said: "The teacher would teach all eight grades. Our principal, Mr. Ring, would come once in a while to give us the State Test, and we would get so excited when he came. He would also bring a movie to show us. We had a wood heater and kerosene lanterns at school that were used for our night plays and other night time activities. Our drinking water was hauled and was put on a little table outside. We had outhouses with lime in them. We had a big school yard, with the bushes acting as the boundaries. We would play tag and baseball, or just build little houses out of rocks." The Underwood School was relocated to Vera Hollaway's home property, on Eagle Mountain Road. Married in 1946, Curtis and Vera eventually had six children: Gary, Bruce, Rickie, Diane, Becky, and Cindy. Curtis died in November 2006. Vera has a deep passion for creating gifts for others and continues to crochet afghans. This 2013 photograph shows her extraordinaire creative skills, as she adds one more afghan to her "hundreds." (Courtesy of author.)

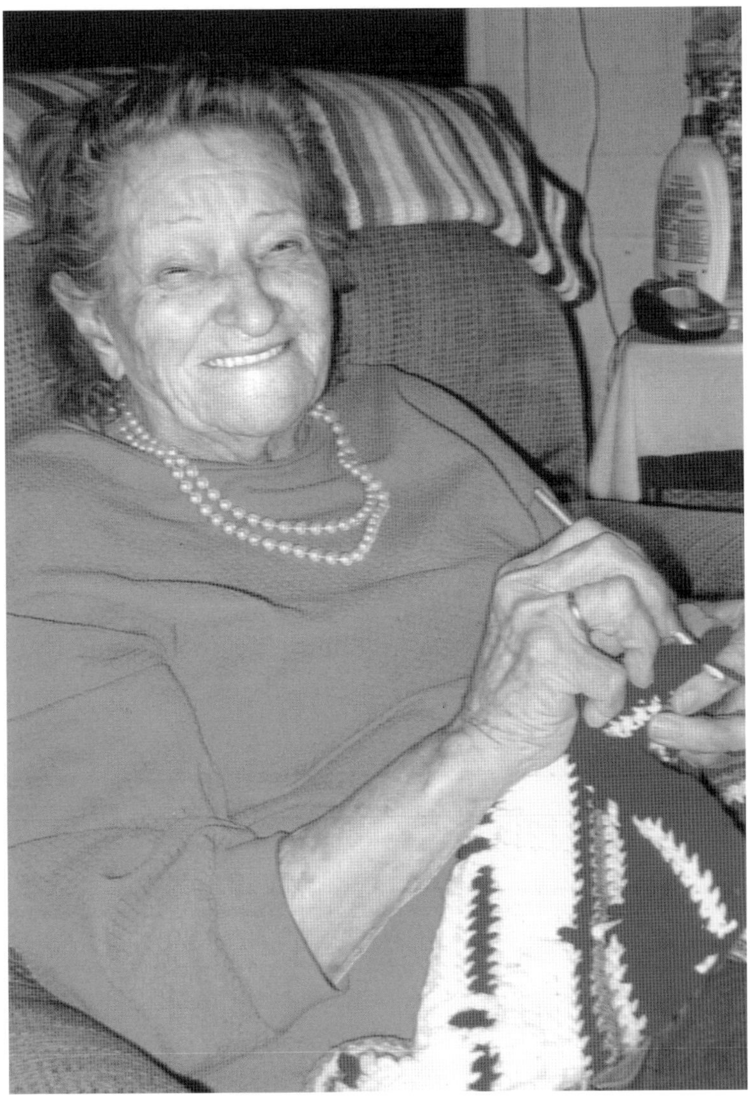

W. Robert Doster, DVM

Traveling west in January 1961 from Ohio, honeymooners Bob and Mary Lou Doster planned to settle in the Phoenix area. They became attracted to Buckeye because of the Ohio nickname. A contact with Dr. Ray Hinshaw, DVM, invited them to Buckeye. After Bob passed the state board examination in July 1961, his Buckeye practice opened in September at 824 Monroe Avenue. Mary Lou offered clinical laboratory services to three local medical doctors as well as the Doster Veterinary Clinic. Garry Strander was the first client, and he took Bob to see the Rodeo Grounds and Currens Feed & Seed and ended with lunch at Mildred's Restaurant. Bob and Mary Lou made three categories to prioritize their time and energy: practice growth; community involvement; and planning family. The practice continued to grow, with calls taking him east to Glendale and Laveen; west to Aguila, Salome, and Harquahala Valley; southwest to Gila Bend and Wellton; and south to Ajo. At 24090 Highway 85, a large animal facility was developed so that livestock and horses could be transported to a central location. Community involvement began and continued. When Dr. Doster became president of the Buckeye Chamber of Commerce in 1965, he suggested a name change to Buckeye Valley Chamber of Commerce. It was agreed, and the name was changed. Bob served on the town council for 10 years (1999–2009), the BES board for three terms, and the BUHS board for eight years. The Doster family goal was also realized. The couple had four children: Karen, Diane, Bill, and Steve. Bob believes the best decision he and his bride made was in July 1961, when they chose to come to Buckeye. They never looked back, and they now express thanks to the Buckeye Valley. (Courtesy of author.)

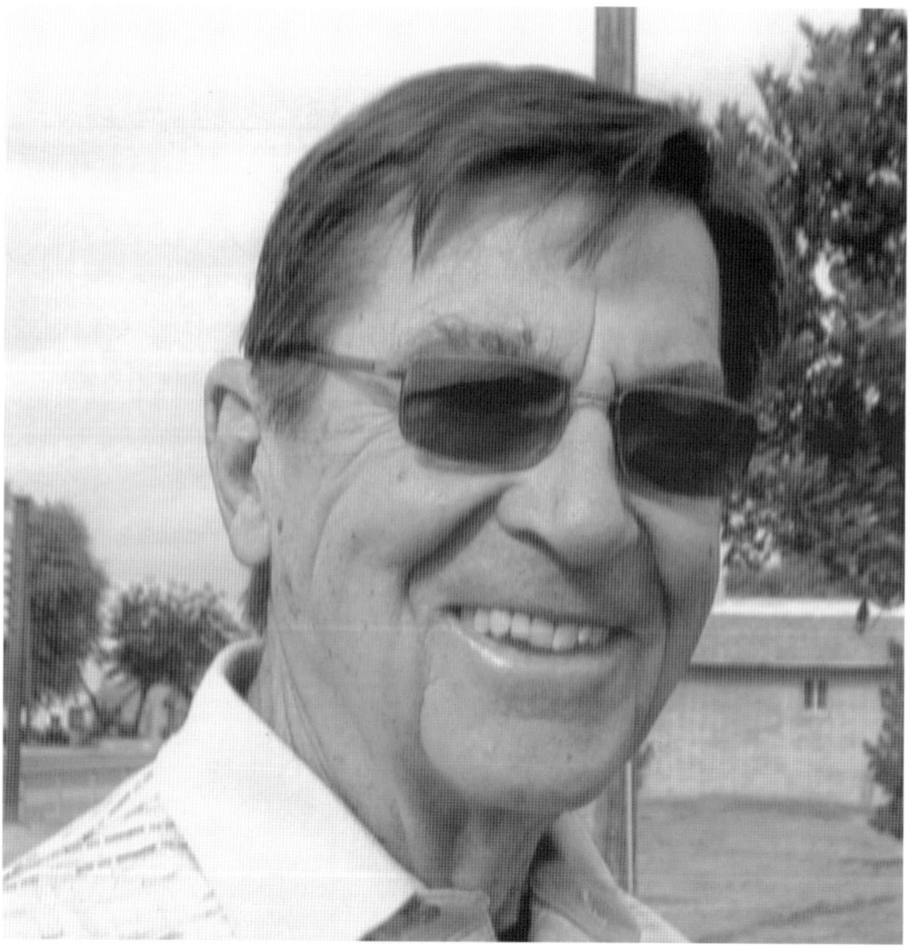

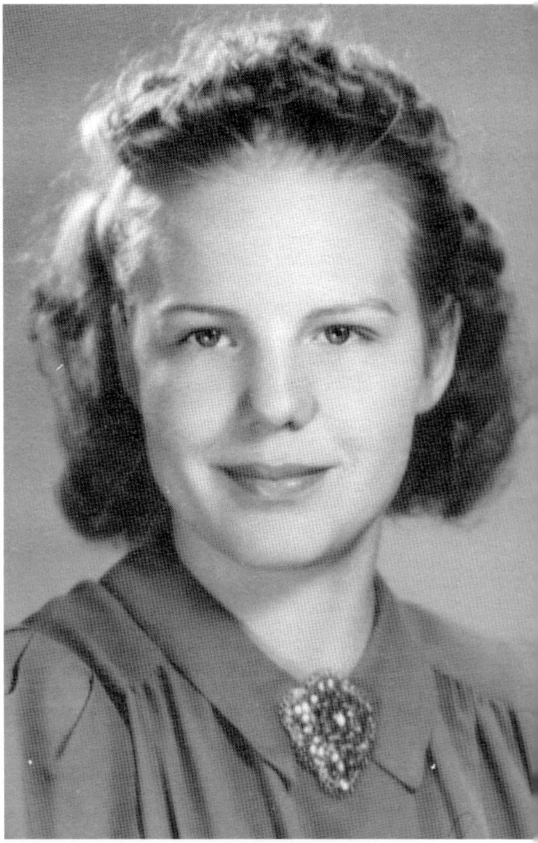

Marie Faver

On November 1, 1922, Marie (Faust) Faver (right) was born in Cheyenne, Wyoming. She arrived in Buckeye from Globe, Arizona, with her mother, Ida Faust, and siblings Evalyne, Violet, and Joe Faust in September 1930. Marie was baptized in an irrigation ditch on April 30, 1932, and became a member of the First Southern Baptist Church, founded in 1925. After her 1940 BUHS graduation, she married Lee "Buddy" Faver on August 31, 1941. The couple is shown below. Marie has been a member of Buckeye's First Southern Baptist Church (FSBC) for the past 82-plus years, under 18 pastors. She has served as a teacher/director of Sunday school, a choir member/leader, a pianist/soloist, and a cook for church suppers, and she served on the Training Union, Vacation Bible School, and Woman's Missionary Union. Marie wrote the original history of FSBC for the 50th anniversary in 1975. Marie's late husband, Lee "Buddy" Faver, became known for "Buckeye" candy. His recipe is as follows: "eight T. butter, one 18-ounce jar crunch peanut butter, one box powdered sugar, three c. of Rice Krispies, one-half bar paraffin, one 12-ounce bag chocolate chips. Blend butter, sugar, peanut butter, and Rice Krispies. Roll into small balls. In double boiler, melt paraffin and chocolate chips until blended. Roll balls in chocolate and place on waxed paper until dry." (Both, courtesy of author.)

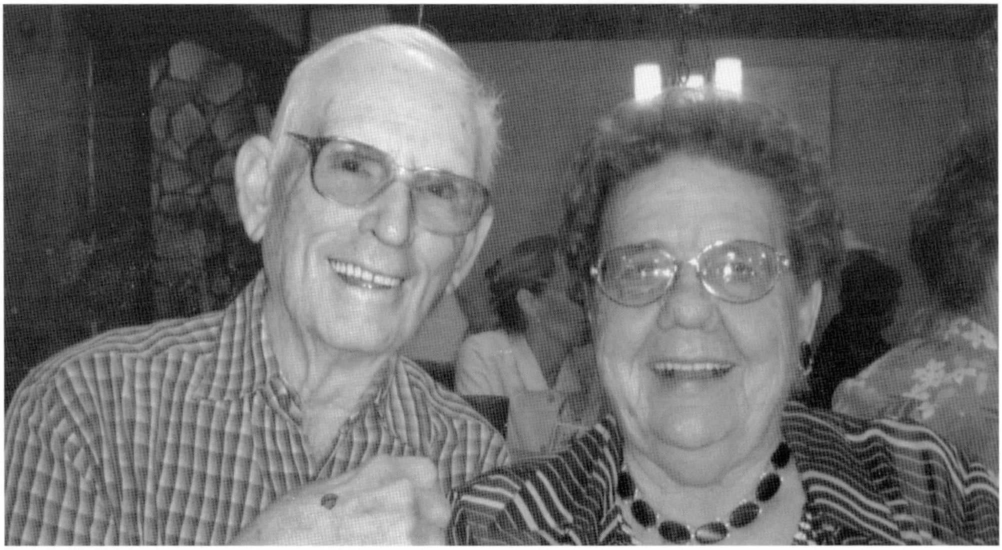

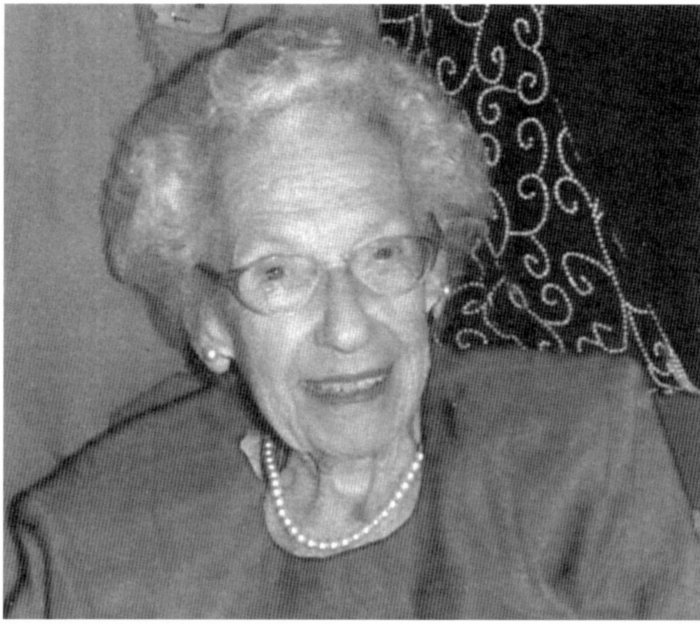

Alice Charman

Alice Charman was born in Carbondale, Pennsylvania, and died on July 9, 2014, at age 90 in Buckeye. She was a lady with many projects. She was first a high school biology teacher in Pennsylvania, then moved to Tempe in 1950 and to Salome in 1955. Charman came to Buckeye in the summer of 1971 with her husband, Bob Charman, and taught eighth grade for 10 years at Ruth Fisher Elementary, retiring in 1988. Among her community services were being an actress and codirector at Pioneer Day Melodramas for 17 years and serving on the Buckeye Town Council (1984–1990, 2000–2004). Her first volunteer job in Buckeye was to help move the library from the old jail to the current building on Sixth Street and Eason Avenue. She was a Friends of the Library member since its beginning in 1991, a member of the Community Church since 1972, and a 50-plus-year member of Buckeye Woman's Club. Alice Charman was given the Buckeye Valley Chamber of Commerce Outstanding Community Service Award in 1999 and was chosen for the Buckeye Valley Chamber of Commerce's Citizen of the Year Award in 2008. In July 2007, the Town of Buckeye named a building for her: Alice Charman Municipal Building (below), at 1101 East Ash Avenue. (Both, courtesy of the author.)

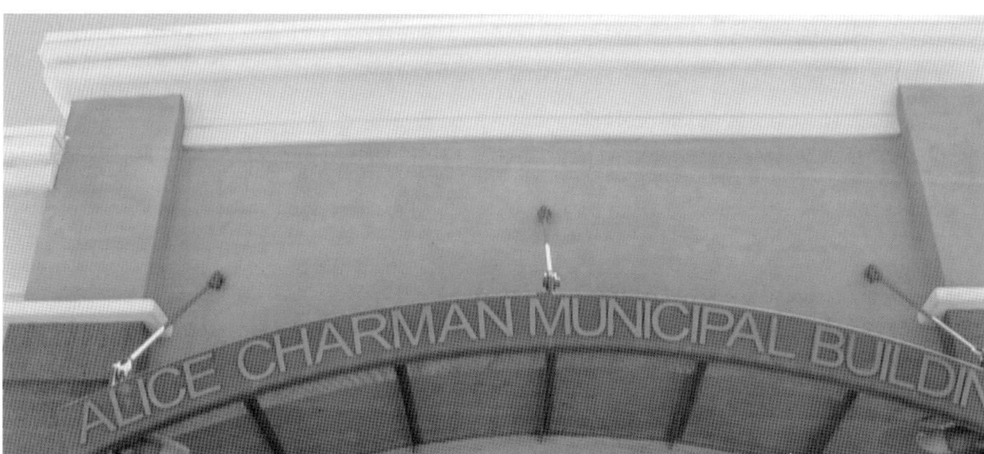

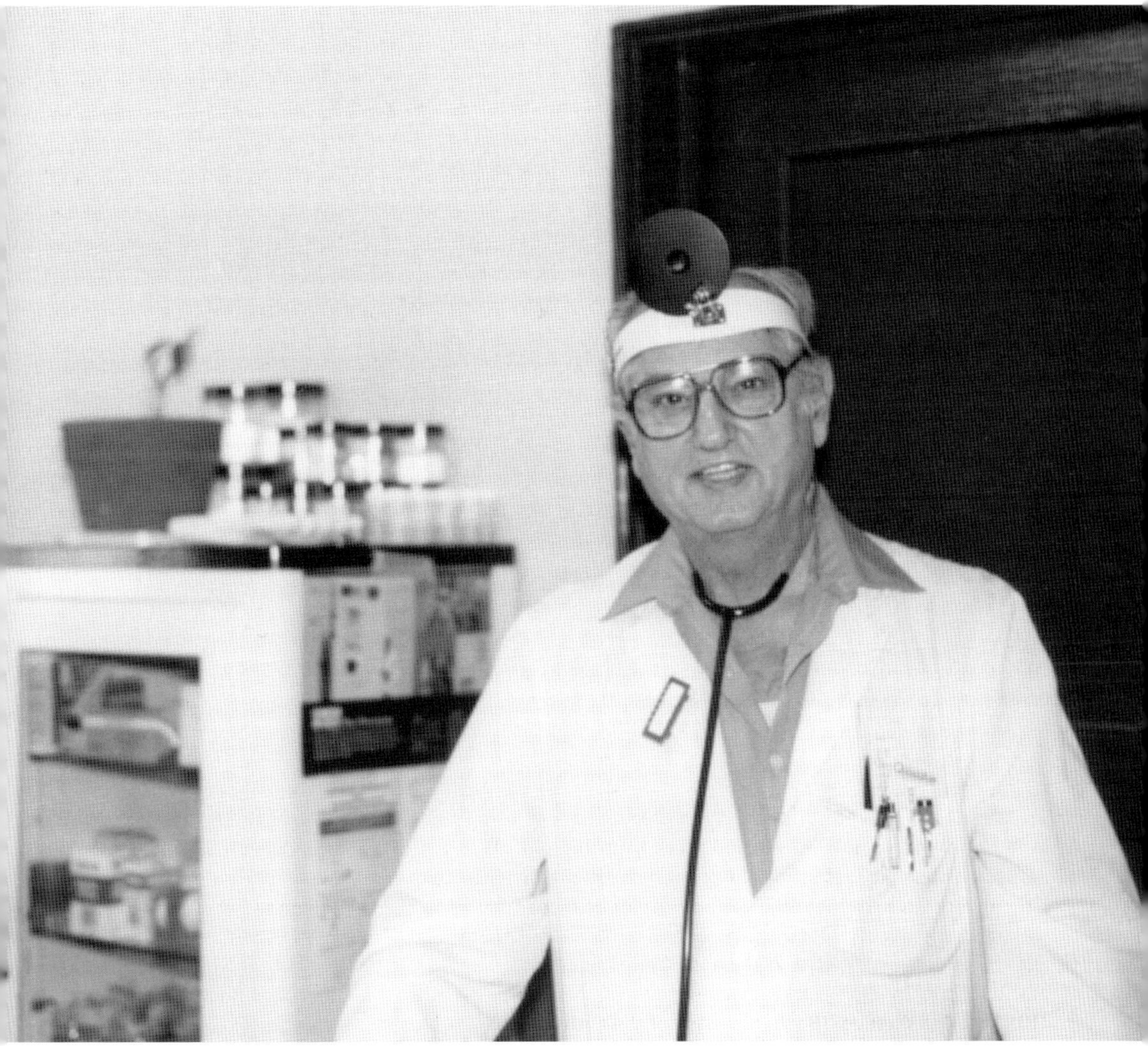

Robert A. Saide, MD
Dr. Saide was born in Detroit, Michigan, in 1915, and died in Buckeye, Arizona, in 2001. He and his wife, Isabelle, moved to the small town of Buckeye in 1951 because Isabelle's family owned a grocery market, known as Abraham's Market. Dr. Saide and Eddie Basha, of Basha's Grocery Store, were first cousins. Robert Saide was honored on "Dr. Saide Day", December 6, 1992, after 42 years of excellent caregiving. He is a doctor who cared and gave effective remedies. He always remembered one's name, and he delivered many babies. Dr. Saide often traveled valley roads to see patients. He was interested in families and had a dedication to the medical profession. Dr. Saide voluntarily stood on the BUHS football field sidelines as the team physician. During his long office hours, many patients heard him sing songs while they were being examined. Dr. Saide was honored with the 1987 Buckeye Valley Chamber of Commerce Citizen of the Year Award. On June 30, 2006, the Dr. Robert A. Saide Recreation Center was dedicated. (Courtesy of author.)

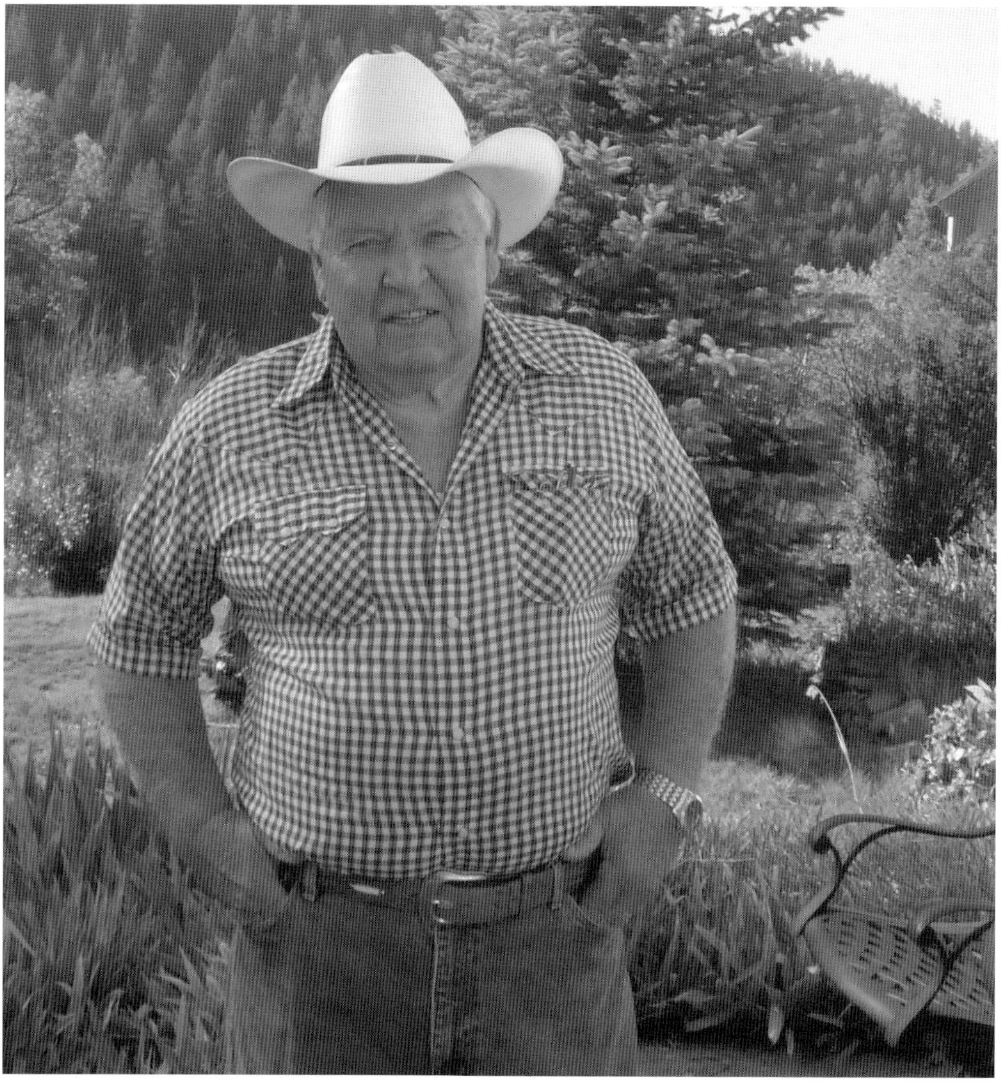

Frank Zellner

The owners of Buckeye Home Supply on South Fourth Street, Ted and Foda Zellner, gave Buckeye a legendary family: Jean, Lettie, Blannie, Ted Jr., and Frank. Frank graduated from BUHS in 1956 and lived in Huntington Beach, California, for 39 years. He has resided in Pagosa Springs, Colorado, for 16 years. Wherever he is, he is involved in community clubs and activities. In 2014, Frank Zellner brought together many "old timers" (BUHS students from around 1948 to 1962) through an "ask and answer" e-mail. It is called the Buckeye Trivia Team. Chairman and CEO Zellner says: "many factors go into making a community special. Hundreds of folks made Buckeye what it was and is today . . . so let's remember them." The following is a sample of trivia questions sent to team members: "What was the name of the clothing store next to the Buckeye Pharmacy?" "What was the Big Dipper?" "On the southeast corner of Fourth and Monroe, there was a huge square hole in the ground. Why was it there?" "How about the Roxy Café?" "Anybody remember rodeo dances at the American Legion Hall?" "Is the Enloe family still around?" "Does anyone have roller skating rink memories?" (Courtesy of Frank Zellner.)

CHAPTER SIX

Only in Buckeye

The author had a brainstorming session with longtime resident Marion Ratlief, and many names were recalled. Nicknames are everywhere, and they reveal who someone is and how they are known. In the following list, a few nicknames include last names: Bea, Bubba, Buddy, Bug, Bull Pasture, Buster, Charlie, Chickie, Chucklebea (Lofton), Cookie, Corky (Narramore), Dat 'n' Der, Duck, Dusty, Fat, Flash, Fletch, Frog, Gooch, Guero, Hank, Heavy, Honey Bun, Honey Dropper, Hook, Jake, Junior, Dutch (Dean), Mama Lucille, Manny, Mig (Miglio), Moppy, Nasty Brothers, Nute, Pig (Carr), Pig (Pittman), Poop (Hardesty), Poozy, Rat (Webb), Red, Red Boy, Rosey (Heiden), Rusty (Hardesty), Short (Carr) Skeeter, Slick, Snake, Snakeman, Snooks (Huff), Sonny, Spud, Stinker (Ray), Stub, Tiger, Til (Hunter), Toad, Toots (Osborn), Tubby, Tuffy (Campbell), Turkey, Whitey, and Yogi. Names like these are found only in Buckeye. This chapter highlights Buckeye legends, such as Billy the Kid, Canal Swimmers, J.D. Steward, Echeverria Sheep Camp, Gerre Rooks, Roman Comer, Dennis Daniel, and "Duck" Ezell.

Carl Baxter

Baxter was born on October 15, 1923, in Buckeye, weighing in at 14.75 pounds on a cotton scale. He was born at Grandma Burke's house (where Duncan Truck Lines now has offices). A Mrs. Couch was the midwife. The doctor came the day after his birth. Carl was the first of four children born to Joe and Sally (Burke) Baxter. The others were Leota, Raymond, and Claude. The youngest child was only five weeks old when Sally passed away of diphtheria in 1929. Carl graduated from BUHS in 1942. According to the *Falcon* yearbook, he was involved in football, basketball, and Future Farmers of America and was the senior class vice president. His pet slang term was "Gee Whiz." Carl recalls that Ted "Dad" Miller lived about 100 yards south of Baxter's home on Dean Road. Carl was Miller's closest neighbor, and Miller was like a big brother to six-year-old Carl. Also, Carl remembers Dad Miller showing him how to shoot a .45-caliber pistol at a turkey feather and to take out only the fluff of feathers—all that was left was the stem. Buckeye lost a part of its legacy when Carl Baxter died on November 19, 2014. (Courtesy of Lorayne Niedermeyer.)

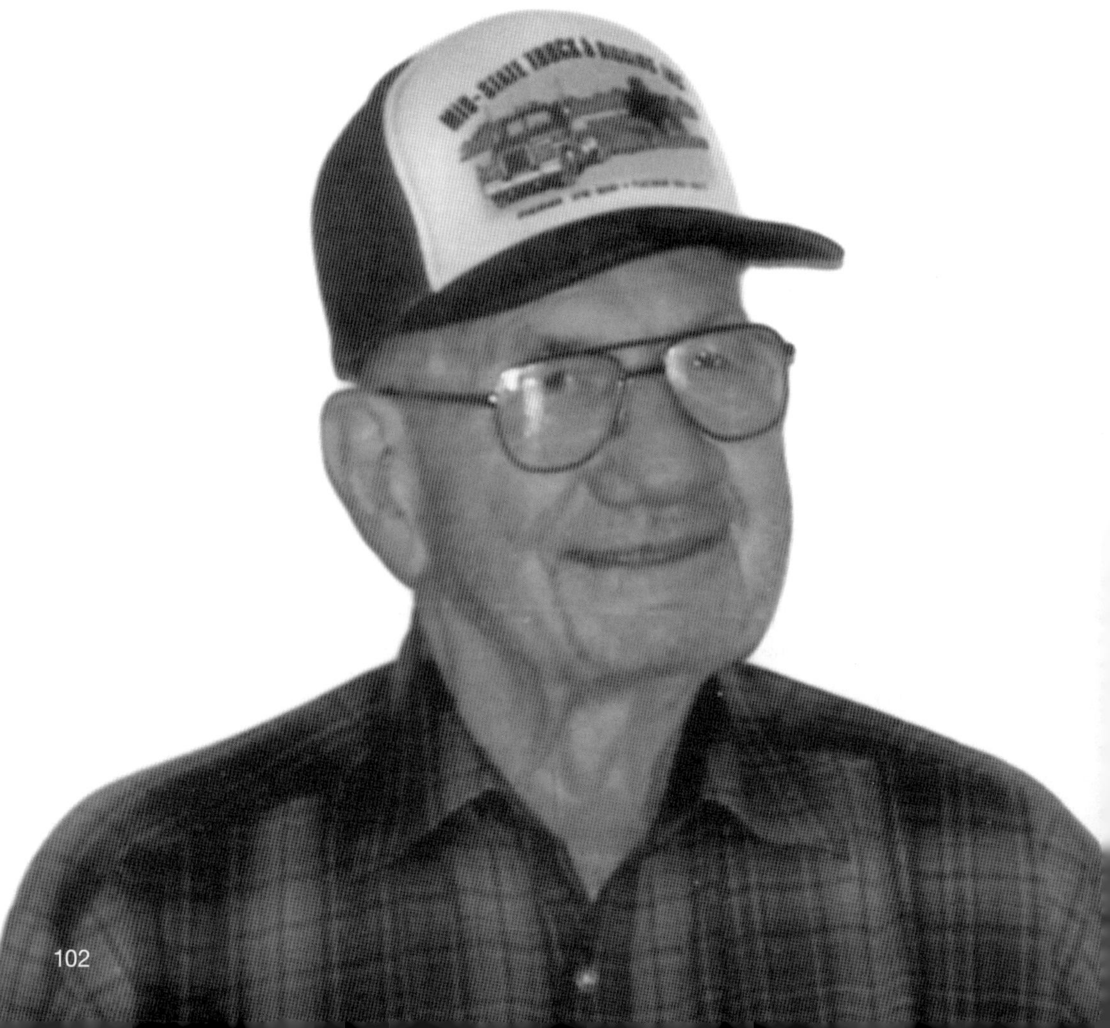

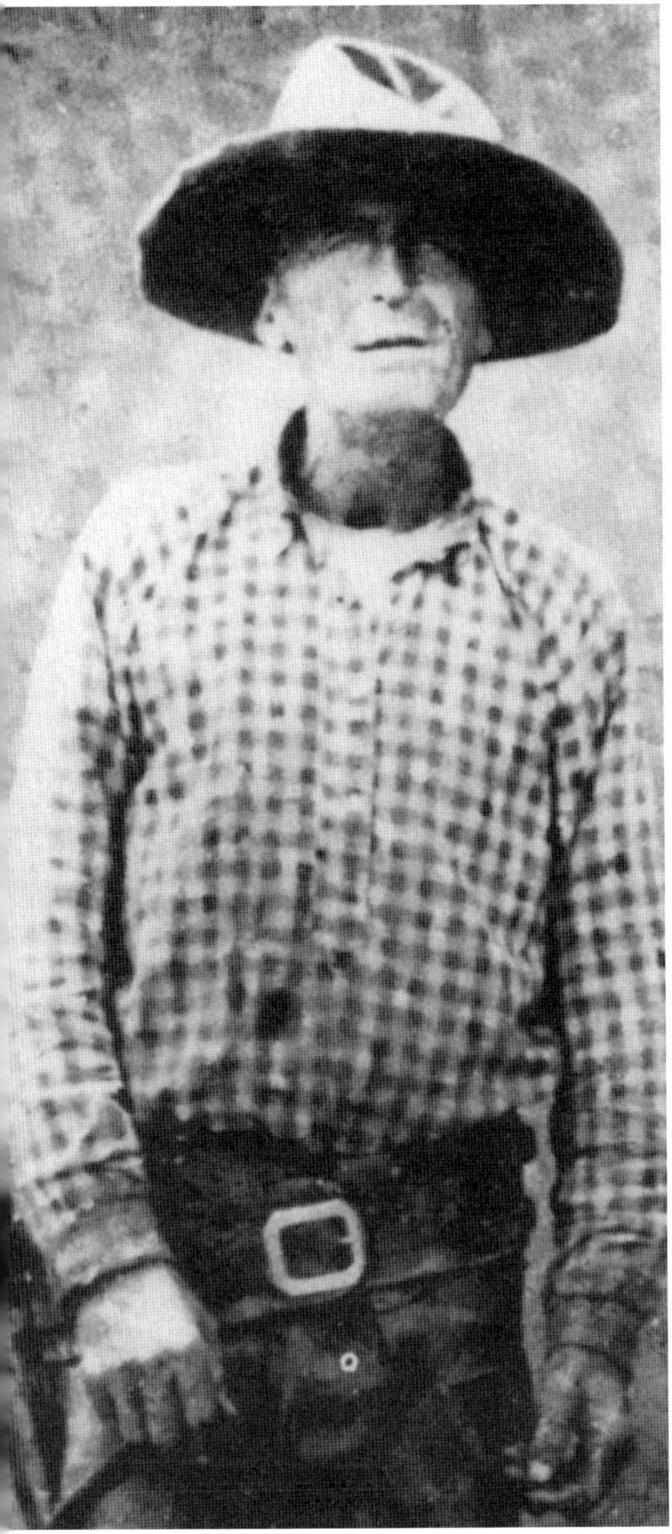

Billy the Kid

This story was written by June Dean in 2008, as told to her by Carl Baxter. History has it that Billy the Kid was gunned down in Fort Sumner, New Mexico, on July 14, 1881, when he was 21 years old, by his old friend Sheriff Pat Garrett. However, doubts about the true identity of the man Garrett killed that night started to pop up immediately after the shooting, and many people believe Billy the Kid escaped to live out his days under an assumed name. Some say that Billy the Kid was Ted "Dad" Miller, who lived one-fourth of a mile north of MC 85 on Dean Road in a home he made of adobe bricks. He made the bricks, laid them up himself, got scrap material from around the neighborhood for roofing, and sprinkled the dirt floor with water to keep the dust down. Miller owned a horse and buggy. His wife had cancer in her nose, and they would take cigarette papers, dampen them, and plaster them over her nose. Because of this, she had to breathe through her mouth. With no electricity, Miller carried water in a barrel with a sled to his house. Once, Dad Miller and Baxter made a *riata* (rope) from deer hides that Miller had obtained from local farmers. They tanned and cut them into one strip in a continuous circle to make one strand from each hide. Then, they braided them and made a rope. Miller asked Carl to look after his wife once the rope was done while he went on a trip. About one month went by, and Miller returned from New Mexico. Baxter asked where he had been and where the riata was. Miller said, "Well, son, I replaced one that a fella broke pulling the bars out of a window for me." Miller also told Carl that he knew the New Mexico territory very well. So, did Billy the Kid live in Buckeye? (Courtesy of author.)

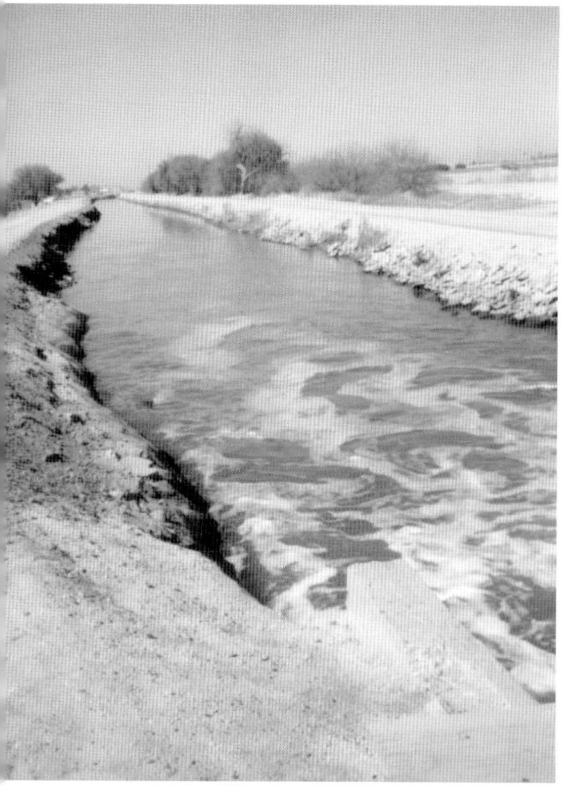

Buckeye Canal People

In the below photograph, Al Makin and his children pose in 1926 at the Buckeye Canal. John Wood of Palo Verde remembers swimming in the canal in the 1930s with Tom Cantrell, Bud and John Roberts, and Virginia and Marie Roberts. In 1935, miles of cool-water canals became summer pleasure centers. Sundays and evenings, canals were filled with swimmers engaging in ducking conflicts or just keeping cool. Buckeye youth rigged one-passenger boats by bending a roofing tin at the ends and filling the ends with tar. With these boats, folks would try to sink each other by either ramming them or swamping them with a bucket of water. William Major's home became a drydock for young shipbuilders, such as Billy Meck, Richard Wetzler, Billy Major, Tudor McClure, Wilmer Harper, Charles Wetzler, Bill Hatch, Robert Weskamp, and Charles Narramore. For "surfing season", all that was needed was a surfboard and about 100 feet of rope. The board was thrown into the canal and connected by rope to the back bumper of a car. The car was then driven down the canal bank at 25 to 40 miles per hour. The rope was kept tight so as to miss headgates. (Both, courtesy of author.)

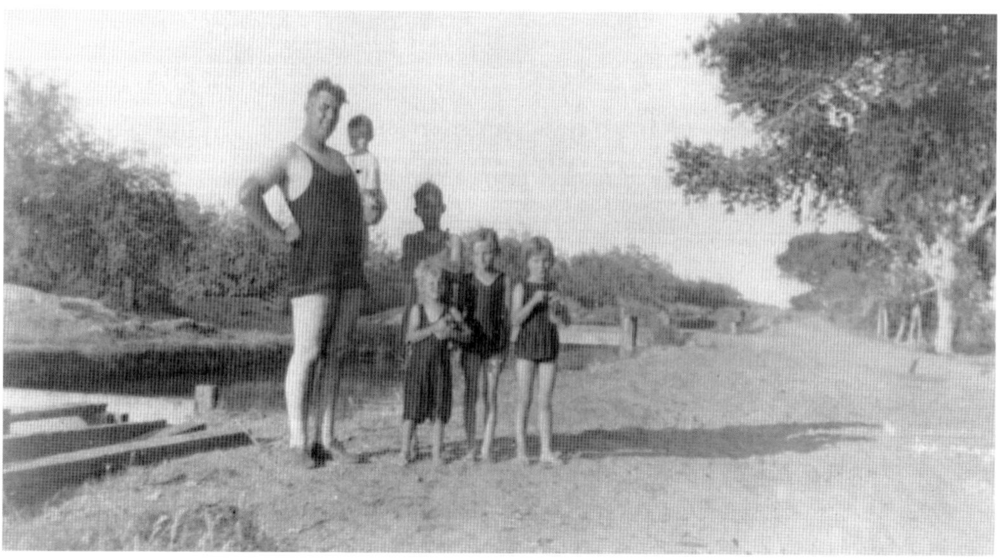

Rowdy Six

Since the first grade, the "Rowdy Six", members of the class of 1960, have been friends. As BUHS juniors in 1958, they convinced their parents to host all of them for a dinner at each other's home. Judge Bill Meck dubbed them the "Rowdy Six", and the name stuck. Mary Ganley called them the "Dirty Half Dozen", after the movie *The Dirty Dozen*. In 1959, they put on a stage production, *Dangerous Dan McGrew*, at BUHS. Each student had a part, and it was an unmemorable event in the eyes of many. But the young men made a pact to participate in each other's weddings, birthdays, anniversaries, and funerals. The vow was sealed with a beer. The Rowdy Six met at all reunions and at least twice a year with wives to celebrate birthdays. Shown here at the Colorado River in 2002 are, standing from left to right, Tommy Meck, Mike Ganley, Earl Webb, Jimmy Wood, and Paul Alva. Kneeling in front is Robert Edgar. Alva died in 2008, and five "Rowdies" served as his pallbearers. (Courtesy of Betty [Gilbertson] Meck.)

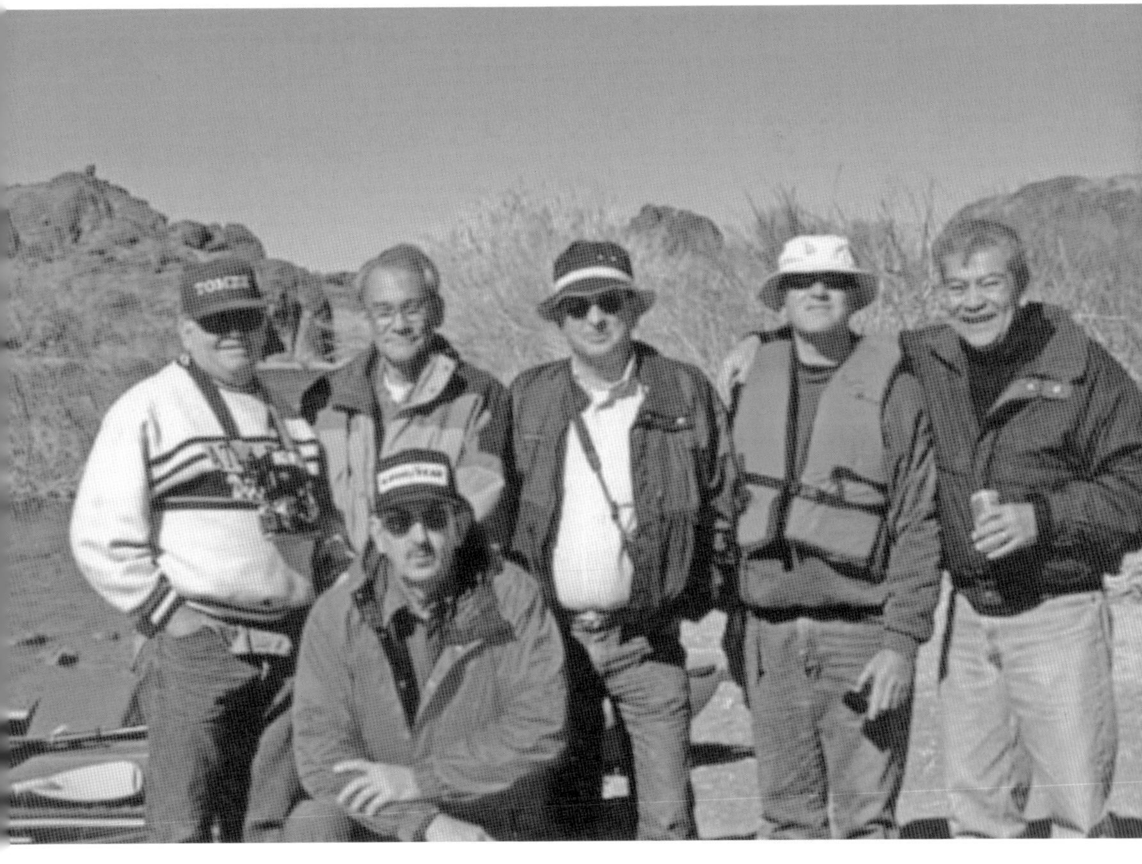

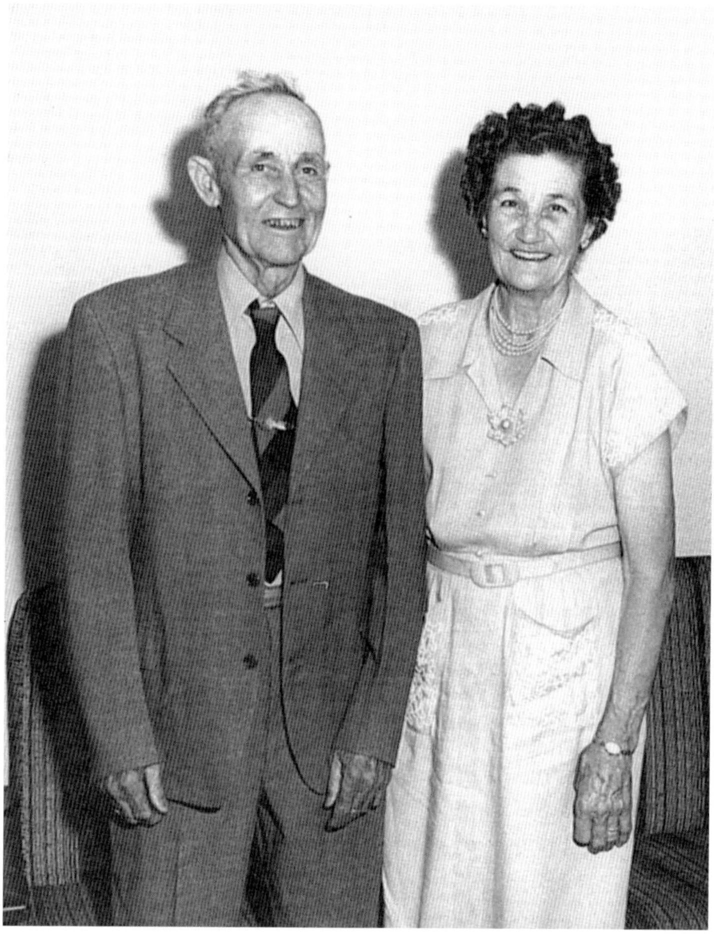

James Steward

James D. "J.D." Steward, a retired Buckeye rancher, was not only lucky. He was smart. "I never was lost," he said. On October 26, 1950, he was separated from his companion, Essie Conley, during a hunting trip on the first day of deer season. A search party reached him 10 days later about 15 miles west of the Black Canyon Highway near Bumblebee in the bottom of Sycamore Canyon. Steward said,

> We went out before breakfast the first day, after making camp near the top of the canyon. I walked to the bottom of the canyon and when my trick right knee started to bother me, I sat down to rest. It was hurting so bad I couldn't climb back up the hill. When no one came to my rescue I decided the best thing was to stay where I was. There was a small pool of water in the bottom of the canyon. How did I survive the ordeal of ten days in the mountains? The presence of moss in the water probably helped to nourish me. I never did feel hungry. I slept on branches beside the water pool and tore a piece of underwear through which I strained the water when wanting a drink. I still had a couple of buckets of water left when Carl Arnold, G.W. Cox, and Norman Wedgeworth, all of Buckeye, found me. My biggest disappointment was that I didn't even sight one buck deer.

J.D. Steward is the grandfather of Doris (Beyer) King, Delbert Beyer, and Sharon (Beyer) Hinkle of Buckeye. J.D. and Maudie Steward (pictured) became residents of Buckeye in 1927. (Courtesy of Sharon [Bayer] Hinkle.)

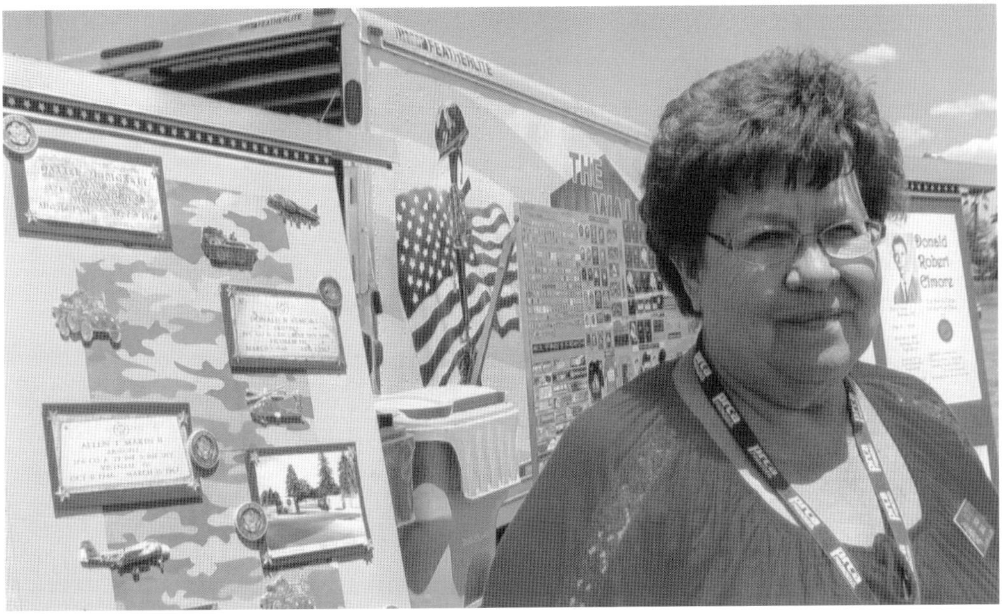

Linda Davis and Karen Goins
Continuing family legacies are two Buckeye native daughters and 1960s BUHS students. Linda (Armstrong) Davis (above) is the granddaughter of Ruth Thompson, Buckeye Museum curator from 1964 to 1976. Thompson lived at the museum. Davis is a volunteer at the museum and is a member and registrar of the local chapter of the Daughters of the American Revolution. She organized and led the Capturing Arizona's Stories grant project as well as a 2011 renovation grant project for the Buckeye Hazelton Cemetery. Karen (Williams) Goins (below) is the daughter of longtime barber H.D. "Hook" Williams and Royleen "Chickie" Balmes. Goins, at the request of her BUHS high school physical education teacher, Mrs. Meck, "volunteered" to input data and illustrations into two Buckeye books that Meck authored. (Both, courtesy of author.)

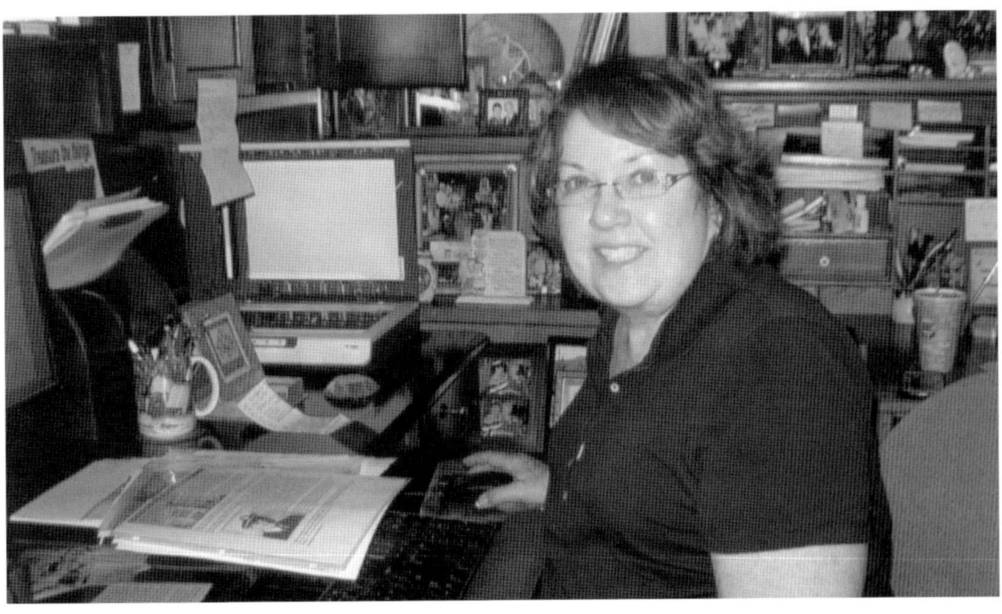

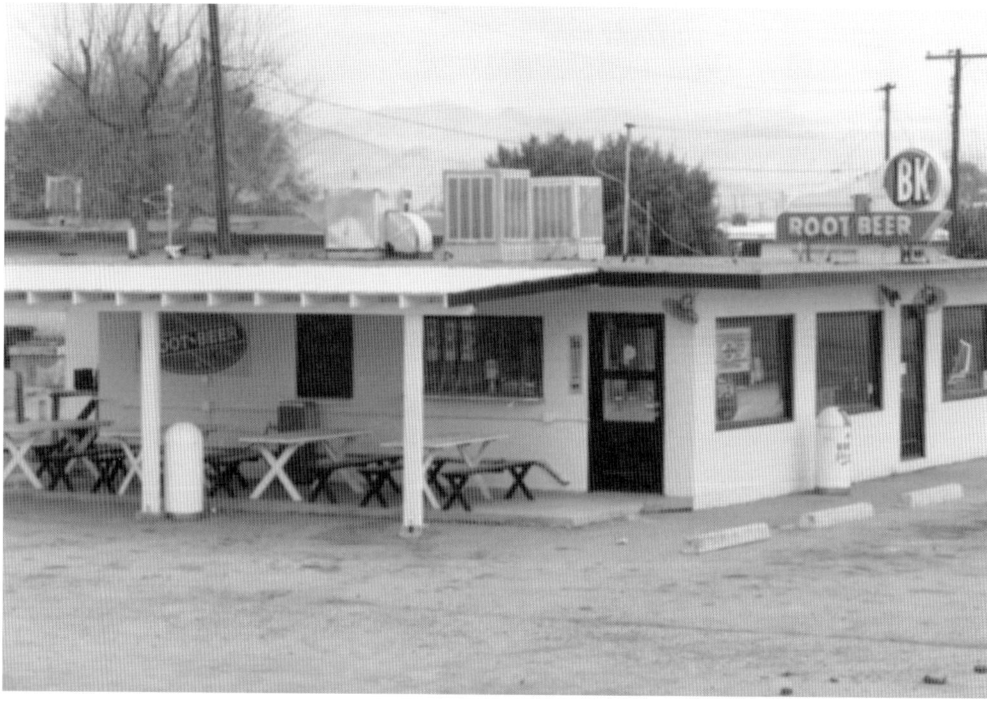

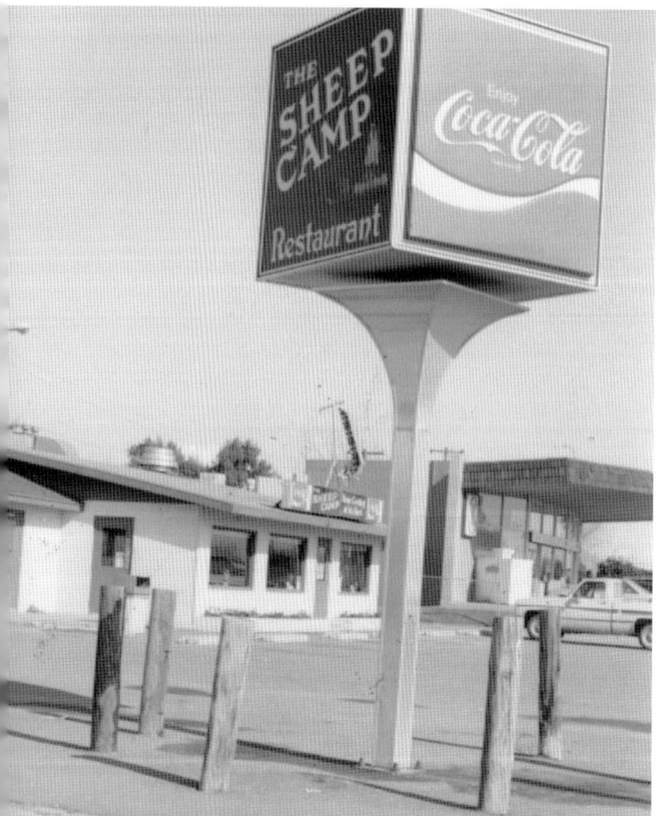

Echeverria Sheep Camp

Manuel and Matilde Aja had six children: Julia, Virginia, Manuel, Basilio, Robert, and Benny. Julia and her husband, Phillip Echeverria, were in the sheep business for many years. Julia remembered that, at one time, they had more than 10,000 sheep. Like her father, Julia's husband died in an accident. While shearing sheep one early morning in 1966, the herders lit a campfire to keep themselves warm. Somehow, Phillip inhaled too much smoke and died at age 43. Julia sold her last sheep 10 years after Phillip's death and bought the Root Beer Stand at East Highway 85 and Watkins Avenue (above) with her daughter-in-law Bonnie, who is married to Julia's son Phillip. The two women converted the Root Beer Stand into a restaurant and called it The Sheep Camp (left). For 18 years, they served breakfast and lunch to Buckeye residents and visitors. Julia passed away in October 2014. With new owners, it continues to be a Buckeye gathering place where legends are told. (Both, courtesy of author.)

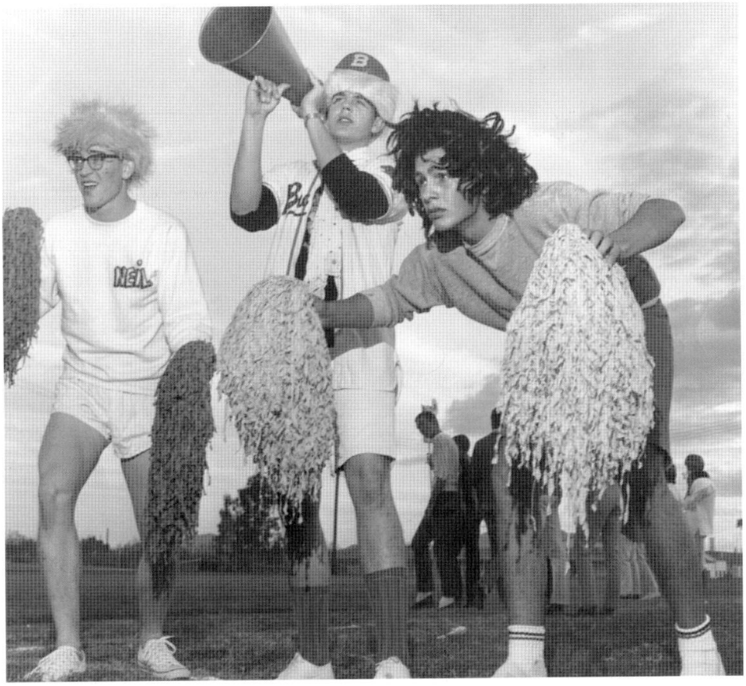

Powder Puff Football

In the above photograph, BUHS cheerleaders Neil Myers (left), Larry Brabbin (center), and Jacky Janda (right) rooted for players in the Pep Club vs. Future Homemakers of America Powder Puff Football game in 1964. Then, 50 years later, on April 14, 2014, the BUHS junior girls defeated the BUHS senior girls 22-21. Again, high school male cheerleaders led the spectators in the very close and exciting Powder Puff game (below). (Above, courtesy of BUHS Archives; below, courtesy of Hawk Staff Photography.)

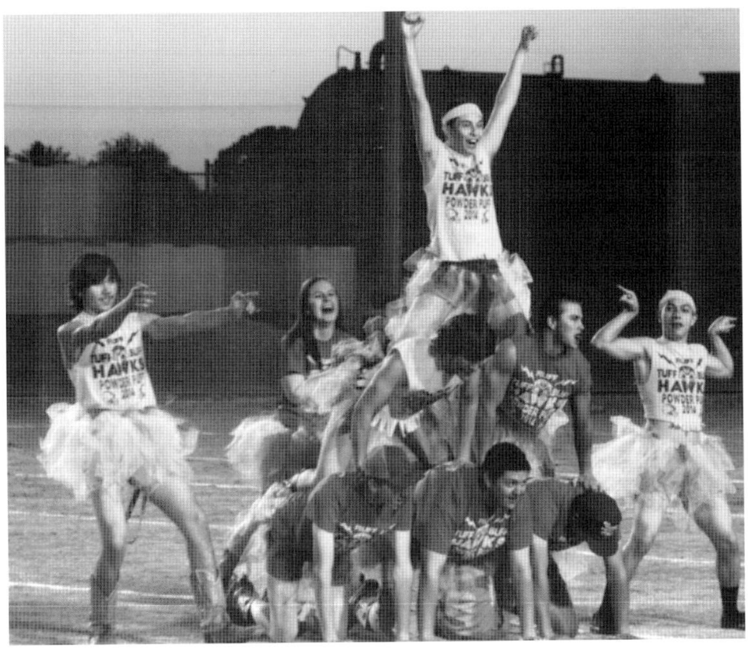

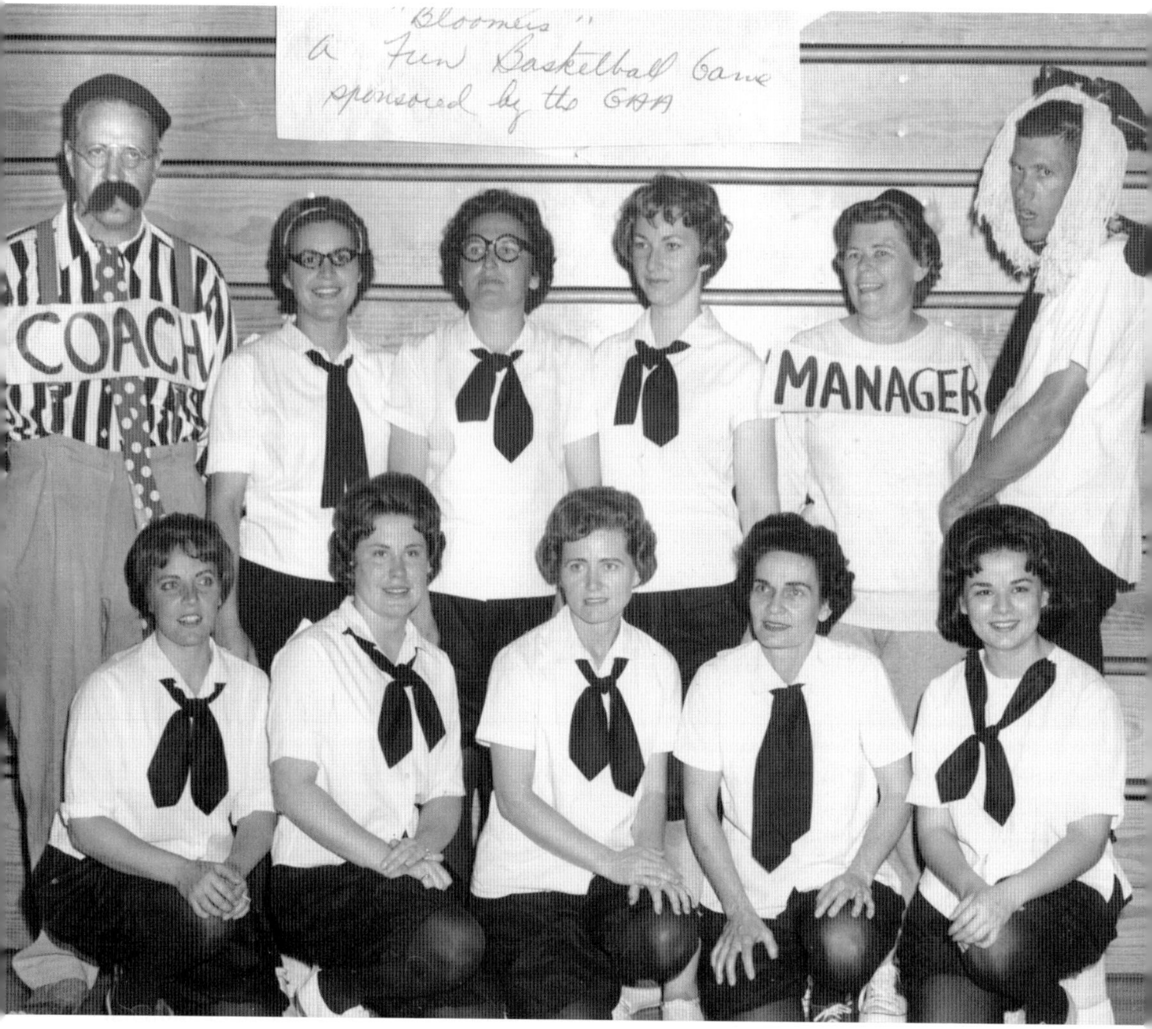

BUHS Bloomers Team

The BUHS Girls Athletic Association sponsored a fun basketball game in 1964 featuring school faculty and staff members. The Bloomers wore "historical" girls' athletic uniforms. Those participating were, from left to right, (first row) Mary Sue Tomlinson, Karen Vannest, Arlyne Turner, Dottie Rausch, and Pat Brinias; (second row) coach Chet McNabb, Verlyne Meck, Mary Jane Hardesty, Pat Rovey, manager Edith Mae Christian, and "Secret Surprise" Miss Jerry (Mabel) Conner. The opposing team was comprised of Girls Athletic Association members. (Courtesy of BUHS Archives.)

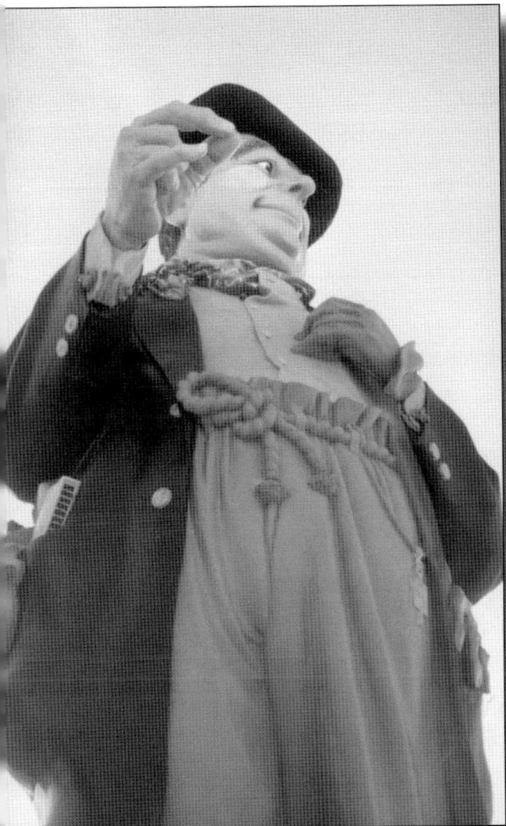

Hobo Joe

Just about the time a driver hits cruise control on Interstate 10 and Watson Road on the way to California, there appears the sign for Buckeye. Taking that exit, a traveler finds a main street, Monroe Avenue (Old Highway 80). Entering Buckeye on the east end, the driver is likely to see the 23-foot, 1,200-pound statue of Hobo Joe. The plaque on its base reads: "Hobo Joe, built by and stands in memory of Marvin Ransdell (1928–1988) by his good friend Ramon Gillum. July 1989." It is a fine statue, full of details, such as a copy of the *Wall Street Journal* stuffed in a back pocket, the watch fob and chain stretched across his chest, and even the shoe with its flap of a sole. Ramon Gillum, owner of Gillum's Meat Locker & Processing Plant, was Ransdell's friend. The fiberglass statue was constructed by Marvin Ransdell in 1967. It possibly served as a mascot for a restaurant chain with outlets in Phoenix, Las Vegas, and El Paso. Questions still exist about its connection to the Hobo Joe Restaurant chain. When Buckeye town fathers decided that the statue was a piece of Americana and not just a sign, it went up in July 1989, the same day that Buckeye dedicated a town hall at 1101 East Ash Avenue. (Both, courtesy of author.)

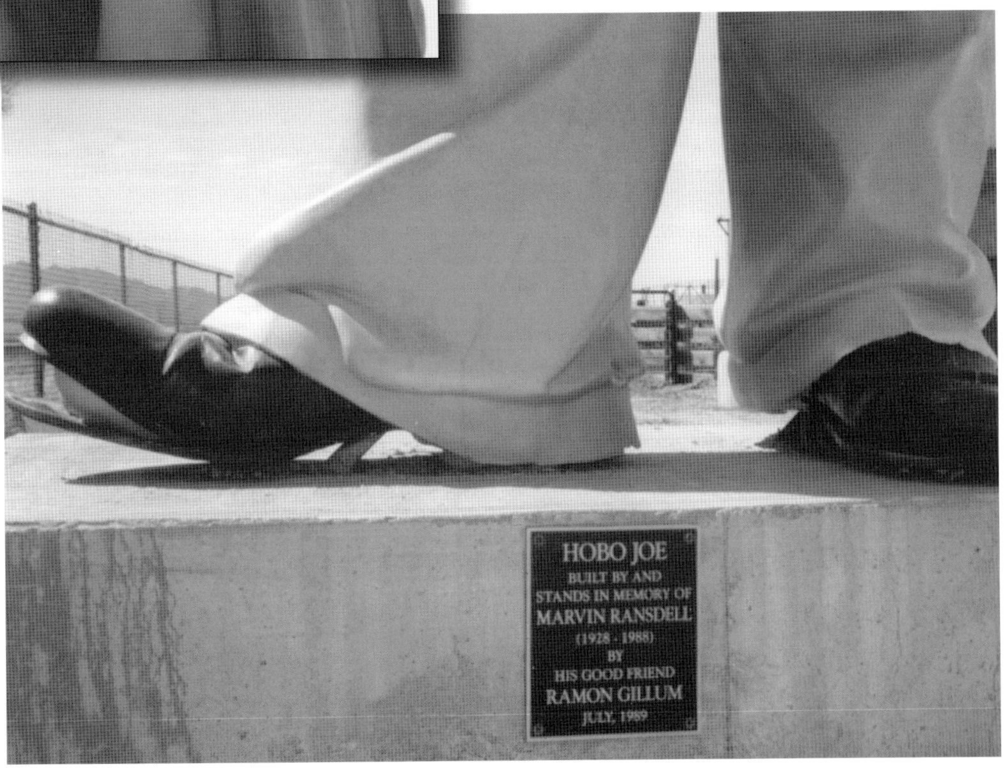

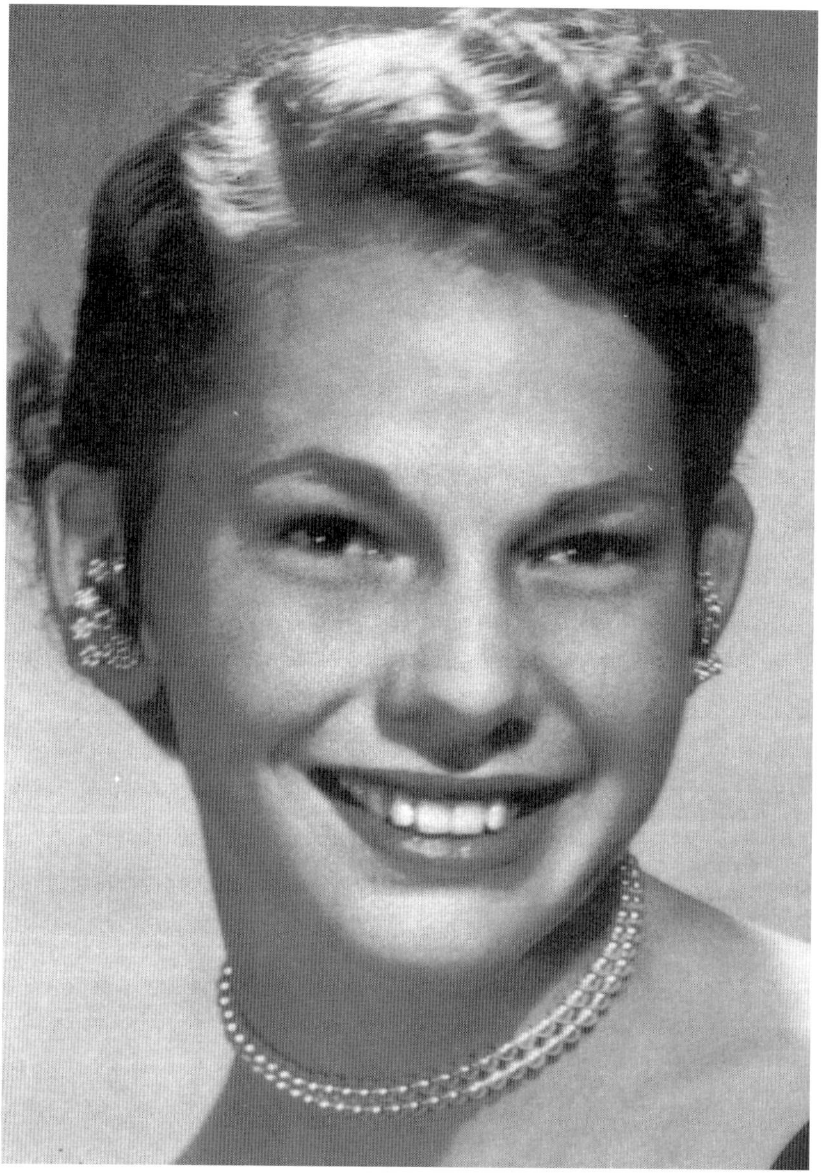

Gerre Rooks

Gerre "Toots" Rooks arrived in Buckeye from New Mexico around 1944 with her parents, Jack and Jerrie Rooks, and brothers Jack and Don. Her dad was a cotton farmer and cattleman on Broadway Road, west of Miller Road. Gerre says she collected chicken eggs, got pecked a lot, and fought with Don about churning cream into butter, as it was a job she did not like. Gerre loved riding horses. In 1952, she was the Helzapoppin Rodeo Queen. During her 1952–1956 BUHS years, other awards came her way. A favorite was being the 1955–1956 Homecoming Queen with King Bill Meck Jr. In 1955 and 1956, Gerre was Buckeye's Salad Bowl Princess and a candidate for Salad Bowl Queen. In 1955, out of 44 candidates, Gerre was one of three runners-up. The Salad Bowl was a postseason college football game played on New Year's Day at Montgomery Stadium in Phoenix between 1947 and 1956. Other BUHS students who were Salad Bowl Princess candidates were Joan Brown (1952), Kay O'Neill (1953), and Raquel Loudermilk (1954). (Courtesy of BUHS Archives.)

Jimmy H. Tracy, Bee Man
For many years, the Buckeye Valley was a tremendous shipper of honey. With many fields of alfalfa and stems covered with beautiful purple flowers, plus huge thickets along the rivers and canal bank, bees were kept busy producing one of the most flavorful honeys imaginable. A July 1918 *Buckeye Valley News* article reported that a valuable carload of food products left the Buckeye Valley. The shipment included 410 cans of honey from shippers Mrs. McDonald of Liberty, P.H. Benson of Palo Verde, T.J. Patterson of Arlington, and J.H. Tracy of Buckeye. The shipment would go direct to France and would be enjoyed by American soldiers. Storytellers Marion Ratlief and R. Bruce Heiden recalled Jimmy Tracy. He was an old bachelor with a stiff leg at the knee. Heiden's father, Bob "Rosey" Heiden, at age 16, worked for Tracy in the summer of 1936. Honey was stored in five-gallon cans and sold once a year. That would account for Tracy's income for the entire year. This 2014 photograph shows the location of Jimmy Tracy's home, built sometime between 1930 and 1940, located east on Rainbow Road, south of the Buckeye Canal. (Courtesy of author.)

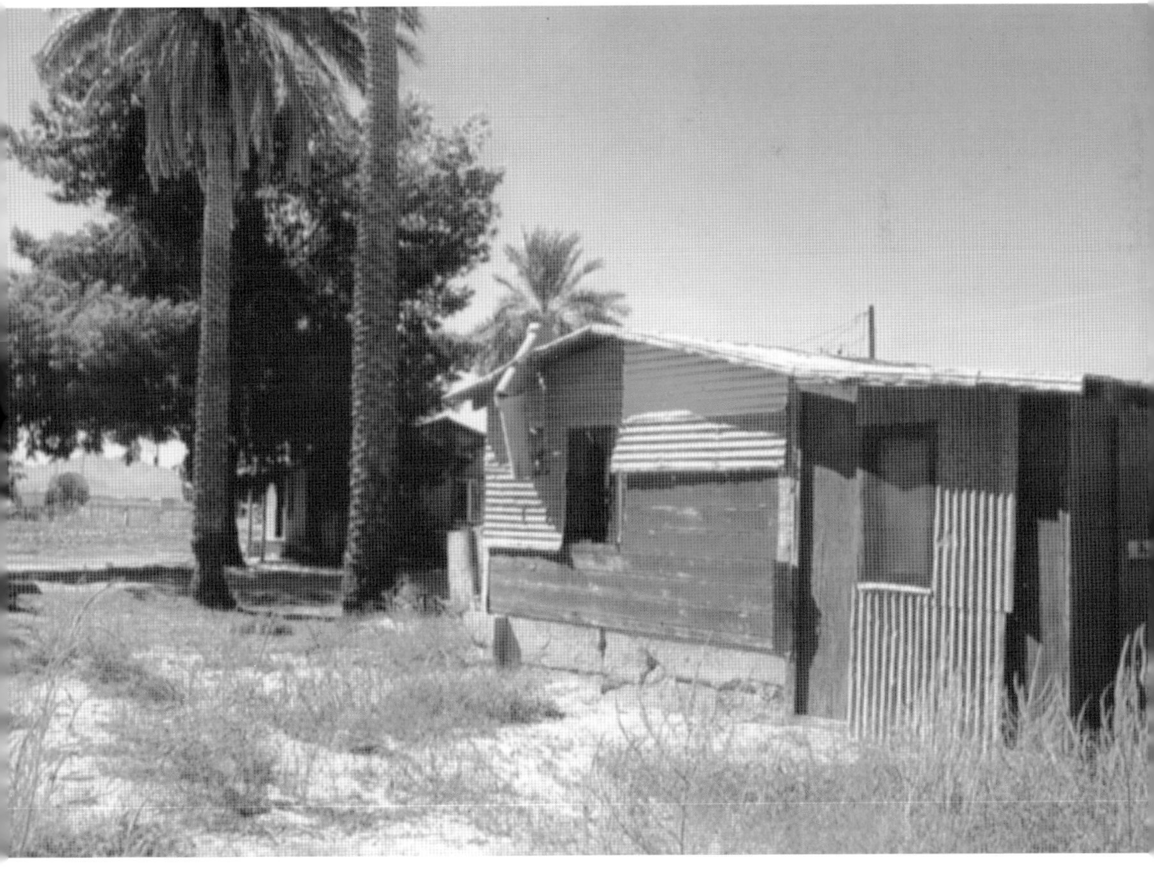

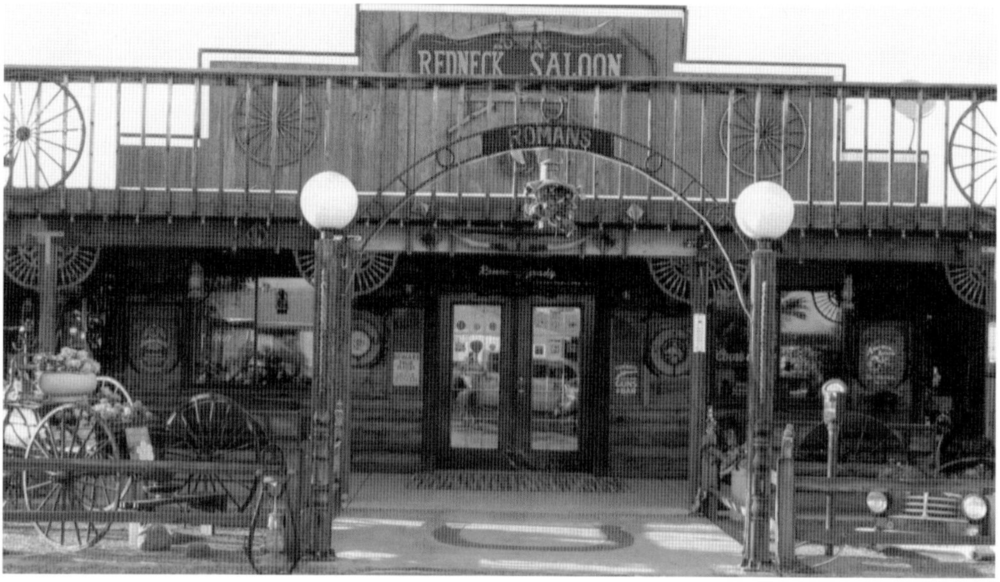

Roman Comer

Comer (1932–2011) (below, left) moved to the Buckeye Valley in 1986 from Oakman, Alabama. His quick wit and fun-loving personality brought joy to all who met him. For more than 25 years, Roman's Oasis on Yuma Road has been the site for the annual chili cook-off that benefits Buckeye Rotary Club's Christmas Angel program. Nowhere is Comer's creative genius more evident than at his homestead, Roman and Grady's Hillbilly Hilton (above and below, right). Located in the Buckeye Valley, their home was the picturesque site for the Buckeye Valley Chamber of Commerce awards dinner for many years. Comer's eclectic collection of memorabilia from across the years takes visitors through decades of history. This Western town boasts a livery, blacksmith, mercantile, barbershop, fueling station, jail, bank, saloon, and, of course, an outhouse. A special Roman Comer legend has it that he once purchased a truck from a widow in downtown Buckeye, paying more for it than he should have, just to help her out. He then sold it to his daughter Myra Curtis for a quarter so that he could tell his sons Steven and Grant that he did not give it to her, but that she bought it. (All, courtesy of the author.)

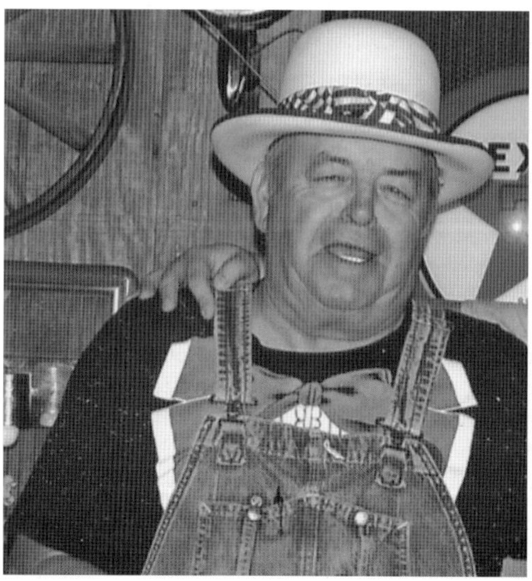

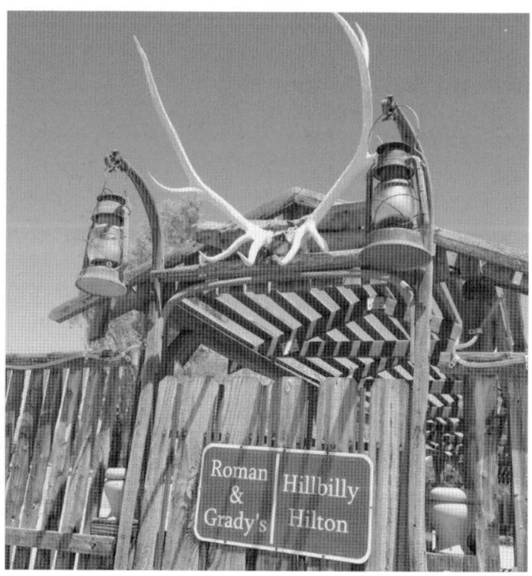

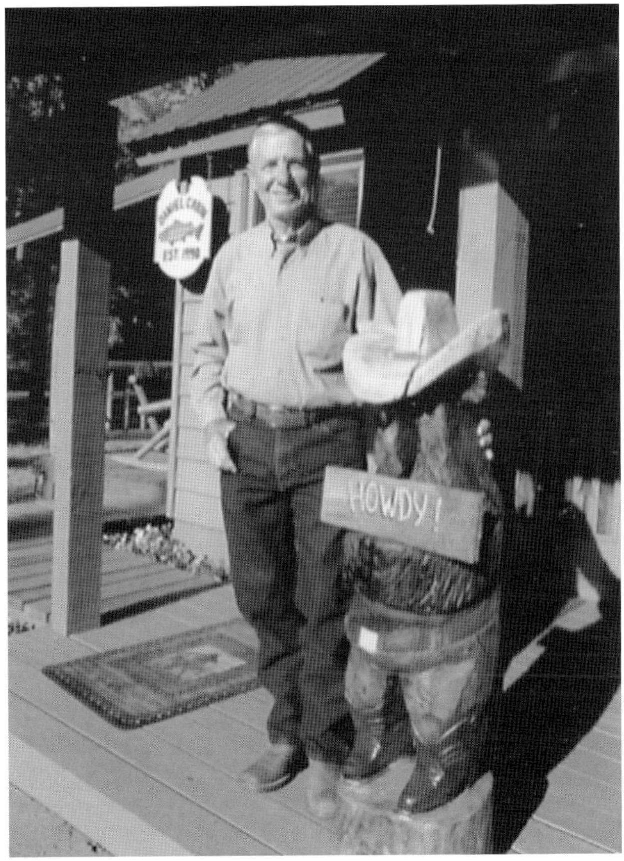

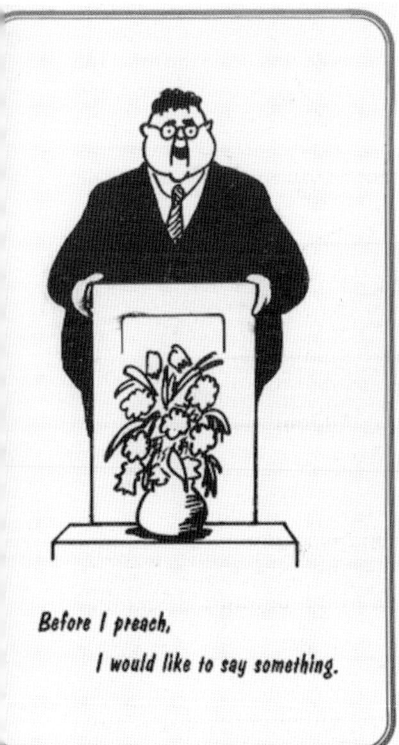

Dennis Daniel

Daniel arrived from Utah in 1972 and pastored for eight years at the First Southern Baptist Church. His wife, Paula, had wanted to move to a warmer climate and to have a house closer to the church. She got both wishes: Buckeye heat and a parsonage on the front lawn of the church. Known for his sense of humor, Reverend Dennis was entering the church campus one day and met several members of Weight Watchers. He greeted them with, "Wow, you have a big group!" Realizing his faux pas, Dennis tried to backtrack, saying, "I mean, there's a lot of you." Finally, he blurted out, "Oh, I'll just shut up!" During his tenure in Buckeye, Daniel began drawing a "Brother Blooper" cartoon character (left). This character became well known and appears in many publications. When asked where he gets his ideas, Daniel just smiles and says, "I just keep my eyes and ears open around the church." Church attendees looked forward to his chalk drawing presentations. He retired after serving seven churches for 38 years. The Daniels returned to the west valley and now attend their "old" church. He says folks have let him return because they have either forgotten or forgiven him. Reverend Daniel is also known as a chainsaw carver of "cowboy bears" (above). (Both, courtesy of Dennis Daniel.)

Roy Clark

Roy Albert Clark was born on March 11, 1917, in Broken Bow, Nebraska. Shortly after his birth, the family moved back to the family farm in Iowa. After being drafted into the Army, he was stationed in Hawaii, where Marie later joined him for marriage. At the end of World War II, they returned to Iowa and farmed. During this time, he attended Iowa State University, receiving his teaching certification. While in Iowa, he became the father of three sons. The family moved to Buckeye in 1952, and Roy taught vocational agriculture and science at BUHS. For the next 30 years, he developed a legacy of an outstanding Future Farmers of American program. As Coach Clark, he assisted with football and was known as "Energy Plus." Gilbert Vasquez recalls that Clark provided on-point counseling that lasted a lifetime. While in Buckeye, Roy's two daughters were born. The first one died shortly after her birth. Roy retired in 1982, after 30 years of teaching. He and Marie then moved to Glencroft Retirement Community. Roy became active in the Arizona State Games and also competed at the Senior Olympics national level. He earned gold in both and won more than 800 medals and awards, including the Arizona State Lifetime Achievement Award. Roy Clark came to the finish line of his last race on May 30, 2008. (Courtesy of author.)

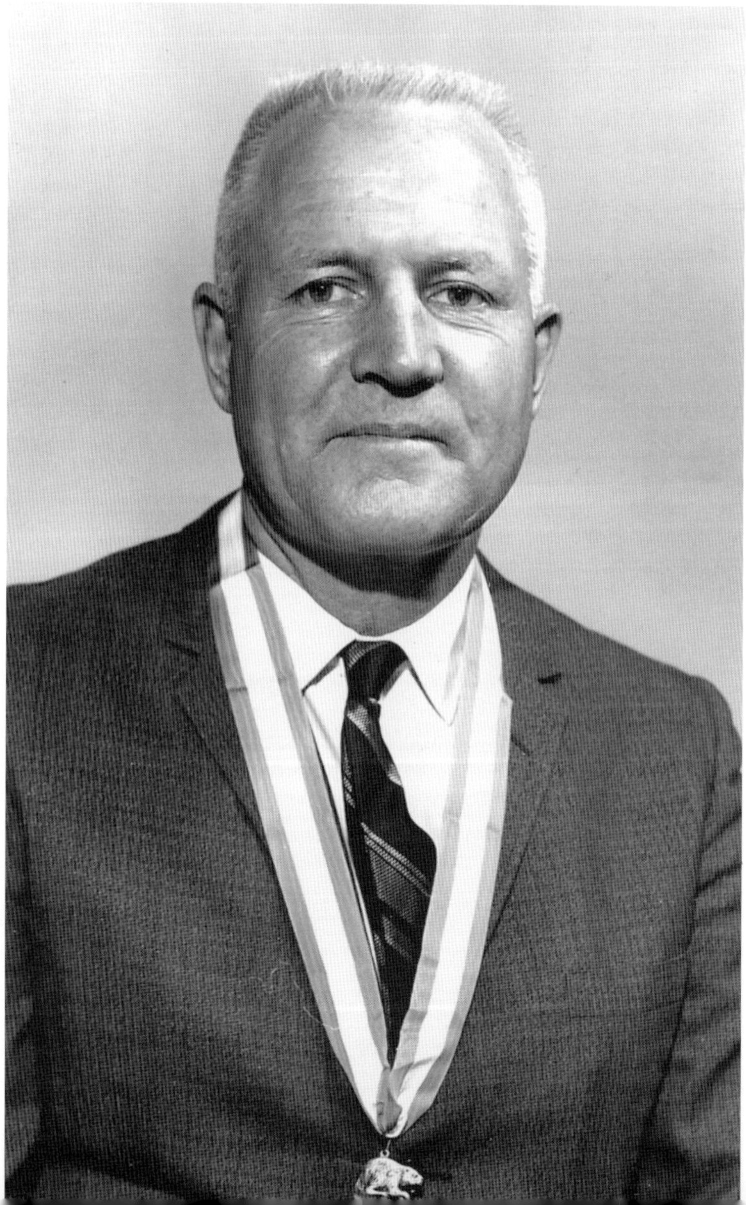

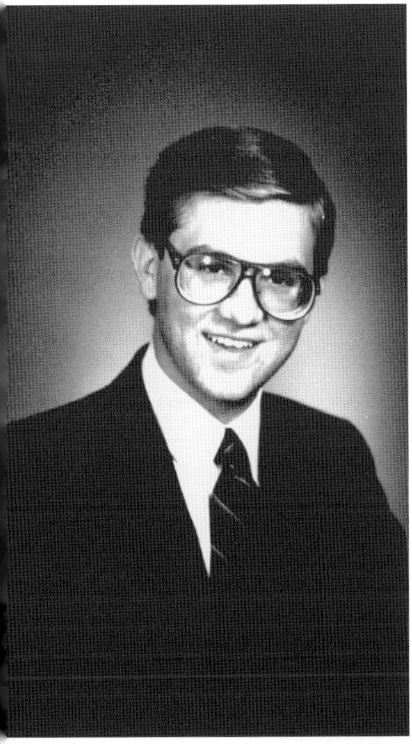

Jackie Meck Jr., Vernon and Irene (Beloat) Butler

In 1983, as a Liberty School eighth grader, Jackie Meck Jr. (left) wrote a letter to *Buckeye Valley News* editor Mark Shepard. This ultimately began the centennial celebration process. "Dear Mr. Shepard, I am wondering what is the proper date of our town's founding. The entrance sign at the west end of town on Highway 85 has '1886' printed upon it. The sign at the east end of Buckeye has '1888' printed upon it. Since our town's Centennial is progressing toward us, I think it would be appropriate if we knew when our town was founded." After settling on 1888 for the founding of the post office, Verlyne Meck, Lola Johnson, and Mary Joslin, on May 30, 1985, were asked by the Buckeye Valley Coordinating Council to start planning a celebration. A meeting was held in the BUHS McNabb Library four months later, and Verlyne Meck was appointed chair of the Buckeye Valley Centennial Commission. At the opening event, on January 9, 1988, Vernon Potter Beloat and Irene (Beloat) Butler (below), brother and sister and the oldest native-born residents, were presented as Centennial Parade marshals, inaugurating a comprehensive, 16-month celebration. For a final centennial event, on May 25, 1989, a time capsule was dedicated at the Town-County Complex at 100 North Apache Road. (Both, courtesy of author.)

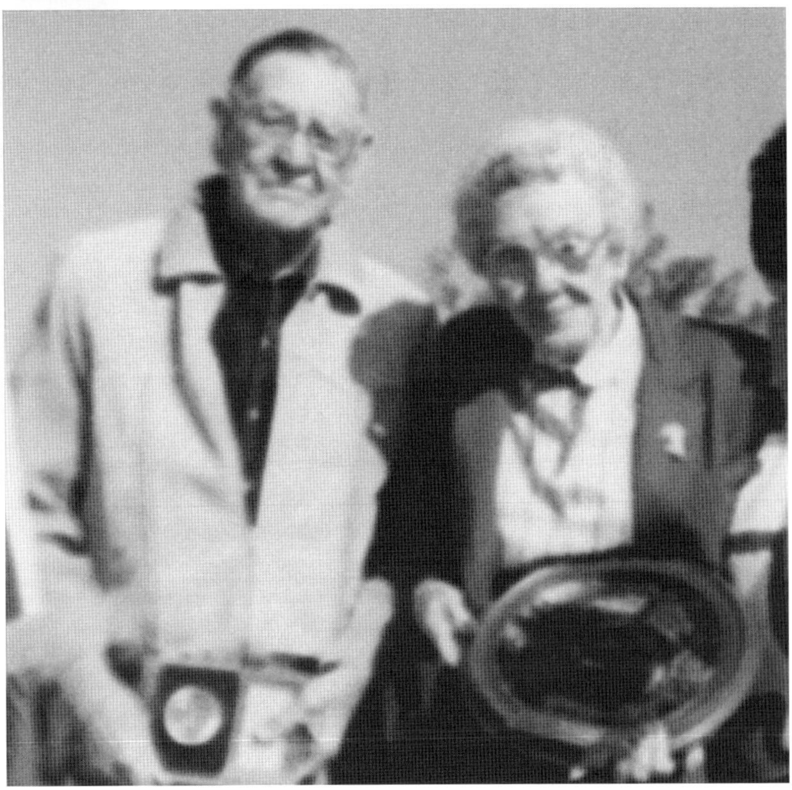

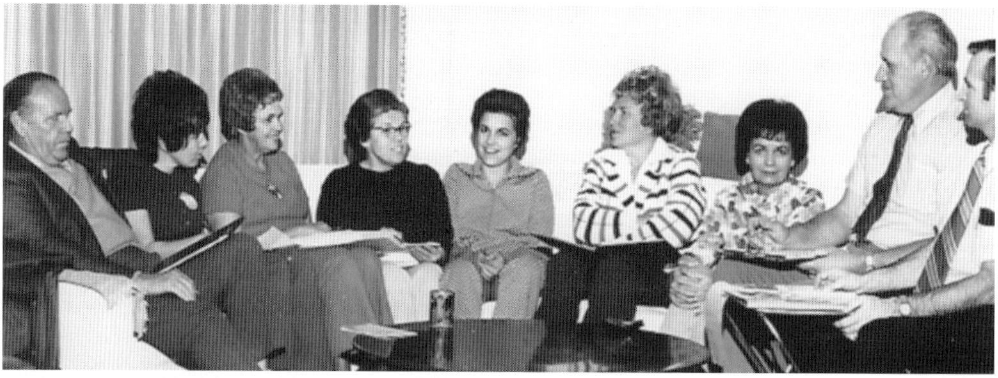

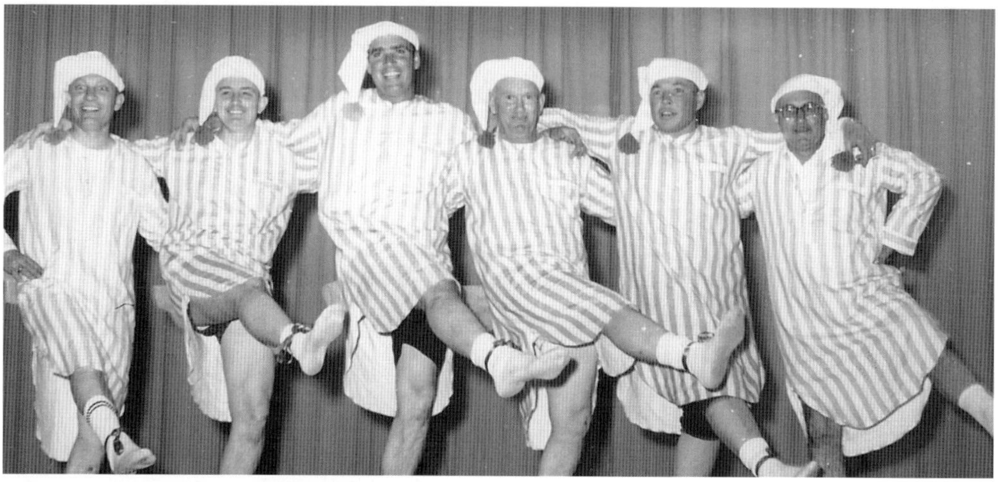

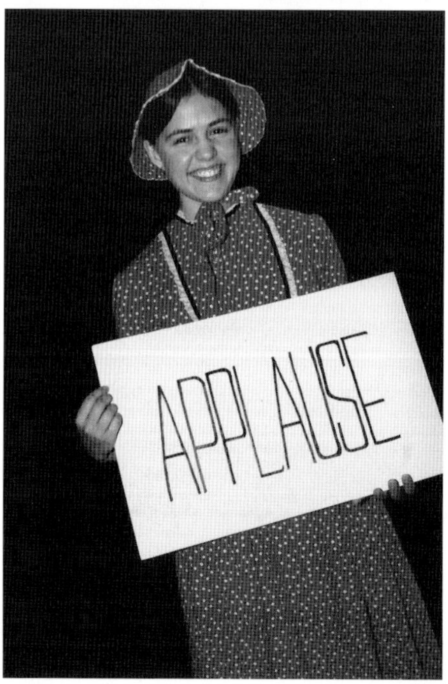

Pioneer Days Personalities

In 1969, at the home of Jackie and Verlyne Meck, a meeting of the Buckeye Valley Coordinating Council (top) involved plans for another Pioneer Days festivity. Pictured are, from left to right, Louis Joslin, Barbara Bales, Lola Johnson, Mary Joslin, Verlyne Meck, Mary Jane Hardesty, Betty Miglio, Chet McNabb, and Jackie Meck. At the first Pioneer Days Celebration (middle), dancers at the olio following the pageant *Tales of Buckeye Valley* on March 11–12, 1967, were, from left to right, Leigh Watkins, Joe Wolf, Ken Wood, LeRoy Turner, Jess Odom, and Wilbur Weigold. In 2000, at the Pioneer Days Melodrama, Denise Navejar (left) tells the audience what they are to do. (All, courtesy of author.)

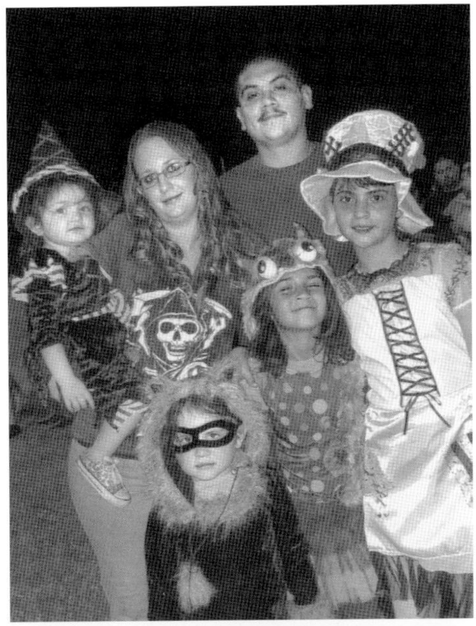

Halloween Carnival Personalities

Through the years, volunteers such as Louis Joslin, Lester Way, Deanna Kupcik, Buckeye Woman's Club, Bill Meck, school clubs, and Boy Scouts have planned and worked to make the Halloween Carnival happen. Buckeye's carnival has missed only one year since 1940. The 70-plus-year history of the event continued on October 25, 2014, at Earl Edgar Park, when the family of Jaime and Christine Rosales (right) enjoyed themselves. People are truly involved in the event, with all funds raised by local charities and nonprofit organizations staying in the community. Among the attractions are creepy carnival games, Krazy Kar rides, and bingo with lots of great prizes. Food booths abound for families to eat and enjoy. For many years, the carnival was held on the BUHS football field and, later, on the baseball field. One goal of the carnival may have been to keep youngsters out of Halloween mischief around town. (All, courtesy of the author.)

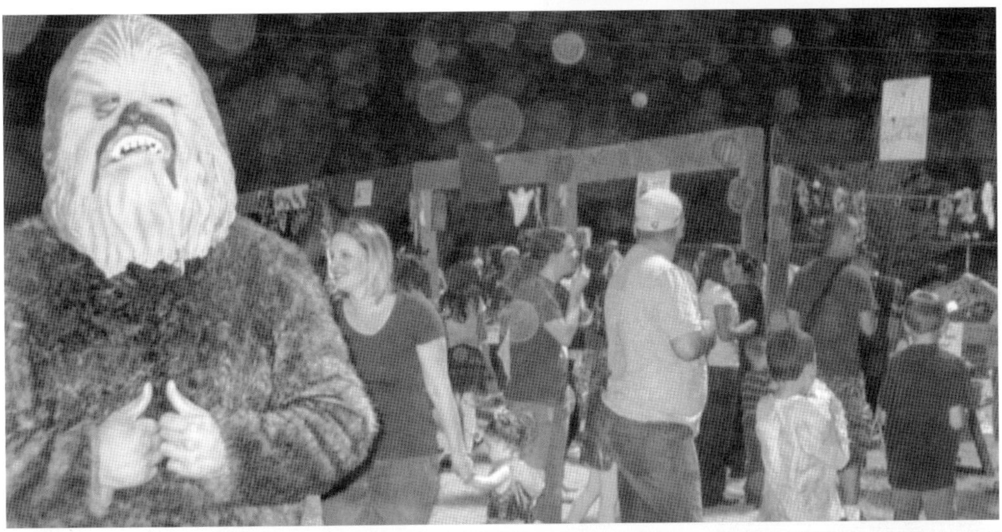

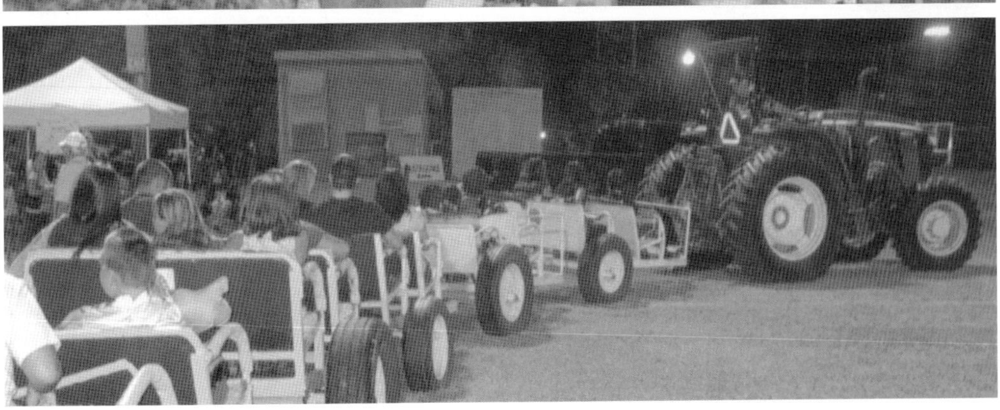

Legendary Cowboys

This 1965 photograph depicts six Buckeye Valley men who had lived in Arizona a total of 350 years. They rode as honorary parade marshals in Buckeye's 19th annual Helzapoppin celebration. All six cowboys were still active in cattle raising and ranching. This signed photograph is from the collection of Jack C. Gable. The men are, from left to right, John Osborne, 78, of Arlington; Jack Gable, 64, of Arlington; Jack Narramore, 60, of Gila Bend; Ross Roberts, 67, of Palo Verde; Carl Arnold, 67, of Buckeye; and John Beloat, 73, of Liberty. *The Little Red Book of Cowboy Wisdom* lists the following pearls: "Sometimes you ride hard, sometimes you ride easy." "Life's never so clear as when seen from the back of a horse." "No hour of life is wasted that is spent in the saddle." "I'm back in the saddle again." "A bad day roping beats a good day at any other work." "Nothing fits better than old boots, old jeans, and an old hat." "You can always tell a cowboy, but you can't tell him much." (Courtesy of Jack C. Gable.)

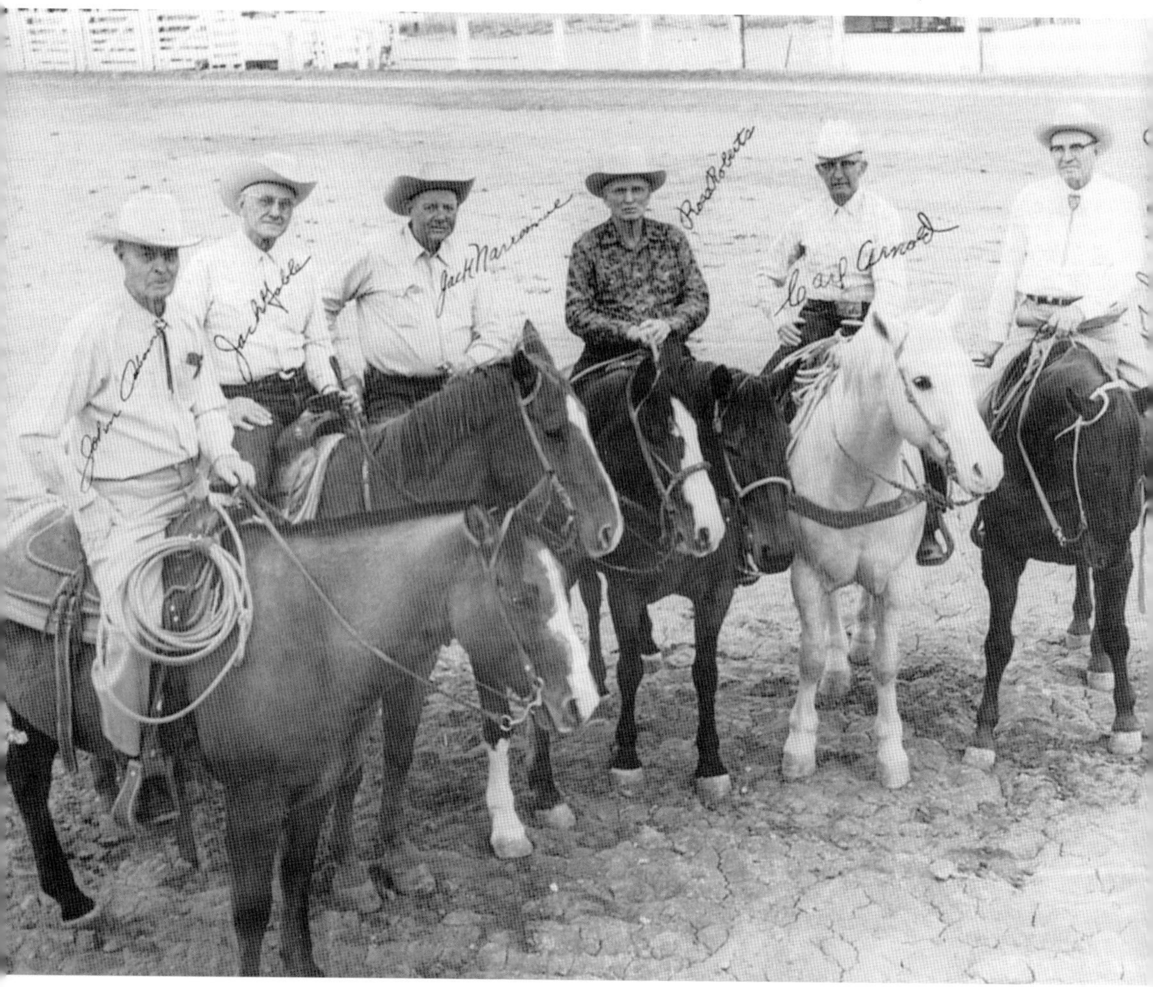

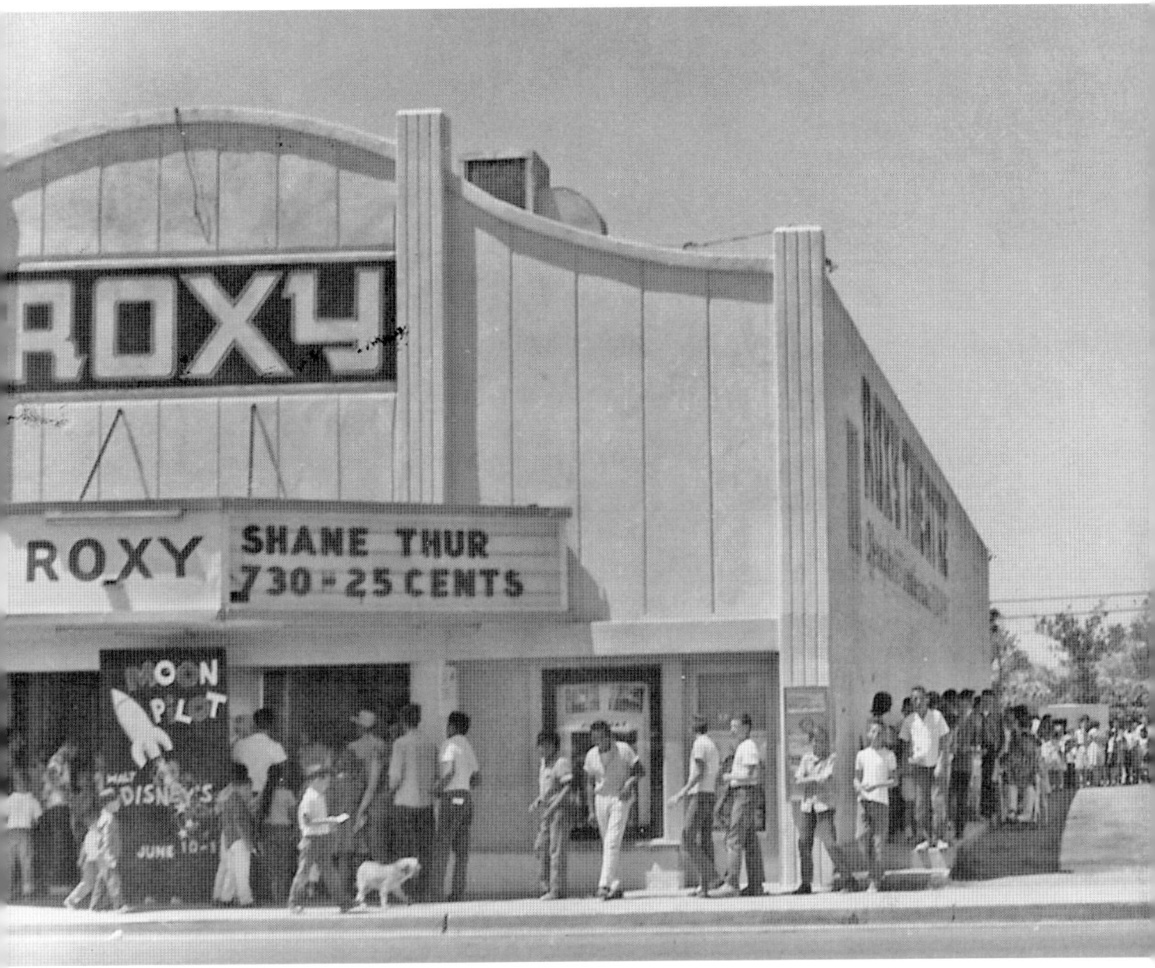

Wade Loudermilk

On December 25, 1935, with fanfare, the new $25,000 Roxy Theatre was opened by owner/manager Wade Loudermilk. The Roxy closed in 1971 and burned down on January 21, 2001. Buckeye City Hall is now located on the site. The Roxy was the main source of entertainment for Buckeye from 1935 to 1971. Youngsters would gather in the first three rows and watch the big show. Every once in a while, a young boy would get assertive and hold hands with a girl during the show. Milk Duds, Big Hunks, Milky Ways, and Cracker Jacks were on the snack menu. The movies in those days were fantastic, and viewers got so into it, cheering when the good guys (Durango Kid, Hopalong Cassidy, the Lone Ranger) came to rescue the gal who was about to lose her ranch to the bad guy. Newsreels, Three Stooges shorts, and serials also kept viewers entertained. All of this could be had for 50¢ (adults) or 25¢ (kids). The movie *Shane*, released in 1953, brought a long line of viewers (pictured). Simple, wholesome entertainment did not need ratings in those days. On either side of the projection booth were the Green Room for smokers (extra charge) and the Cry Room for crying babies (no extra charge). Many young people worked as projectionists, marquee changers, popcorn makers, and ticket takers. General managers included Wade Loudermilk, George Hamner, Bill Kee, Sid Davis, and Bill Johnson. (Courtesy of author.)

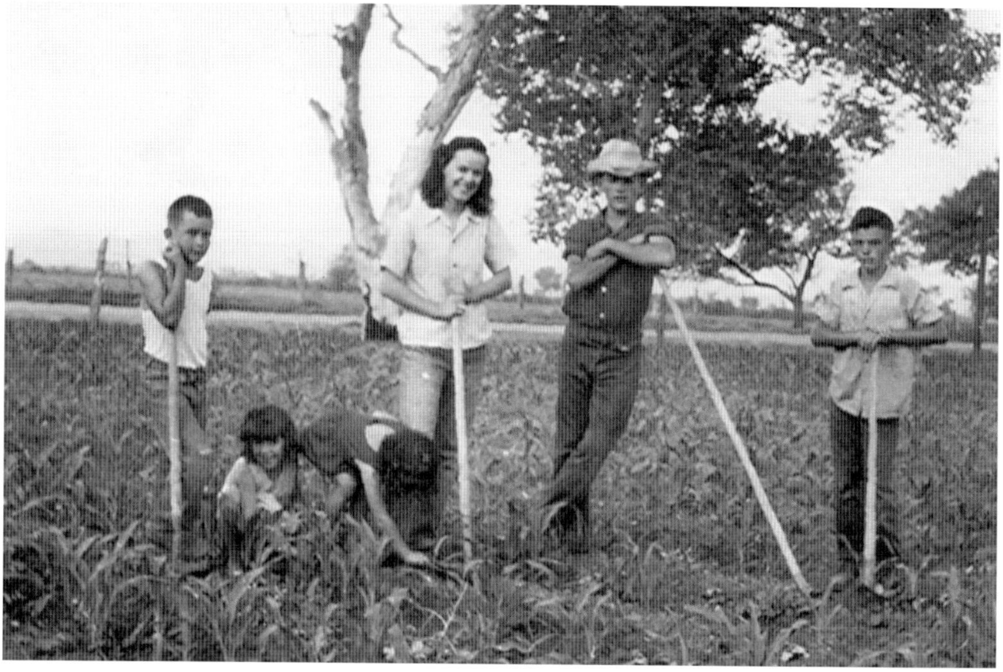

Don M. Balmes

Don Balmes was born in Phoenix on August 25, 1930. His parents were Roy W. Balmes and Arleen (Miller) Balmes. The family included four brothers and four sisters: Mary Val, Bill, Royleen "Chickie", Neal "Hank", Don, Dale, Sharon, and La Rae. Roy and Arleen were farmers, and all of the children grew up and attended schools in Palo Verde and Buckeye. Pictured in August 1943 are, from left to right, Dale, Sharon, La Rae, Dorothy Fillerup, Hank, and Don. Don has written many of his memories:

> Buckeye—Founded 1888—Includes surrounding communities, places and times: *3H Mercantile*—Downtown Buckeye; Arch Grocery—Two miles west of Buckeye; The Ice Plant—Started 1914; Carmoney's Grocery and Gas—1-1/2 mile west of Buckeye; Desert Rose—Between Arlington and Gila Bend; First Baptist Church—Inception in 1890, oldest in Buckeye area; Hassayampa Store—West of Palo Verde at the river crossing; Arlington Store—Arlington; Palo Verde Baptist Church—Inception in 1894; Major's Pharmacy—Downtown Buckeye (afterschool hangout); Buckeye Pharmacy—Downtown Buckeye (afterschool hangout); American Legion Hall—North Buckeye—Fourth Street and Edison; Trucker's Paradise—East side of Buckeye at the curve; Tamarack—East of Liberty at the curve; Oasis—Between Perryville and Avondale (old Highway 80); Allenville—One mile south of Buckeye; Helzapoppin Days—Started in 1935; Old Swimming Pool—North of Buckeye on Apache at Southern Ave.; Long's Dairy—Best chocolate bottled milk ever; Colored School—Palo Verde—Started in 1929 and closed in 1954; Liberty Store—Owned by Bob Sapp's father; Prisoner of War Camps—You could often see German and Italian prisoners going by on farm trailers to/from the fields and they were most always singing; Nucco—Looked like lard and you had to stir in coloring so it would look like butter; Some Memorable People of the Buckeye, Palo Verde & Liberty Area: John Allen—Allenville; John Rutledge—Allenville; Jack Currens—Buckeye Feed and Seed; Audre Chapman—BUHS; Florence Mickelson—BES; Bonnie Jean Cowart—BUHS—My Favorite Teacher; Herschel Hooper—BUHS; Dr. Jeffery—Good Doctor; Hi Parkman—Zanjero for Buckeye Irrigation Company and Historian and Tommy Lara—Buckeye Bakery.

(Courtesy of Don Balmes.)

Verlyne Meck

Verlyne (Henry) Meck is a native of Buckeye. Born in 1940, her life in the country on Broadway and Dean Roads was filled with horses, chickens, cotton, brothers, cousins, neighbors, and Sunday dinners. She married her teenage sweetheart, Jackie Meck, in 1962. Verlyne graduated from Liberty School, BUHS, and Grand Canyon College. She earned a master's degree from ASU and a library endorsement from the University of Arizona. Meck taught girls' physical education at BUHS from 1962 to 1966. Then, with three children, Teresa, Sara, and Jackie Jr., she was a full-time homemaker for 20 years. From 1985 to 2006, she worked at BUHS as a librarian and yearbook advisor. An extensive collection of timelines, reunion gatherings, yearbooks, sports records, photographs, and memorabilia was preserved. In addition, Meck taught a Southwest literature class, coached track and field and tennis, and cosponsored the National Honor Society. Since the 1960s, she has served as librarian and organist/pianist at First Southern Baptist Church, and she has been the charter secretary/treasurer for the Arizona Baptist Historical Society since 1989. Meck has a special passion for collecting and preserving Buckeye history and is a board member of the Buckeye Valley Museum Historical Society. She served as chair of Buckeye's 1988 Centennial Commission. Meck assisted with anniversary celebrations for First Southern Baptist Church at 50 and 75 years, Buckeye Union High School at 75 years, Buckeye Valley Museum at 50 years, and Liberty Elementary at 100 years. In 1984, Grand Canyon University selected her as Alumnus of the Year. After she retired from BUHS in 2006, the library was named Verlyne Meck Library. She became one of 100 persons named for the Arizona Culture Keeper Award in 2009. At her retirement, a fellow teacher described her as "an important part of Arizona . . . a woman who is welcoming, gentle, yet tough as the State itself." Since 1998, Verlyne Meck has been known as the "hat lady" for her fun and unique hats. (Courtesy of author.)

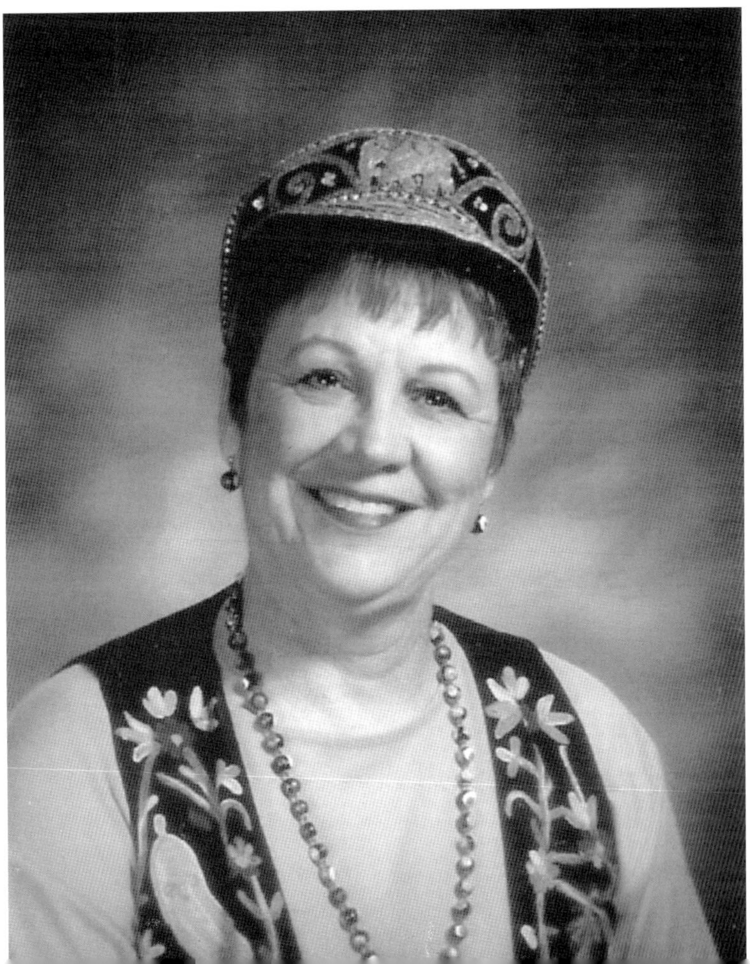

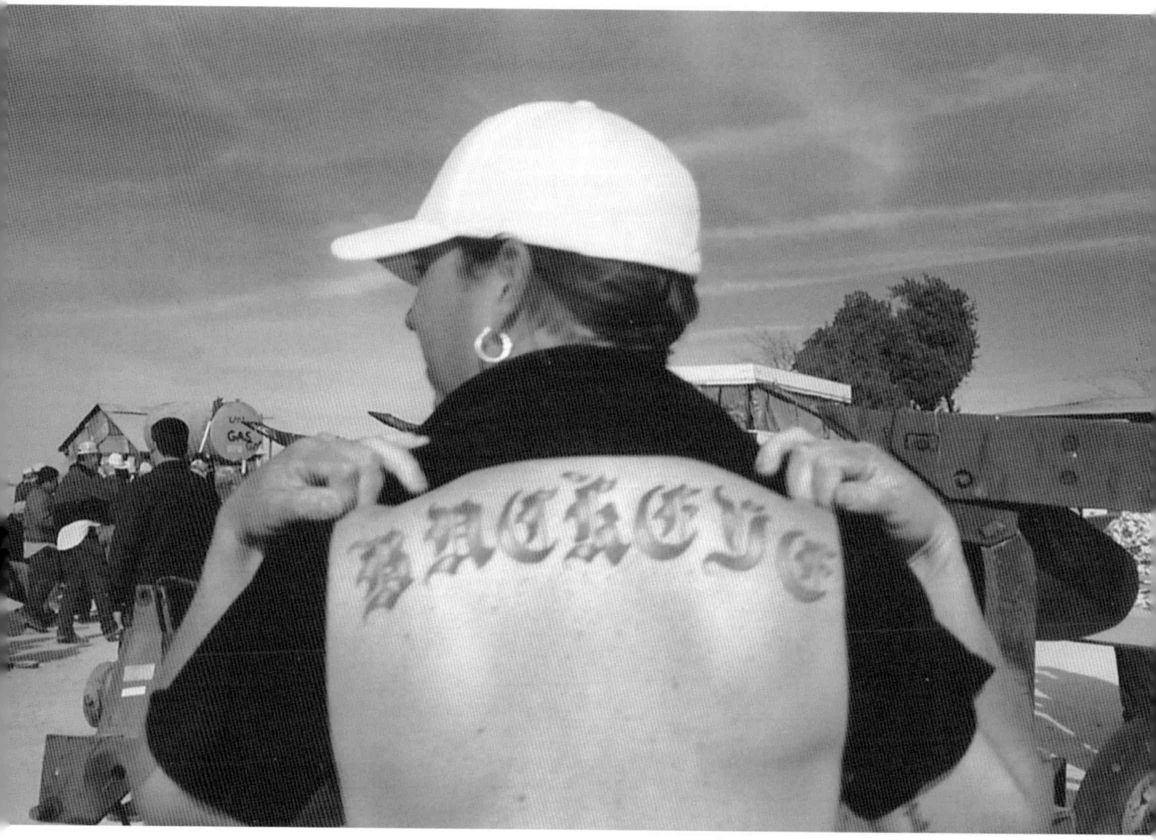

Dustin Ezell

Former resident J.C. Moore once said, "You can take the boy out of Buckeye, but you can't take Buckeye out of the boy." Here, Dustin "Duck" Ezell shows that truth on January 28, 2006, with a "Buckeye" tattoo. Ezell, a Buckeye native, owns Duck's Septic Pump & Install business. The Ezell family's roots are entwined with those of the Calvert family, and both are important parts of Buckeye. (Courtesy of author.)

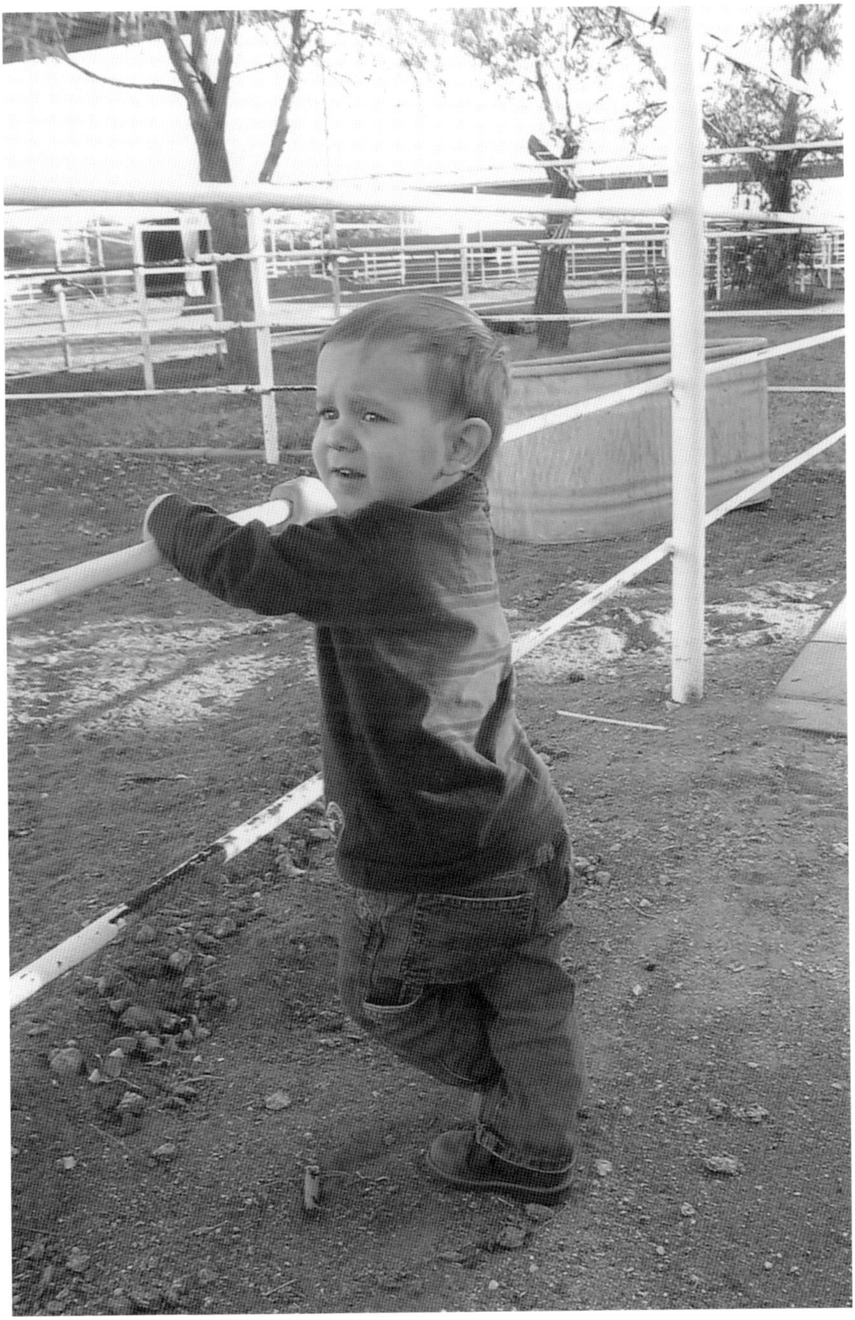

Jackson Faccio
Verlyne Meck, as grandmas do, took this photograph of her grandson Jackson Faccio in 2009. She never dreamed that it would be incorporated into a book. The expression on Jackson's face seems to ask the question on everyone's mind: "I wonder what the future holds?" Jackson is the son of Buck and Sara Faccio. Buck is a genuine part of Buckeye, as he is "Voice of the Hawks", the announcer for BUHS athletic events. Sara has been a teacher in Buckeye schools and is currently a Cancer Fighter Ambassador for the Cancer Treatment Center of America. (Courtesy of author.)

INDEX

LEGENDARY LOCALS

AN IMPRINT OF ARCADIA PUBLISHING

Find more books like this at
www.legendarylocals.com

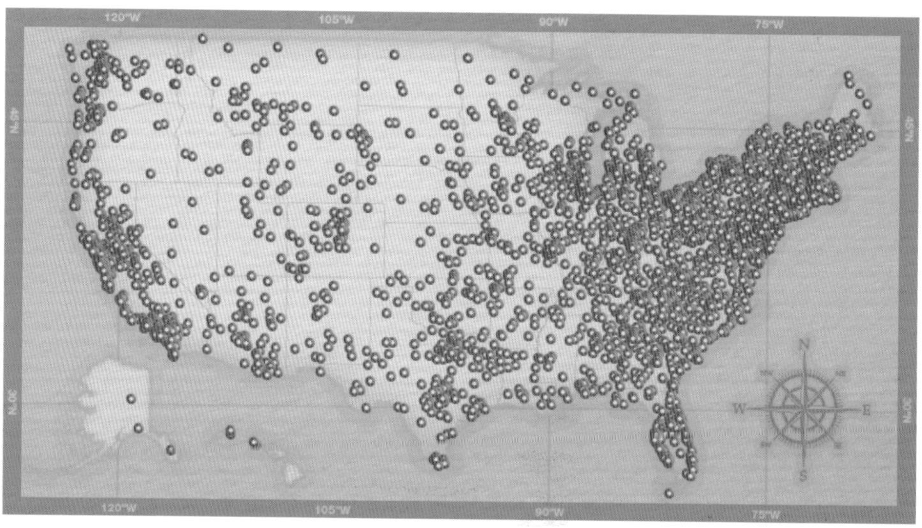

Discover more local and regional history books at
www.arcadiapublishing.com

Consistent with our mission to preserve history on a local level, this book was printed in South Carolina on American-made paper and manufactured entirely in the United States. Products carrying the accredited Forest Stewardship Council (FSC) label are printed on 100 percent FSC-certified paper.

MADE IN THE USA